Legislative Development in Africa

What explains contemporary variations in African legislative institutions – including their strengths and weaknesses? Compared with the more powerful executive branches, legislatures throughout the continent have historically been classified as weak and largely inconsequential to policy–making processes. But, as Ken Ochieng' Opalo suggests here, African legislatures actually serve important roles, and under certain conditions, powerful and independent democratic legislatures can emerge from their autocratic foundations. In this book, Opalo examines the colonial origins of African legislatures, as well as how postcolonial intra–elite politics structured the processes of adapting inherited legislative institutions to local political economies. Through detailed case studies of Kenya and Zambia, Opalo offers comparative longitudinal analyses of the evolution of legislative strength and institutionalization in the two countries. In addition, the book presents a regional survey of legislative development under colonial rule, postcolonial autocratic single-party rule, and multiparty politics throughout Africa.

KEN OCHIENG' OPALO is an assistant professor in the School of Foreign Service at Georgetown University. He received his PhD from Stanford University and BA from Yale. His work has been published in journals such as the *British Journal of Political Science,* the *Journal of Democracy,* and the *Journal of Eastern African Studies.* His research interests include historical institutional development (with a focus on legislatures), the political economy of development, and the politics of the provision of public goods and services. Opalo's research has been supported by Stanford University's Susan Ford Dorsey Fellowship, the United Kingdom's Department for International Development (DFID), and the Omidyar Network.

Legislative Development in Africa

Politics and Postcolonial Legacies

KEN OCHIENG' OPALO
Georgetown University

CAMBRIDGE
UNIVERSITY PRESS

CAMBRIDGE
UNIVERSITY PRESS

University Printing House, Cambridge CB2 8BS, United Kingdom

One Liberty Plaza, 20th Floor, New York, NY 10006, USA

477 Williamstown Road, Port Melbourne, VIC 3207, Australia

314–321, 3rd Floor, Plot 3, Splendor Forum, Jasola District Centre, New Delhi – 110025, India

79 Anson Road, #06–04/06, Singapore 079906

Cambridge University Press is part of the University of Cambridge.

It furthers the University's mission by disseminating knowledge in the pursuit of education, learning, and research at the highest international levels of excellence.

www.cambridge.org
Information on this title: www.cambridge.org/9781108492102
DOI: 10.1017/9781108684651

© Ken Ochieng' Opalo 2019

First published 2019

Printed and bound in Great Britain by Clays Ltd, Elcograf S.p.A.

A catalogue record for this publication is available from the British Library.

Library of Congress Cataloging-in-Publication Data
Names: Opalo, Ken Ochieng', 1983– author.
Title: Legislative development in Africa : politics and postcolonial legacies / Ken Ochieng' Opalo.
Description: New York, NY : Cambridge University Press, 2019. | Originally presented as the author's thesis (doctoral)–Stanford University, 2015. | Includes bibliographical references and index.
Identifiers: LCCN 2019005630 | ISBN 9781108492102 (hardback : alk. paper) | ISBN 9781108710350 (pbk. : alk. paper)
Subjects: LCSH: Legislative bodies–Africa–History. | Legislative power–Africa. | Africa–Politics and government.
Classification: LCC JQ1877 .O63 2019 | DDC 328.6–dc23
LC record available at https://lccn.loc.gov/2019005630

ISBN 978-1-108-49210-2 Hardback

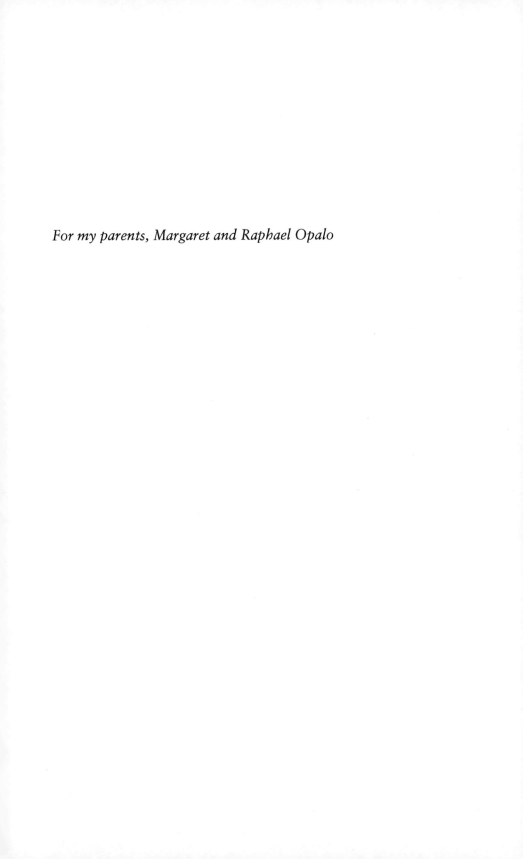

For my parents, Margaret and Raphael Opalo

Contents

Figures

Tables

Preface

Premised on the notion that the study of institutions is critical for understanding both political and economic development, this book seeks to answer two simple questions: What explains both cross-sectional and longitudinal variation in legislative strength under autocracy? And, under what conditions do democratic institutions emerge from their autocratic foundations?

My answer to the first question is that autocrats' specific strategies of legislative control determine the extent of organizational development and institutionalization of autocratic legislatures. Under autocracy, legislatures typically lack *ends independence* – the ability to pursue any legislative outcome that can garner majority support. In other words, legislative outcomes invariably conform to chief executives' preferences. However, autocratic legislatures may differ in how they arrive at statutory outcomes that are consistent with the preferences of chief executives. Some do so through direct executive direction, while others may have room for intra-legislative bargaining. Direct autocratic meddling in legislative processes denies legislatures opportunities for internal differentiation and general organizational development. Indirect and extra-legislative means of legislative control creates room for legislators to develop organizational mechanisms for handling intra-elite bargains typical of legislative processes (independent of the executive branch). Under these conditions, much of the lawmaking process takes place *within* legislatures that have *means independence* – defined as the ability of legislators to choose the specific intra-legislative bargaining arrangements through which to achieve statutory outcomes that are consistent with chief executives' preferences, including through logrolling. Without means independence, legislatures exist as mere constitutional rubber-stamps of executive action. But, those with means independence serve as significant arenas for intra-elite bargaining over policy and the sharing of governance rents (access to public resources for private benefit).

Notice that under autocracy the outcomes of these two strategies are observationally equivalent. Both types of legislatures lack ends independence and produce statutes that reflect chief executives' preferences. But, while legislative statutes under both conditions invariably conform to chief executives' preferences, the different strategies of legislative control have differential implications for long-run legislative development. The lack of means independence stunts legislative institutional development. Independence over means creates incentives for legislators to invest in internal differential and general organizational development of legislatures.

A subsidiary concern is why some autocrats choose one strategy of elite control over the other. I argue that secure autocrats are more likely to grant legislatures means independence relative to their insecure counterparts. In other words, that the subjective security of tenure of the autocrat provides an implicit upper limit to legislative institutionalization and strength. This leads to the counterintuitive conclusion that strong autocrats are more likely to rule with strong legislatures.

I answer the second question by showing that levels of legislative organizational development and institutionalization under autocracy determine the trajectory of institutional development following a democratic transition. Received wisdom in the literature depicts regime transitions as the founding moments of strong democratic institutions. I argue that institutional development after transitions tends to be marked by important continuities, rather than sharp discontinuities. New legislative institutional forms and functions are typically informed by persistent ideas about *how legislatures work*. Therefore, to understand postautocratic legislative development, one must first examine the dynamics of pretransition legislative development. In sum, strong autocratic legislatures create the organizational foundations for the emergence of strong democratic legislatures.

I provide empirical evidence to back these claims with material from Kenya and Zambia. The two countries are excellent comparative cases on account of their similar backgrounds, but also divergence in key outcomes. Both are former British colonies that inherited a Westminster system and gained independence under multiparty democracy. Both countries also went through periods of single-party rule before readopting multipartyism in the early 1990s. In exploring the cases of Kenya and Zambia, two general strands of analyses guide my discussion throughout this book.

First, I focus on legislative development under autocracy in both the colonial and postcolonial eras. In doing so I highlight the differences in institutional development between the Kenyan and Zambian legislatures. In Kenya, political development in the colonial period was fragmented (largely along ethnic lines) and institutionalized (within the colonial Legislative Council). In Zambia, political development was territorial (and largely multiethnic) and, especially in the late colonial period, extra-institutional. Kenya achieved independence under a fragmented elite party, while Zambia's independence movement spawned a multiethnic mass party. These differences conditioned presidents' strategies of controlling elites serving in the two countries' postcolonial legislatures. In Kenya, control was extra-parliamentary and through the apparatus of the Provincial Administration. In Zambia, it was through the ruling party, and involved extensive meddling in intra-legislative processes. Both legislatures lacked ends independence. However, the Kenyan legislature enjoyed a fair amount of means independence, while its Zambian counterpart did not. In Kenya, parliament was *the main game in town*, while in Zambia the ruling party reigned supreme. These differences explain the contrasts in the observed organizational strength and capacity of postcolonial autocratic legislatures in Kenya and Zambia.

Second, I explain how democratic legislatures can emerge from their autocratic foundations. In this part of my analysis I focus on changes in legislative characteristics and outputs in Kenya and Zambia around the time of transition to multiparty politics in the early 1990s. I show how the level of legislative institutionalization at the point of transition – from autocracy to democracy – impacts further institutional development in the posttransition period. In other words, that autocracies with strong legislatures on the eve of transition are more likely (relative to those with weaker legislatures) to have strong posttransition legislatures. The data show that compared to their Zambian counterparts, Kenyan legislators had greater bargaining power following the transition to multipartyism – as indicated by the increase in budget allocation to the legislature, remuneration of legislators, the share of executive bills passed, the electoral performance of incumbent legislators, and the general rebalancing of executive-legislative relations.

The idea that strong autocratic legislatures beget strong democratic legislatures is at once obvious and important. Much of the extant literature on institutional development emphasizes institutional discontinuities at the point of transition as the sources of strong institutions of limited government under democracy. In other words, that inclusive and constraining institutions emerge primarily out of the contractarian bargains around the time of transition. In this book I show in great detail that continuities during the transition process (from autocracy) matter for the emergence of strong legislatures after transition. An overarching idea in my analyses is that history matters because institutions develop *over time*. The material evidence in this book – both from across Africa and in detailed case studies of Kenya and Zambia – documents legislative development in Africa from the colonial period to the present, and shows how historical contingencies structured the observed variation in legislative institutionalization and strength in Africa.

This book makes several important contributions to the study of institutions. First, the theoretical and empirical approach herein offers a coherent theory of institutional development both under autocracy and after transition to democracy. My analyses link and synthesize the disparate literatures on autocratic institutions on the one hand, and democratic institutions on the other. Second, by providing a rich array of data on African legislatures, this book expands the field of Legislative Studies to include material evidence from non-Western democracies. Thus far the literature on legislatures has been dominated by material evidence from the North Atlantic, and in particular, the United States Congress.

I bring new data to bear in answering important questions – such as why some presidents choose to rule by decree while others rule by statutes, how fluctuations in the executive-legislative relations and balance of power impact legislative activities and output, the role of parties in conditioning legislative institutionalization and development, and how intra-legislative politics explain the observed variation in the proportion of executive initiatives that get passed. Lastly, by focusing on electoral legislative politics in Kenya and Zambia, this book explains the dynamics of incumbency (dis)advantage in low-income democracies. Incumbency advantage (over challengers) is an established fact in wealthy advanced democracies. But, in emerging democracies incumbents tend to be disadvantaged. This book provides a simple political economy explanation for this difference.

An important policy contribution of this book is to highlight possible avenues for strengthening legislatures in emerging democracies. Democratic consolidation crucially hinges on the emergence of stable systems of horizontal accountability. This book argues that legislative strengthening should go beyond technical assistance and organizational capacity building (currently favored by donors) and include the political empowerment of legislators. This is for the simple reason that politically independent and electorally autonomous legislators make for politically independent legislatures. In the same vein, this book cautions against uncritical party strengthening initiatives in emerging democracies. Through the capacity to instill party discipline and deny legislatures means independence, strong political parties in contexts with weak legislatures can stunt legislative organizational development and institutional strengthening.

Acknowledgments

I have benefited immensely from the mentorship, guidance, and support from many people throughout the process of writing this book. I am deeply indebted to my dissertation committee members, David Laitin, James Fearon, and Stephen Haber. Throughout my time in graduate school, David, James, and Steve constantly encouraged me to think differently and creatively about African politics. It is partially because of their encouragement that I ended up writing a book on the predictable and institutionalized regularities of politics in Africa, a region that has thus far been characterized as dominated by singularly uninstitutionalized personalist politics.

I am also grateful to Lisa Blaydes, who was not only a great academic adviser but also provided me with practical guidance on how to navigate graduate school. I thank Gary Cox, Francis Fukuyama, Stephen Stedman, and Larry Diamond for their insights and advice throughout my time at Stanford. Dr. Laura Hubbard, Associate Director of the Center for African Studies, deserves special recognition for pushing me to be a methodologically rigorous and well-rounded Africanist. I am grateful for her continued mentorship and friendship.

This project began as my dissertation at Stanford University. Friendships at Stanford provided a rich intellectual environment in which to develop the ideas that resulted in this book. I thank Jennifer Haskell, Kara Downey, Melissa Lee, and Melina Platas-Izama for their comments at different stages of writing my dissertation. I thank the Program of African Studies at Northwestern University for hosting me as a predoctoral fellow.

The process of data collection for this book immensely benefited from the generosity of the staff at the National Assembly libraries in Nairobi, Kenya and Lusaka, Zambia. I am particularly grateful to Joab Amagola and Chama Mfula in Nairobi and Lusaka, respectively. I thank Dr. Luis Franceschi for hosting me at Strathmore University in Nairobi, and Dr. Marja Hinfelaar for helping me navigate the research terrain in Zambia. I thank my colleagues at Georgetown University, James Habyarimana, Lahra Smith, and Scott Taylor, for their support and mentorship. I also thank Bethania Michael, Zachary Scherer, and Evan Waddill for excellent research assistance. My fieldwork was made possible by the Susan Ford Dorsey Fellowship from the Center for African Studies at Stanford University.

Finally, I would like to thank my family for their patience and support throughout this journey. I am immensely grateful to my father Raphael and late mother Margaret Opalo for having nurtured my intellectual curiosity from an early age. I thank my father for supporting my decision to pursue higher education away from home. I thank my sister Rose and brothers Collins, Bernard, and Michael for their support, insights, and encouragement. I also thank our family friends, Anne and Emmanuel Nyabera and Mary and Art Hunt for their invaluable mentorship and guidance. Last, but not least, I would like to thank my partner, best friend, and lifetime travel companion, Vanessa Watters for her intellectual companionship, edits, and for making our life together a fountain of intellectual growth, happiness, and stability.

1 | Introduction

1.1 A Tale of Two Legislatures

On August 14, 2001 Kenya's president, Daniel arap Moi, walked into *Bunge* (parliament) as an ordinary representative for Baringo Central constituency with the express purpose of casting a crucial vote. This was a first in Kenya's history, and highlighted the president's desperation in lobbying recalcitrant Members of Parliament (MPs). Moi needed the legislators to pass a constitutional amendment establishing an anticorruption authority as a precondition for the release of over 25 billion Kenya Shillings (approximately US$300 million at the time) in promised donor funds. But, the MPs had other plans, and handed the president a narrow loss by 15 votes.[1]

Moi's loss on this particular Tuesday afternoon was not an isolated incident. Since the reintroduction of multiparty politics in 1991 he had faced an increasingly hostile legislature. For the first 14 of his 24 years in office (1978–1991), 89.14 percent of executive bills introduced in parliament got passed. During this period Kenya was a single-party state under the Kenya African National Union (KANU). However, following the transition to multiparty politics (1992–2002), only 57.22 percent of executive bills got passed in the legislature. This dramatic change in Moi's legislative success rate is particularly noteworthy since during this period KANU and allied parties commanded majorities in the legislature. KANU alone held 56 percent and 51 percent of seats in the seventh and eighth parliaments, respectively.

Why did the Kenyan legislature pass a smaller proportion of executive bills after 1991 despite the fact that KANU held a majority in the legislature? Under standard assumptions of rationality, Moi ought to have exercised his legislative proposal powers strategically, only introducing bills that were likely to pass in the legislature. Therefore,

---

[1] Republic of Kenya, *Kenya National Assembly Official Record*, August 14, 2001, Cols. 2248–2249.

the significant drop in the share of executive bills passed signaled a precipitous decline in Moi's ability either to accurately predict Kenyan legislators' policy preferences, or to convince them to vote for his legislative agenda. In other words, the transition to multiparty politics occasioned a shift in the executive-legislative balance of power in favor of the Kenyan parliament. And as a result Moi's ability to orchestrate legislative outcomes that were consistent with his preferences was significantly curtailed.

But, elsewhere in Africa the end of single-party rule was not a sufficient condition for a decline in the share of executive bills passed. For example, over the same period in Zambia (1992–2001), and following the transition to multiparty electoral democracy, the National Assembly passed 90.12 percent of executive bills introduced. This rate of passage of executive bills was not dissimilar to what obtained under single-party rule (1964–1991) when parliament passed 91.04 percent of executive bills. Measured by the proportion of executive bills passed, Zambia's democratic transition scarcely altered the executive-legislative balance of power.[2]

Clearly, the end of single-party rule empowered legislators to a greater extent in Kenya than in Zambia. This differential effect of regime transition on executive-legislative relations in Kenya and Zambia manifested itself beyond the proportion of executive bills passed. It was also evident in other standard measures of legislative strength and institutionalization, including the control over legislative budgets and calendars, the size of legislative staff, oversight of public finances, control over discretionary development funds, and the political autonomy of individual legislators.

This is a puzzling outcome. Conventional wisdom holds that competitive elections strengthen political institutions, including representative legislative institutions.[3] Yet, in the present examples of Kenya

---

[2] Note that for much of the period covered in this book nearly all bills introduced in the Kenyan and Zambian legislatures originated from the executive branch. In addition, the offices of the Attorneys General in both countries monopolized the legislative drafting process. Bills at variance with presidents' preferences often died a slow death in the chambers of the respective Attorneys General in both countries.

[3] The key assumption here is that the reelection motive incentivizes political elites to invest in strengthening institutions with a view of making them better able to cater to voters' interests and to protect their political careers (Barro, 1973; Mayhew, 1974; Ferejohn, 1986; Besley, 2006).

and Zambia, the introduction of competitive multiparty electoral institutions appears to have strengthened the legislature in one case and not the other. This outcome is even more intriguing because Zambia's 1991 election ended Kenneth Kaunda's 27 years in power at the helm of the United National Independence Party (UNIP), ostensibly putting the the country on the path toward greater democratic consolidation. This raises the question, what explains the divergent trajectories of the Kenyan and Zambian legislatures?

This book engages this question by examining both postcolonial legislative development in Africa under autocracy and the conditions under which strong and effective democratic legislatures can emerge from their autocratic foundations. Motivated by the idea that legislatures are critical for democratic consolidation and the realization of limited government, it seeks to answer two specific and empirically tractable questions: (i) What explains the observed variation in the strength and level of institutionalization of autocratic legislatures? and (ii) Under what conditions do transitions to competitive electoral democracy result in the strengthening of legislative institutions?

Given the considerable attention that social scientists have given to the study of institutions and the process of democratization over the last three decades, one might expect existing works to have ready answers to these questions. Yet, very little research exists to explain divergent outcomes in levels of legislative strength and institutionalization in low-income emerging democracies.[4] Indeed, much of our knowledge of the evolution and development of legislatures is informed by research on the high-income established democracies of Western Europe and North America, despite significant differences in the development of contemporary postcolonial legislatures.[5]

In Europe and North America, legislatures emerged out of the political economies of the late medieval or early modern periods to reflect the existing balance of power between chief executives

---

[4] A notable exception is Joel D. Barkan's pioneering research on legislative development in Africa. See, for example, Barkan (1976, 1979); Barkan and Okumu (1980); Barkan et al. (1984); Barkan (2009b), and Barkan and Mattes (2014).

[5] For canonical works on legislative development in Western Europe and North America see Thompson (1953), Cox (1987), North and Weingast (1989), Stasavage (2003), Maddicott (2010), and Squire (2012).

(monarchs or presidents) and fellow elites (wealthy aristocrats and/or property owners). Importantly, chief executives became accountable to legislatures due to the former's dependence on the latter for material resources (the origins of the legislative *the power of the purse*). Furthermore, the restriction of political participation to an exclusive club of wealthy males ensured that those best able to wield both economic and political power were granted the institutional means of providing checks and balances vis-à-vis chief executives. Broadly speaking, legislative institutional forms and practices mirrored the de facto distribution of power among elites.

Take the the stylized account of the origins of the English parliament. King John conceded powers to a proto-legislature in Runnymede in order to stave off a baronial rebellion and to secure material support for his war effort. The *Magna Carta*, in a sense, merely codified the existing intra-elite balance of power in thirteenth-century England. At the time the English King was in a position of weakness vis-à-vis fellow elites acting collectively as a proto-legislature. And, perhaps most importantly, the *Magna Carta* was enforceable. Clause 61 expressly granted the king's barons the right to elect 25 of their number to wage war against King John if he violated the charter. The Provisions of Oxford (in 1258) were backed by the implicit threat of force from barons who commanded armies, and the weight of established custom and religion.[6]

This conventional depiction of legislative development – characterized by chief executives making concessions to powerful elites around the founding moment of legislatures – does not accurately portray the history of legislatures in the postcolonial states that emerged after World War II.[7] In these states, imported legislatures were grafted onto incongruous social and political terrains. Departing European colonialists left "overdeveloped" executive branches

[6] In one account, King John's "opponents [rebelling barons] asked a plain acceptance of their plainly expressed demands. Before nightfall, John, overawed by their firmness and by the numbers of the armed force behind them, was constrained to surrender, and signified his acceptance of the barons' demands" (McKechnie, 1914, p. 38). See also Holt (1992) and Maddicott (1994) on the baronial efforts to constrain the English monarchy.
[7] By "legislative development" I mean the process through which legislatures become internally differentiated, develop greater organizational capacity, and acquire operational and political autonomy from chief executives.

(relative to legislatures and judiciaries) that held considerable auto-cratic power.[8] As Ojwang (1980) observes, "the dominant feature of colonial government ... was invariably the executive" (p. 298). Legislative institutions in these colonies did not coevolve with the consolidation of executive power. Unlike in Europe, legislative devel-opment under colonialism did little to engender the emergence of strong legislatures rooted in local political economies and capa-ble of effectively balancing chief executives. Postcolonial African chief executives inherited nearly all of autocratic colonial governors' powers – that fused executive, legislative, and judicial functions (Mamdani, 1996). This reality doomed postcolonial African legisla-tures to evolve in the shadow of much stronger chief executives.

These specific distinctions between North Atlantic and postcolonial legislatures are important. To understand the evolution of postcolonial legislatures is to understand that separation of powers and legislative strength is endogenous to the prevailing intra-elite balance of power. Legislative independence and strength necessarily implies constrained executive powers. Assuming that chief executives desire to maximize their power while in office, it follows that they have strong incentives to limit legislative independence and strength. Therefore, legislative development in contexts where elites are weak relative to the chief executive is fundamentally different from contexts where elites pos-sessed both material and coercive capacities to constrain the chief executive.

The histories of the Kenyan and Zambian legislatures demonstrate these facts. Both countries' legislatures (Legislative Councils) were founded under British colonial rule with the sole objective of balancing immigrant European interests against those of the crown in London. Their basic Westminster orientation notwithstanding, institutional engineering guaranteed the dominance of colonial governors over the

---

[8] By the term "overdeveloped" I mean an executive branch whose coercive and bureaucratic powers are exogenously imposed and not the result of gradual coevolution with other branches of government and related sociocultural and economic institutions within a given polity. The idea of "overdeveloped" executive branches resulting from the colonial experience has long been a staple of postcolonial studies. For example, Alavi (1972) provides an exposition of the idea with application to Pakistan and Bangladesh. See also Leys (1976) for a critical review of this idea. As used in this book, executive overdevelopment signifies the relative interbranch power differential, and the resulting inability of legislators to check and balance chief executives.

Legislative Councils (LegCos) in the two colonies. At independence, Kenya and Zambia inherited this lopsided pattern of executive-legislative relations intact, with presidential powers akin to those of colonial governors. This imbalanced executive-legislative distribution of power enabled chief executives to actively limit the emergence of politically independent legislatures in the two countries in the first three decades of independence.

Despite their common origin, the Kenyan and Zambian legislatures differed in important respects. In Kenya, the contingencies of decolonization resulted in a strong administrative apparatus and a relatively weak ruling party. A strong administrative structure enabled Kenya's founding president to cede a modicum of independence to fellow elites in the legislature without fear of losing his own power and influence. The weakness of the ruling party reinforced this relationship, permitting the legislature to function as the focal arena of intra-elite bargaining over public policy and allocating access to public resources for private benefit. Things were different in Zambia. There, the decolonization process resulted in a relatively strong ruling party and a ruling class committed to the dismantling of the colonial administrative apparatus. After independence, the ruling party, and not the legislature, emerged as the locus of intra-elite bargaining. In addition, a weakened administrative structure limited the Zambian founding president's willingness to cede any powers to fellow elites in the legislature. Unsure of his ability to effectively control and regulate elite political activity in the institution, the Zambian president chose to curtail legislative independence.

The dynamics of intra-elite politics influenced the localization of inherited colonial legislative institutional forms and practices. In Kenya, relative legislative autonomy as a result of the chief executive's subject sense of security of tenure enabled the emergence of an organizationally strong institution with a tradition of open debate and political relevance. On a number of occasions, the Kenyan legislature went as far as passing resolutions opposed by the president (Hakes, 1970; Gertzel, 1970; Opalo, 2014). In Zambia, the president's subjective insecurity and the subordination of the legislature to the ruling party stunted its organizational development (Tordoff, 1977a; Alderfer, 1997). And, so while both legislatures were weak relative to chief executives, their underlying organizational capacities differed – a fact that became evident after the end of single-party rule. In the early 1990s, the Kenyan legislature was organizationally strong enough to take advantage of its new-found political freedom under multiparty politics. The same was not true of Zambian legislature, which remained largely subordinate to the executive branch despite the regime change.

1.2 The Challenge of Governing with Legislatures

Political contestation over the adaptation of inherited colonial legislative institutional forms and practices to local political economies was not limited to Kenya and Zambia. Across Africa, autocratic postcolonial presidents fought to subordinate legislative institutions to their will. Due to their colonial inheritance of "overdeveloped" powers, many succeeded, thereby stunting legislative development in their respective states. But, as I show in Figure 1.1, in a number of cases

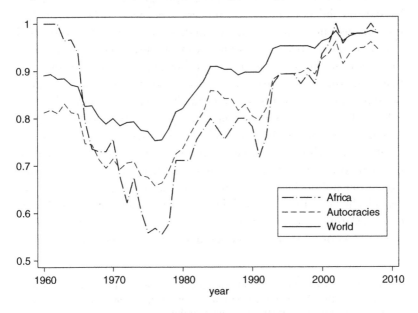

Figure 1.1 The decline and rise of postcolonial legislatures
Notes: Graph indicates the share of extant states with open legislatures. Note the rapid decline in the share of African states with open legislatures in the first two decades of independence (1960–1980). Graph based on author's calculations using data from Cheibub, Gandhi, and Vreeland (2010).

these contestations resulted in a complete breakdown of intra-elite relations and the closure of legislatures. Beginning in the early 1960s, there was a precipitous decline in the share of African countries with open legislatures due to elite political instability. African presidents that could not control legislatures simply disbanded them. It was not until the late 1970s that this trend was reversed, as African elites learned to structure stable forms of intra-elite relations on the back of legislative institutions.

But, why did African chief executives seek to adapt colonial legislatures to their respective local political contexts? The answer is twofold. First, at the end of the colonial era the Montesquieuian ideal of three branches of government (Legislative, Judicial, and Executive) had become widely accepted across the globe as a means of organizing legitimate political action among elites. Thus, many postcolonial states either inherited colonial legislatures (with expanded non-European membership) or saw the creation of these institutions right before independence. The lack of economic, social, or political bases for strong legislatures did not hinder this process. The need to be accepted as fully-fledged independent and legitimate states both domestically and internationally drove these countries in the direction of institutional isomorphic mimicry, and to the establishment of legislative institutions that, for the most part, were incongruous with local political economies, social structures, and intra-elite balance of power.[9]

Second, and perhaps more importantly, legislatures provided chief executives in the newly independent states with a mechanism for credible intra-elite commitment and cooperation in the sharing of political power and governance rents.[10] In order to be able to preside over stable political environments in the immediate postindependence period, chief executives needed the cooperation of fellow elites. To this end legislatures provided a ready mechanism for organizing credible intra-elite coordination over policy, allocation of political power, and

---

[9] See DiMaggio and Powell (1983) for a discussion of "institutional isomorphic mimicry" – the idea that organizations adopt specific forms in order to gain legitimacy in their external environment and not necessarily to improve internal coherence and effectiveness. In the specific case of postcolonial states, the colonial inheritance of three branches had a strong influence on common knowledge ideas and assumptions of *how politics works*.

[10] For a discussion of the functional importance of autocratic legislatures, see Gandhi (2008) and Myerson (2008).

the distribution of governance rents. In addition, legislatures enabled postcolonial regimes to institutionalize ascriptive representation at the center (whether ethnic, religious, or geographic) and recruitment of new members into the governing class. It is therefore not surprising that throughout the period under study the majority of countries in Africa (and the world) had open legislatures in any given year (see Figure 1.1).

It is worth noting that from the perspective of postcolonial African chief executives, legislatures came with significant risks. By bringing elites together, they served the crucial function of coordinating intra-elite collective action, thereby raising the cost of reneging on intra-elite pacts. But, while this might have been beneficial in situations where pivotal legislators' preferences coincided with those of chief executives, it was also a threat whenever intractable intra-elite differences arose. In theory, coordinated action among elites serving in a legislature could result in the ouster of unwitting chief executives.

Herein lay the strategic dilemma facing chief executives. As outlined above, legislatures were critical for the maintenance of political stability. However, to secure their tenure in office, chief executives also needed to ensure that the same institutions never became too strong to control. The resultant balancing act, typified by diurnal political contestations over the political autonomy and organizational independence of legislatures, determined the developmental trajectories of postcolonial legislatures. As I show above, chief executives did not always succeed in negotiating this balancing act, and in some cases went as far as abolishing legislatures altogether and ruling by decree.

The fact that only a minority of countries went off the equilibrium path and experienced the abolition of legislatures underscores the importance of this book. The choice for most postcolonial chief executives was seldom whether or not to abolish legislatures. Rather, chief executives sought to control these institutions while also delegating power to them. This historical fact calls for a study of how relatively powerful postcolonial chief executives managed intra-elite politics within legislatures, and how this in turn led to a variation in the observable levels of legislative strength and institutionalization.

Chief executives' strategies of elite control determined the institutional independence and powers of postcolonial legislatures, and their development *over time*. Invariably, chief executives protected their hold on power by only tolerating legislative outcomes that were consistent with their preferences. They did this by exploiting both constitutional and extra-constitutional powers. Through the strategic use of their proposal powers they could limit the feasible set of statutory legislative outcomes. Constitutions also allowed them to formally veto any adverse legislative outcomes. Lastly, they could influence the composition of legislatures by calling for fresh elections, or manipulating the membership of ruling parties that acted as gatekeepers to legislatures. When all failed, some simply abolished legislatures altogether.

1.3 Distinguishing between Means and Ends

To explain the institutional evolution of African legislatures in the shadow of preponderant chief executives, this book distinguishes between legislative *means* and *ends*. My point of departure is that due to the significant power and resource differentials between postcolonial chief executives and legislatures, most African legislatures lacked the ability to compel chief executives to action through statutes. Invariably, these legislatures lacked *ends independence* – the ability to arrive at any legislative outcome that could garner majority support. Stated differently, the feasible set of possible statutory outcomes was predetermined by chief executives.

However, not all postcolonial chief executives were created equal. Specifically, differences in the nature of postcolonial autocratic rule and strategies of legislative control generated variance in the processes through which legislatures produced outcomes that were consistent with the preferences of chief executives. In some countries, legislatures had *means independence* – the ability of legislative majorities to choose specific intra-legislative bargaining arrangements through which to achieve statutory outcomes prescribed by chief executives. Under these conditions, postcolonial legislatures served as focal arenas for intra-elite bargaining, where legislators sought to manage intra-legislative conflicts that ineluctably arose from attempts to negotiate and ultimately aggregate varied interests.

Importantly, means independence incentivized individual legislators to invest in the requisite legislative organizational capacity – rules and procedures and organizational structures – for resolving intra-elite conflicts. From a strategic standpoint, collective bargaining with the chief executive promised to produce commitments that were more credible than individual arrangements. Therefore, individual legislators sought to lower the cost of collective action within legislatures. The result was internal differentiation of legislatures, marked by the development of mechanisms to facilitate and manage intertemporal bargaining in the process of enacting statutes. The reverse was true in contexts where legislatures lacked means independence. In these states chief executives routinely inserted themselves into intra-legislature bargaining processes in attempts to engineer specific statutory outcomes. This constant meddling obviated the need for elites to come up with institutional mechanisms of handling intra-legislative bargaining processes (e.g., enforceable logrolling) and, by extension, to invest in the organizational development of legislatures.

Notice that the statutory outputs from legislatures with means independence and those without were observationally equivalent: they were invariably consistent with the preferences of chief executives (on account of the shared lack of ends independence). But, the process of achieving these outcomes differed. Means independence made legislatures *the main political game in town* among elites, and in turn incentivized elite investment in their organizational and institutional development. Such investments included demanding for more financial resources, increasing the number of legislative sessions, hiring more staff, and the adoption of universalistic parliamentary rules – many of which were inherited from the colonial period. These efforts fostered the evolution of a corporate identity among legislators, and facilitated the process of legislative internal differentiation.

The lack of means independence reduced the political stature of legislatures, and incentivized elites to focus on other loci of power – be they the executive branch, the military, or ruling parties – at the expense of legislatures. Legislatures lacking means independence were organizationally stunted and functioned as constitutional rubber-stamps for extra-legislative bargains. The fact that these legislatures effectively functioned as mere extensions of the executive branch created strong disincentives for elite investment in their organizational development.

Legislative development in postcolonial Kenya and Zambia mirrored these dynamics.[11] For much of their history, both countries'

---

[11] See Gertzel (1970), Mueller (1984), Widner (1992), and Opalo (2014) on legislative development in Kenya; and Scott (1976), Bates (1971), Tordoff (1977*a*), Bratton (1980), and Alderfer (1997) for the case of Zambia.

legislatures lacked ends independence. But, they differed on the dimension of means independence. In Kenya, the decolonization process – marked by the need to counter a war of independence and the proliferation of fractious ethnic parties – resulted in a strong administrative state and a weak independence party. These factors predisposed Kenya's founding president to regulate elite political activity through the administrative structure (and not the party) and to grant the legislature a fair amount of means independence. As such, for much of the first 15 years of independence the Kenyan legislature functioned as an arena for open intra-elite debates over public policy. During this period outcomes of specific parliamentary debates were not necessarily binding on the president. But, they served to structure the bargaining relationship between the legislature and the president. More importantly, having means independence allowed legislators to invest in the organizational capacity of the legislature.

Things were different in Zambia. The decolonization process – marked by racial tension and an intransigent settler population – produced a strong mass party that strengthened Kaunda's ability to not only regulate entry into the legislature, but also to substitute the legislature with the ruling party. As such, much of the lawmaking process occurred within the higher echelons of the ruling party, with the legislature merely existing as a rubber-stamp institution. The ruling party, as opposed to the legislature, was the main game in town. The party served as a focal point for intra-elite bargaining and distribution of rents, and strictly regulated entry into the legislature. Incumbent legislators had therefore very little incentive to invest in the organizational development of the institution.

Across Africa, the general lack of ends independence among post-colonial legislatures led many scholars to dismiss these institutions as uniformly weak and inconsequential to the policymaking process. This conclusion resulted in the scholarly abandonment of legislative studies in Africa for the following four decades. The contention of this book is that while African legislatures shared a general lack of ends independence, they differed on the dimension of means independence. Variations in means independence, and the concomitant variation in legislative organizational development, became apparent following the regime changes that occurred in the region in the early 1990s. The advent of multiparty politics provided legislatures with outside options and reduced chief executives' ability to dictate the political careers of legislators.

The degree to which postautocratic legislatures took advantage of this new-found freedom varied. In countries with a history of legislative means independence, these institutions were able to take full advantage of the political opening and become even stronger and better able to constrain chief executives. Legislatures that lacked means independence before transition lagged in this regard, on account of their organizational underdevelopment. Simply put, organizationally strong autocratic legislatures begat strong democratic legislatures.

1.4 Measuring Legislative Strength

A core claim in this book is that in order to understand the dynamics that drive legislative development in young democracies, we must first understand their development under autocracy as well as the persistent institutional forms and functions that survive democratic transitions. In other words, that historical institutional development matters and regime changes seldom produce the far-reaching institutional discontinuities that most scholars currently assume.

But, studying a slow-moving variable like "institutional development" over time comes with unique challenges. Chief among them is the absence of cross-national panel data on legislative strength. And, even when these data are available, it is often difficult to ascertain the validity of cross-country measures of legislative strength. For example, the existence of de jure separation of powers or legislative control over the budget is often not a guarantee of de facto legislative empowerment. History and political culture typically intervene to produce the realized executive-legislative distribution of power.

In this book I provide a partial solution to this problem by collecting detailed longitudinal data on the Kenyan and Zambian legislatures covering 50 years. I complement these data with different cross-national measures of legislative strength in Africa. At the same time, whenever possible, I disaggregate the available cross-national indices in order to examine specific component measures of legislative strength across different African states.

My dependent variable is the level of legislative strength. My primary independent variable is means independence, as determined by the set of specific strategies that chief executives employ to control and regulate the actions of legislators and legislative outcomes. To identify the effects of means independence on legislative strength in Kenya and Zambia, I rely on two critical junctures precipitated by two main quasi-exogenous factors. These are (i) the decolonization process resulting from the "winds of change" that ended European colonization after World War II; and (ii) the spread of multiparty politics in Africa in the early 1990s that was, in part, driven by domestic protests, the collapse of the Soviet Union and a push for political liberalization by Western donors.

In operationalizing my dependent variable, I focus on both organizational and political measures of legislative strength and institutionalization. In the specific cases of Kenya and Zambia, I collected comparable data on these measures. I measure and quantify legislative strength as (i) the share of executive bills that get passed in the legislature; (ii) the levels and proportions of annual budgetary allocations for the legislature – that includes allocations toward capital investments, staff, research, and remuneration of legislators; (iii) the number of legislative sittings (daily sessions) in a given calendar year – that is an indicator of the amount of plenary time available for parliamentary debates over legislation and other oversight inquiries; (iv) the political independence of individual legislators and their ability to win reelection; and (v) the incidence of presidential rule-making under delegated powers – that is an indicator of the ability of the legislature to regulate unilateral executive action. In addition to these measures, I also compiled cross-national measures of legislative strength from various sources that quantify legislatures' ability to constrain chief executives – including via regulation of the public finance system, calendar autonomy, levels of direct influence on the executive, and overall institutional capacity. In my analyses I use these cross-national data to demonstrate the external validity of the conclusions I derive from the country case studies of Kenya and Zambia.

These micro-level measures map onto broader measures of legislative institutionalization identified by Polsby (1968). These include: (i) *relative boundedness* – the degree of differentiation from the external environment, internal control over budgets and calendars, and barriers to entry (incumbency advantage); (ii) *organizational complexity* – the degree of internal differentiation and division of labor into committees and other organizational organs such as parliamentary budget offices; and (iii) *adherence to internal rules and a universalistic criteria* – the degree to which internal decision-making and procedures are rule-bound and specific parliamentary procedures predictable. I document legislative powers over legislative calendars and budgets, legislators' ability to win reelection, the functional forms of committee systems, and the extent to which Standing Orders and established norms govern the behavior of legislators in Kenya and Zambia.[12]

Using these quantifiable indicators of legislative development and a number of statistical identification strategies, I show how different tactics of autocratic domination influenced legislative development in Africa in general, and Kenya and Zambia in particular. The longitudinal data on legislative development in Kenya and Zambia allow me to examine how predemocratic dynamics of institutional development in turn influenced the posttransition trajectories of the two countries' legislatures. Throughout the book I augment the various statistical analyses with careful qualitative accounts of how differing strategies of presidential domination over fellow elites in Africa structured the conduct of everyday politics in the region. Specifically, I show how elite political behavior in reaction to autocratic presidents influenced legislative development in the region during and after the end of the autocratic period following independence.

This book is therefore also about political development in Africa. The analytical narratives herein illuminate the conditions under which the conduct of everyday intra-elite politics can alter the executive-legislative balance of power in favor of legislatures, despite deliberate attempts by relatively more powerful chief executives to limit legislative development. It is an account of *legislative agency in tight corners* – characterized by constant political contestation to define and redefine the functions and political significance of African legislatures

---

[12] Although this book discusses the logics governing the internal organization of African legislatures, it is not about legislative structure and organization. Nor is it about the specific rules that govern legislative processes. This is not to say that interrogating the industrial organization of African legislatures is not a worthwhile academic exercise (future research should definitely focus on these topics). Rather, this book is about a more elementary aspect of legislatures as institutions: the contested relationship between legislators and chief executives and how these contestations structure legislative institutional development over time. Unlike other students of legislative politics, my analytical approach does not assume the existence of de facto separation of powers. Instead, I endogenize separation of powers in order to explain the emergence of strong and institutionalized legislatures in low-income emerging democracies under the shadow of preponderant chief executives.

over the last 50 years. Beyond the region, the mix of quantitative and detailed qualitative analyses in this book serve to illuminate the nuances of contemporary legislative development in low-income democracies that emerged at the end of European colonization in the mid-twentieth century.

Kenya and Zambia are ideal comparative cases for this study. The two countries have a shared history as British settler colonies with significant Westminster influence on their respective legislatures. Following independence, both countries experienced autocratic single-party rule between the early 1970s and the early 1990s. The two countries are also among a small group of African states that enjoyed relative elite political stability characterized by regular and competitive legislative elections throughout the postcolonial period. Yet, despite these commonalities, the two countries' trajectories of observable levels of legislative development diverged in the early 1990s following the end of single-party rule. The goal of this book is to make sense of this divergence.

1.5 Literature Review

1.5.1 Bringing African Legislatures Back In

The study of legislatures is particularly pertinent in sub-Saharan Africa. While scholars of early postcolonial African politics realized the important role of these institutions (Proctor, 1965; Tordoff, 1965; Stultz, 1968; Hakes, 1970; Helgerson, 1970; Hakes and Helgerson, 1973; Tordoff, 1977*a*), the spread of autocratic rule in the region after the mid-1960s led a shift away from legislatures and an almost exclusive scholastic focus on presidential politics. As a result, much of the African politics literature portrays African presidents as omnipotent centers of power and patronage presiding over personalist neopatrimonial regimes devoid of any institutional checks and balances. Africa's political institutions, and the dynamics of their development, received little attention.[13]

---

[13] As indicated above, the notable exception is the work of Joel D. Barkan and his collaborators. There is a vast literature on personal rule in Africa and the inherent weakness of the region's institutions. See for example Ake (1966); Bretton (1966); Jackson and Rosberg (1982); Callaghy (1984) and Chabal and Daloz (1999).

Yet, as I show in Figure 1.1, even at the height of autocracy in the late 1970s, more than half of African states had functional legislatures in any given year. In other words, African presidents sought to make these inherited legislative institutional forms and practices work in local contexts. In examining legislative development in Africa, this book contributes to the small but growing literature on institutions and the institutionalization of politics in Africa (Posner, 2005; Salih, 2005; Posner and Young, 2007; Barkan, 2009*b*; Opalo, 2012, 2014, 2019).

More broadly, this book uses material evidence from Africa to make two major contributions. First, within the field of Legislative Studies, I expand the scope of analysis of executive-legislative relations to include low-income emerging democracies. In the process, I go beyond current studies that mainly focus on high-income established democracies and explore the motivations behind the industrial organization of legislatures.[14] My account of legislative development in Africa primarily focuses on conceptual issues concerning the nature of interbranch relations and how they structure contemporary legislative development in low-income emerging democracies. Unlike many of these existing works, I do not take separation of powers for granted. Instead, I endogenize legislative independence and examine the conditions under which politically and functionally independent legislatures can emerge out of contested interbranch relations, over time. My approach is informed by the empirical reality that in many emerging democracies the realized nature of interbranch relations does not always mirror formal constitutional separation of powers.

Second, the cases from Africa in this book allow me to synthesize two strands of literature in Comparative Politics that seldom overlap – studies of autocratic institutions on the one hand (Gandhi, 2008; Wright, 2008; Blaydes, 2011; Svolik, 2012); and works on institutional development following transitions to democracy on the other hand (North and Weingast, 1989; O'Donnell, 1998; Acemoglu and Robinson, 2006; Cox, 2012). Consistent with the autocratic institutions literature, I show that autocratic African legislatures were not epiphenomenal. However, my analysis goes

---

[14] See, for example, Mayhew (1974); Weingast and Marshall (1988); Krehbiel (1991); Sin (2015).

further and examines the sources of variation in the strength of autocratic legislatures in Africa. As a contribution to the literature on democratic transition, I show how pretransition patterns of institutional development impacted the posttransition trajectories of continued legislative strengthening and institutionalization in Africa. In other words, that the transition moment is seldom as discontinuous as is currently portrayed in much of the literature on political development.

1.5.2 Contextualizing Legislative Development in History

Another important contribution of this book is to situate legislative development in Africa (and other postcolonial contexts) in historical perspective. Existing works on legislative development overwhelmingly use cases from early modern Western Europe. As such, despite their insightful contribution to our understanding of institutional development in the *longue durée*, they are limited in the extent to which they can explain contemporary legislative development in the new states that emerged out of the decolonization process at the end of World War II.

A brief historicization of legislative development and the associated academic literature is useful in illustrating the need for studies focusing on postcolonial legislatures. Early Modern European parliaments (be they *cortes, diets, estates, sejms, rikstags*, or *bundestags*) emerged out of the political economy of the Middle Ages (Thompson, 1953; Holt, 1992; Maddicott, 2010). The stylized narrative of European parliamentary development is one of kings conceding powers to fellow landowning elites (in proto legislatures) in exchange for their financial and military cooperation. The adoption and development of these legislatures was therefore gradual, organic, and reflected existing balance of power between the monarch and the nobility within the realm. Importantly, the demands of the "fiscal-military state" of the early modern period exposed chief executives to checks and balances from fellow elites who controlled material resources, including those serving in the newly empowered legislatures (Edling, 2003). Mass politics (through the extension of suffrage) followed after centuries in which the object of legislatures (intra-elite political and fiscal accountability) was consistent with the actual distribution of political power (only property owners had the vote).[15] In other words, the development and maturation of intra-elite accountability through legislatures preceded the spread of mass politics under universal suffrage.

This was not the case in postcolonial states, many of which inherited overdeveloped executive branches of government largely modeled on the United States presidency, but without the strong powers of the United States Congress (Loewenstein, 1949; Ojwang, 1980; Mezey, 2013). The political economies of these countries also worked against the emergence of strong legislatures. Whereas in an earlier time in Europe the monarch needed fellow elites for revenue, in the new post-colonial states the chief executives controlled the flow of patronage to fellow elites (Joseph, 1987; Arriola, 2009). To compound matters, the early adoption of mass politics meant that chief executives could circumvent any checks from fellow elites by engaging in direct vote-buying while at the same time limiting the ability of the same elites to establish independent bases of political power.[16] Without relying on chief executives, few legislators could meet the demands of clientelistic politics that characterized postcolonial Africa (Barkan, 1979).[17]

---

[15] In a comparative review of the rise of legislatures, van Zanden, Buringh, and Bosker (2012) note the importance of fragmented sovereignty in shaping the evolution of European parliaments. In particular, they show how control over revenue empowered these institutions. Even in these formative stages, rulers with independent access to resources – such as Spain after 1500 (riches from the Americas), France after 1439 (local taxes), and Denmark after 1497 (proceeds from the Sound toll) – tended to severely limit legislative powers or simply abolish parliaments relative to their less fiscally-autonomous counterparts.

[16] Huntington (1968) was the first to highlight the dangers of mass political mobilization in a context of weak institutions. The same dangers obtain in the case of legislative politics. Under certain conditions mass-based politics can serve to weaken rather than strengthen legislative institutions.

[17] In this regard Japan's domestication of European legislative institutional forms and functions is instructive. According to Fraser, Mason, and Mitchell (1995), part of the reason the young legislature (established in 1890) was able to effectively check the executive branch was because early Japanese parliaments were a "genuine culmination of Japanese as well as Western experience" (pp. 5–8). In other words, in Japan, and unlike in African colonies, European institutional forms and practices were grafted on top of entrenched Japanese ideas of dynastic sovereignty and social hierarchies. For example, under Japan's founding legislature 60 percent of government revenue came from land taxes; and property qualifications meant that at least half of elected legislators were landlords. This situation meant that those with the most economic power also had the political means to keep the Japanese prime minister in check (p. 31).

These differences in intra-branch relationships between Early Modern Europe and the postcolonial era call for a different model of legislative development in low-income emerging democracies. Building on existing works, this book historicizes legislative development in postcolonial states, while at the same time shedding new light on the dynamics of legislative evolution under mass politics in the shadow of fiscally autonomous and structurally "overdeveloped" executive branches.

Finally, this book emphasizes the importance of understanding the time dimension of legislative development. Following the introduction of new institutions, it takes time for important actors to internalize the rules and develop the organizational and political culture needed to make them work (Pierson, 2004). And, even when institutional discontinuities occur at critical junctures, continued legislative development builds on existing cognitive models and political habits developed prior to discontinuities. Established fundamental principles of *how politics works* are seldom suspended even amidst tumultuous periods of rapid change. New institutional forms and functions are often layered onto or in parallel to the old (Thelen, 2004, p. 217).[18]

1.5.3 Legislative Development under Autocracy and Democracy

This book also contributes to the literature on autocratic institutions. Partly in response to the (over)emphasis of mass-based electoral democracy as a precondition for legislative institutional development, the last decade saw the emergence of a sizable literature on autocratic institutions. The emerging consensus is that autocratic institutions are not mere window dressing, but matter for a variety of reasons. Autocratic institutions serve as arenas for policy negotiation (Lust-Okar, 2005; Gandhi, 2008), help enhance regime durability and the control of elites (Geddes, 1999; Sassoon, 2012), provide opportunities for the

---

[18] For instance, the much-celebrated ascent of the English parliament following the "Glorious Revolution" of 1688 had deep historical antecedents spanning centuries of baronial efforts to constrain the English monarchy – including by men like Simon de Montfort and Oliver Cromwell who went as far as waging war against the monarchy (Maddicott, 1994; Pincus, 2009). Indeed, the consolidation of the revolution's achievements went on for decades well after 1688. In the African context, Barkan (2009a) observes that "the legislature rarely matters as an institution until after the second or third multiparty election, and thus after the transition from authoritarian to democratic rule has been underway for an extended period" (p. 2).

sharing of power and governance rents (Blaydes, 2011), and are ready mechanisms for enhancing intra-elite collective action and general credible commitment in nondemocracies (Magaloni, 2006; Myerson, 2008; Svolik, 2009). The importance of autocratic institutions is borne out in the data. Dictatorships that have legislatures engage in relatively lower levels of rent-seeking (Boix, 2003); face a lower risk of regime collapse (Brownlee, 2007; Gandhi and Przeworski, 2007; Svolik, 2012; Boix and Svolik, 2013); and exhibit higher rates of private investment and economic growth (Wright, 2008; Gehlbach and Keefer, 2012). This strand of research has increased our knowledge of why some autocrats govern with institutions while others do not.

Building upon this important body of work, this book examines both the causes of variation in the strength of autocratic institutions and the conditions under which strong democratic institutions can emerge from their autocratic foundations. As Figure 1.1 shows, for most autocrats the question is whether or not to govern with an institution (such as a legislature). Rather, most autocrats have had to decide how much influence to grant to these institutions in everyday affairs of state. Put differently, *institutionalized autocracy is a continuous, not dichotomous, variable.* Why do some autocrats tolerate legislative organizational development – by allowing for means independence – while others do not? And, how does legislative development under autocracy impact posttransition trajectories of these institutions? The answers to these questions provide an important bridge across the current analytical gap between scholars of autocratic and democratic institutions.

Consider the example of the Chilean legislature. In the decade after transition to democracy "authoritarian enclaves" persisted and "the president [was] the most important legislative actor, and perhaps the most important legislator" (Siavelis, 2002, p. 84). After Augusto Pinochet seized power in a coup in 1973 he set about consolidating his hold onto power and normalizing his rule through the establishment of institutions. For example, between 1973 and 1987 the share of civilians in his cabinet rose from 13% to 71% (Remmer, 1989, p. 158). In 1980, Pinochet inaugurated a new constitution whose effects would last beyond his dictatorship. Designed to keep the legislature weak, the 1980 constitution protected presidential prerogatives. For instance, presidential monopoly on the origination of money bills kept the

Chilean legislatures "starved for staff and infrastructure" (Londregan, 2000, p. 66).

In addition, various articles of the Organic Law of Congress granted the president significant powers in the lawmaking process. The president could amend laws once passed. He could also apply a deadline to force a vote on presidential initiatives in the legislature. This robbed the institution of the option of allowing unfavorable legislation to die in committee, a strategy common in most legislatures.[19] Pinochet's more democratic successors in the *Concertación por la Democracia* found these robust presidential powers irresistible, and used them to effect greater coordination between the executive and the legislature (Fuentes, 2015). It is only in 2005 that significant constitutional reforms of the post-Pinochet institutional dispensation became possible.

The Chilean experience shows that in order to understand the underlying dynamics behind legislative institutional development, one needs to go beyond the transition moment. The developmental trajectory of the post-1989 Chilean legislature had deep roots going back to both the democratic (1925–1973) and autocratic (1973–1989) periods (Zucco, 2007).[20] Even after the end of autocracy, Chile maintained its "exaggerated presidential system" – albeit tempered by moderate postauthoritarian presidents – due to developments in the preceding authoritarian period (Siavelis, 2002). It is also worth reiterating that the reform process leading up to 2005 took place largely within the institutional framework established by Pinochet. Chile's democratic legislature had deep autocratic roots.

The example of Chile reinforces one of the central claims of this book: that in order to understand legislative development in emerging democracies, we need to interrogate their autocratic foundations. Therefore, while the empirical evidence and analytical narratives

---

[19] For example between 1990 and 1993, 70.2 percent of presidential initiatives were completed by the legislature compared to only 13 percent of initiatives originating from Congress. A total of 63.4 percent of presidential initiatives became law, compared to just 6.8 percent of Congressional initiatives (Siavelis, 2002, pp. 85–86).

[20] Internal rules of the Chilean legislature grant the president substantial influence over specific issue areas like salaries, taxes, budgets; as well as ability to set the legislative agenda both directly and indirectly via expansive urgency provisions and veto-amendment powers (Londregan, 2000).

in this book primarily come from postcolonial African states, the model of legislative development herein has external validity in other contexts outside the region. In the next section I summarize the argument that motivates the empirical project in this book.

1.6 The Argument

1.6.1 A Two-Way Intra-Elite Balance of Power

Organizationally strong and politically independent legislatures necessarily limit the discretionary powers of chief executives. In presidential systems, chief executives' interest in maximizing their discretionary authority (regardless of regime type) creates incentives for limiting legislative organizational strength and political autonomy. This means that for horizontal accountability to obtain, legislatures must be in a position to resist attempts by chief executives to limit legislative strength and political autonomy. The realized degree of constitutional separation of powers relies on the enforceability of legislative political autonomy from the executive branch.

This reality creates two basic problems for chief executives. First, it is costly to govern without legislatures. This (as argued above) is primarily due to the established *Montesquieuian* norm of separation of powers along functional lines, and the need for credible intra-elite commitment in order to elicit cooperation from fellow elites. Second, by governing with legislatures – and thereby giving an institutional expression to intra-elite cooperation – chief executives expose themselves to the risk of ouster by fellow elites. This is because legislatures effectively lower the cost of intra-elite collective action, a fact that makes it easier for elites to plot against chief executives that renege on their promises. In summary, while chief executives need legislatures to govern, they also have strong incentives to limit the power and influence of these institutions. The quotidian politics that underly this contested intra-elite relationship conditions the realized interbranch balance of power and the nature of executive-legislative relations.

Elites serving as legislators have strong incentives to stay in office and to strengthen their collective bargaining power. While in office, they get direct remuneration, potential preferential access to public resources for private gain, and general psychic benefits of being a representative of their respective constituencies. These specific benefits make it such that there is a nontrivial opportunity cost to not being in office. Thus, once in office elites make the requisite investments among the electorate (i.e., perform constituency service) with a view to retaining their seats in the legislature. The dual goals of working to retain membership in the legislature and bargaining for access to shared governance rents create incentives for incumbent legislators to invest in the organizational strength and political independence of legislatures. This is for the simple reason that outcomes of collective bargaining with the chief executive are more credible than bilateral deals. Chief executives stand to incur greater costs for reneging on the former deals relative to the latter.

Investing in legislative organizational strength and political independence entails ensuring that the institutions have adequate material resources for remuneration of legislators and constituency service, the financing of legislative activities such as drafting of bills, committee sittings, and research, and the hiring of well-trained staff. Legislative political independence encompasses calendar autonomy (time is a valuable resource in the legislative process), internally determined parliamentary rules governing intertemporal bargains, selection of the legislative leadership, and general intra-legislative agenda control. Organizational strength and political independence provide elites with the requisite resources to balance chief executives and strengthen the credibility of the established bargains governing intra-elite and interbranch relations.

Given these competing incentives, executive-legislative relations are inherently conflictual. Two key logics drive this outcome. First, individual legislators and chief executives have separate mandates. In states with presidential systems of government and low legislative district magnitudes, the modal legislator is typically elected from a localized constituency. Chief executives on the other hand are elected by the entire national electorate. By construction, the preferences of the pivotal voters at the constituency and national levels seldom coincide. And, as a corollary, the policy preferences of chief executives and individual legislators do not always converge. Second, the system of horizontal accountability that underpins interbranch relations is inherently zero sum. Strong legislatures necessarily limit the discretionary authority of chief executives. The reverse is also true. Executive preponderance invariably comes at the expense of legislative influence on public policy and on the distribution of governance rents between the chief executive and fellow elites.

At the same time, chief executives enjoy immense structural advantages over legislatures. Their control over large bureaucracies results in significant informational and expertise asymmetries relative to legislatures. Their stature as heads of state grants them agenda-setting powers in the eyes of the electorate. And, in the case of most low-income countries, weak institutional checks on public finance systems mean that chief executives typically have unfettered control over state budgets. These structural advantages mean that enforcement of horizontal accountability is often met with resistance by chief executives from a position of relative strength. And, so while the electoral imperative incentivizes individual legislators to invest in legislative organizational empowerment and political autonomy, the need to maximize executive discretion incentivizes chief executives to limit legislative empowerment and political autonomy. The outcome of this contestation determines the realized interbranch separation of powers and, by extension, legislative independence and strength.

From the foregoing discussion it is obvious why legislative strength hinges on the relative balance of power between elites (particularly those serving as legislators) and chief executives. It is also obvious why legislatures founded under the shadow of strong chief executives may have a harder time acquiring the organizational capacity and political independence that is required in order to be able to enforce intra-elite horizontal accountability. In other words, the institutional development of legislatures mirrors prevailing patterns of intra-elite balance of power.

Time and timing also matter. Organizational development and general institutionalization take time. Older legislatures are more likely to enjoy significant powers vis-à-vis chief executives relative to their younger counterparts – in part due to the constraining effects of established processes and political culture. In addition, due to institutional path dependence, the prevailing intra-elite balance of power around founding moments of legislatures matters. Legislatures founded in periods when power is sufficiently dispersed among elites (like in medieval England) are likely evolve into institutions capable of enforcing horizontal accountability, despite the structural informational and agenda-setting imbalances outlined above. Those founded in periods of executive branch ascendance (like in most postcolonial states) face the challenge of having to play catch-up against chief executives that control the very resources (material resources and political autonomy) that they need to achieve interbranch political parity.

1.6.2 Means Independence and Institutional Development

Chief executives' strategies of managing the threat posed by elites in legislatures determine the trajectories of their development under relatively "overdeveloped" executive branches. Some predominantly focus on engineering incentive-compatible outcomes *within the legislature* – for instance, by inserting themselves in internal legislative processes or directly influencing the composition of legislatures by manipulating elections. By treating legislatures as extensions of the executive branch, such chief executives deny legislatures means independence. This is in contrast to chief executives that predominantly use *extra-legislative* strategies of monitoring and regulating legislators – such as vetoes or promises of development projects. Legislatures facing such chief executives operate under relative internal autonomy. Importantly, the lack of direct executive interference enables legislative means independence and incentivizes individual legislators to invest in the development of legislative organizational capacity.

The outcomes of both strategies are observationally equivalent. Under conditions of executive preponderance, legislatures in both scenarios lack ends independence and legislative outcomes invariably mirror the preferences of chief executives. Yet, their respective effects on legislative institutional development are different. In the former case, routinized executive interference produces organizationally stunted legislatures. Under these conditions, legislators see now value in investing in issue expertise in committees, institutional memory, predictable internal rules and mechanisms for aggregating policy preferences, or legislative careers. In short, the lack of means independence militates against legislative institutionalization.

Means independence and the lack of direct executive interference incentivizes individual legislators to invest in internal organizational mechanisms for handling intra-elite debates, coalition politics, and intertemporal bargaining arrangements. Operational autonomy – even without ends independence – allows legislatures to develop a corporate identity distinct from the executive branch. And, over time, legislatures with means independence become the main arenas of intra-elite bargaining, acquire greater political significance, and hence see improvements in institutional strength. Individual elites have incentives to increase their collective institutional authority for the simple reason that it is costlier for chief executives to abrogate agreements with the legislature than with individual legislators.

Chief executives' ability to effectively monitor, regulate, and balance fellow elites acting collectively in legislatures (executive power), determines their willingness to grant legislatures means independence. Moderately independent legislatures come with significant risks. Empowered elites acting collectively in the legislature may vote to reduce the power of chief executives, redistribute governance rents, override their vetoes, or remove them from office. Thus, only politically secure chief executives – confident in their ability to win any open conflicts with legislators – are able to take the risk of granting legislatures means independence. For this reason, legislative means independence is positively correlated with levels of executive power. Factors that may enhance executive power and bolster chief executives' political security include established political culture, regime legitimacy, or effective administrative means of elite monitoring and regulation as well as coup-proofing.

Critical junctures, such as when countries transition from autocracy to democracy, may reveal these underlying organizational differences among autocratic legislatures. In theory, democratic politics facilitates legislative strengthening by reducing the power of chief executives. Under democracy, executive-legislative relations are typically governed by the dictates of persuasion rather than coercion. However, the historical organizational strength of legislatures conditions the impact of democratic transitions on legislative strength and independence. Legislatures with a history of means independence under autocracy are more likely to exhibit greater strength and independence following transition to democracy. This is for the simple reason that it takes time to develop the requisite organizational and operational capacity and intra-elite political culture needed to elevate the stature and influence of legislatures. Established notions of *how legislatures work* often survive democratic transitions. And, it is for these reasons that strong autocratic legislatures often beget strong democratic legislatures.

1.6.3 Empirical Implications

This analytically straightforward conceptualization of legislative development, over time, has important advantages. First, it coherently explains legislative development under both autocracy and democracy. Second, it models legislative development in postcolonial contexts under fiscally autonomous and "overdeveloped" chief executives. Finally, it synthesizes the literatures on autocratic institutions and democratic transitions. This increases our understanding of the important role of legislatures as institutional anchors of democratic consolidation.

A number of empirically testable implications emerge from this conceptualization of legislative development. Autocratic chief executives capable of effectively regulating extra-legislative elite political activity and credibly vetoing legislative outcomes should be more likely to preside over relatively autonomous legislatures (with means independence). These legislatures should also have relatively higher levels of organizational development – including higher budgets and remuneration of legislators, relatively more sessions per year, and bigger staff. In addition, we should observe lower rates of passage of executive bills in such legislatures. This is because the process of intra-legislative debates and bargains may reveal new or unanticipated information on the demerits of executive bills, leading to their abandonment. In this manner means independence reduces chief executives' ability to perfectly predict the outcomes of intra-legislative bargains. Finally, chief executives who are confident enough to grant legislatures means independence should also be less likely to interfere in legislative elections or engage in unilateral executive actions through rule-making.

Following transition from autocracy to electoral democracy, we should observe a greater likelihood of legislatures that enjoyed means independence under autocracy to emerge relatively stronger and independent. Relatively high levels of organizational capacity and autonomy at the moment of transition ought to increase the likelihood of legislatures taking advantage of the greater political freedoms available under electoral democracy. In other words, we should observe a faster shift toward the deepening of means independence and attainment of ends independence among these legislatures relative to their counterparts that lacked means independence under autocracy.

Throughout this book I empirically evaluate these claims as well as other ancillary observable implications with cross-country data from Africa as well as detailed qualitative and quantitative examinations of the Kenyan and Zambian legislatures.

1.7 The Plan of the Book

The rest of this book expands on the questions and arguments presented in this chapter. In Chapter 2, I document the variation in legislative institutionalization and strength in Africa and interrogate the historical and political causes of this variation. In Chapter 3 I outline a model of legislative development under autocracy and democracy, specifying the logics of executive-legislative relations, the associated incentive schemes, and how everyday intra-elite politics impacts legislative development.

Building on the insights in Chapter 2 and the theoretical grounding of Chapter 3, the next three chapters focus on the empirical evidence and specific causal mechanisms driving observed differences in legislative strength and institutionalization in Kenya and Zambia. The analytical narratives in Chapter 4 provide a detailed comparative study of the colonial origins of the Kenyan and Zambian legislatures. The chapter also examines the specific ways in which political developments in the late colonial period put the two countries' legislatures on different trajectories of institutional development. Chapter 5 focuses on postcolonial legislative development in Kenya and Zambia and documents how presidents' ability to monitor, regulate, and balance fellow elites' political activity impacted their willingness to tolerate legislative means independence. To this end I analyze the effectiveness of ruling parties and provincial administrative apparatuses – two important institutions used by presidents in both countries to propagate their power and balance fellow elites.

In Chapter 6 I present original data on legislative characteristics and outputs in Kenya and Zambia. These include the number of legislative sittings, the number of bills introduced to the legislature and the share passed, the remuneration of legislators, budget allocations for legislative functions, and the exercise of delegated executive rule-making authority. These data highlight two important facts. First, the Kenyan legislature enjoyed means independence under autocracy and was relatively more autonomous compared to its Zambian counterpart. As such, it enjoyed a higher level of organizational development on the eve of transition to democracy. Second, significant structural breaks occurred around the time of transition to democracy in both countries. However, the postautocratic transition toward a more institutionalized democratic legislature was faster in Kenya than in Zambia. I attribute this to the difference in levels of organizational capacity between the two legislatures on the eve of transition to multiparty electoral politics.

Chapter 7 examines the electoral origins of legislative strength. Being the primary means of gaining membership in legislatures, elections are an important pillar of legislative strength. Politically independent legislators are more likely to use legislative institutional authority to check executive power. In this chapter I examine how changes in executive-legislative relations in the early 1990s impacted Kenyan and Zambian incumbents' ability to cultivate independence bases of political support (i.e., a personal vote), and to win reelection. To do so I employ a regression discontinuity design to estimate the electoral advantage accrued by incumbents on account of being in office (incumbency advantage), relative to comparable challengers. I find that the transition to multiparty electoral politics enabled some legislators to cultivate a personal vote independent of presidents in both countries, thereby entrenching the political independence of the two legislatures.

In Chapter 8 I conclude with discussions of both the scholastic and practical implications of the findings in this book. I begin by providing a framework through which social scientists ought to study contemporary legislative institutional development in postcolonial states. I then discuss practical implications of this book for democracy promotion programs focused on legislative strengthening, and emphasize the need to invest in both the organizational (capacity) and political bases of legislative institutionalization and strength.

2 | *Legislative Development in Africa*

2.1 Common Origins, Divergent Outcomes

African legislatures, in their contemporary institutional expression as elective national institutions, are colonial transplants.[1] As such, many exhibit similar institutional forms and functions as European legislatures. These include the manner of their composition (electoral rules), their specific constitutional powers, the rules and norms governing executive-legislative relations, and internal parliamentary rules of procedure (as outlined in Standing Orders or *Réglement Intérieur*).

At the same time, after half a century of independence, these imported legislatures have become African by evolving to reflect the realities of their local contexts and political economies.[2] This chapter examines the historical development of African legislatures with a view of showing how postcolonial states localized imported European

---

[1] The assemblies of precolonial African states and chiefdoms were largely superseded by the legislative institutions created during European colonization. To the extent that these precolonial assemblies survived the colonial experience, they existed as subordinate subnational institutions with limited influence over policy. Many of these institutions also maintained their specific subnational ethnocultural characters. See, for example, Kuper (1983), Wrigley (1996), Evans-Pritchard (1971), and Tibenderana (1988) for descriptions of different precolonial councils in present-day South Africa, Uganda, South Sudan, and Nigeria, respectively.

[2] Fletcher-Cooke (1966) makes the useful distinction between contemporary states where European legislative institutional forms went as "accompanied baggage" and states where they went as "export[s]" (p. 145). The former signified European offshoots in the Americas and the antipodes. The latter included European colonies in much of the Global South, including much of Africa (with the exception of South Africa). This distinction is important. As noted in the previous chapter, the literature on legislative development is dominated by studies of either European legislatures or states where these institutional forms were transplanted as "accompanied baggage." This book examines the development of exported legislatures in relatively unfamiliar sociopolitical terrains.

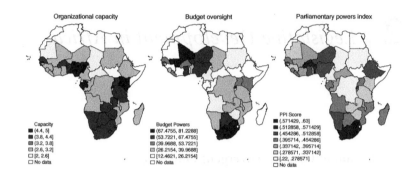

Figure 2.1 Variation in capacity and legislative powers

Notes: Darker shades represent higher levels of legislative capacity and powers. The indicator of organizational capacity captures calendar control and access to resources. Budget oversight covers the level of legislative input in the national budgetary process, and is an average score between 2006 and 2012. The parliamentary powers index covers legislative capacity, autonomy, constitutional powers, and levels of executive influence. These data are from Fish and Kroenig (2009) and the International Open Budget Surveys, available here: www.internationalbudget.org/.

institutional forms and practices. I provide a qualitative comparative account of the key dynamics that informed the adaptation of inherited colonial legislatures and quantitatively analyze the determinants of legislative institutionalization and strength in Africa. My goal here is not to provide an exhaustive historical account, but rather to adumbrate the general principles that have driven legislative development and institutionalization in Africa over the last 50 years.

Figure 2.1 shows the variation in levels of legislative institutionalization and strength generated by the processes of adapting inherited colonial legislative institutional forms and practices in different African states. These variations exist whether measured by de jure or de facto indicators of legislative institutionalization and strength. A core goal of this book is to explain this variation and situate legislative development in Africa in a historical context. As I show below, the observable levels of legislative institutionalization and strength in the region are a result of the interaction between colonial legacies and postcolonial intra-elites politics.

2.2 Colonial Origins of Modern African Legislatures

After their establishment, territory-wide colonial legislatures quickly superseded existing precolonial African elite-level assemblies or councils. A number of centralized precolonial African states and chiefdoms had assemblies or councils that kept their respective rulers in check – through established rules governing the leadership selection process, norms of intra-elite political accountability, or, in some extreme cases, impeachment powers. However, because of the blurred lines between religious, executive, and lawmaking authority in most of precolonial Africa, these institutions operated very differently from contemporary conventional notions of executive-legislative relations and balance of powers. They were also largely limited to specific ethnic and cultural groups.

Examples of precolonial African legislative institutions include the Baganda *Lukiiko*, the councillors of Nguni chiefdoms in Southern Africa, the *Kgotlas* of the Tswana chieftaincies in Botswana, the Lozi *Khotla* (National Council) in western Zambia, and the Kotoko Council in the Ashanti Confederacy, to name a few.[3] In nearly all cases membership to these institutions was through appointment or inheritance. In addition, their policy input was fairly minimal on account of the limited capacities and administrative scope of Africa's precolonial states (Saad, 1983; Vansina, 2004).[4]

European invasion and colonization in the late nineteenth century necessitated the creation of colony-wide advisory councils, including exclusively African assemblies and European-dominated legislative councils. The majority-African assemblies typically existed at the subterritorial level were modeled on essentialist European notions of "traditional" African institutions, and dealt primarily with African

---

[3] For discussions on precolonial states, chiefdoms, and assemblies in Africa, see Arhin (1967), Proctor (1968), Twaddle (1969), Chanaiwa (1980), and Hjort (2010). A number of African countries have constitutions that recognize these historical institutions by having ceremonial Upper Houses of legislatures populated by chiefs. For recent studies of the role of chiefs in contemporary African politics, see Koter (2013) and Baldwin (2015).

[4] It is worth noting that a number of precolonial African assemblies had considerable power and influence over policy positions taken by kings. Perhaps the best example of this was the Ashanti Confederacy in which the King had to consult fellow elites before major policy decisions, and "aristocrats could interfere in all foreign politics, and even possessed the right to veto the king's decision" (Tordoff, 1962, p. 409). As a reflection of the power of precolonial chiefs in Ghana, in 1852 they reacted to the creation of a colonial Legislative Council two years earlier by establishing the "Legislative Assembly of Native Chiefs upon the Gold Coast" that claimed to make laws binding upon everyone in the protectorate (Wight, 1947).

affairs.[5] In both the settler and nonsettler colonies, the official territorial legislative councils were initially dominated by European immigrants and commercial interests (see Table 2.1). In French West Africa people of mixed race, "métis," were also granted rights of political participation (Jones, 2013). In the ensuing six decades parallel political development among Africans and European immigrants took place under the shadow of colonial institutions, including legislatures. Racial segregation in the early colonial legislatures triggered African political mobilization for direct representation and against discriminatory laws and policies. European majorities in colonial legislatures invariably supported policies that gave them access to subsidized land and conscript African labor and protected their monopsonies. These policies were in conflict with African interests. As chief executives, colonial governors adjudicated competing interests among Europeans and Africans and between them (Berry, 1992). Their commitment to advancing European interests in the colonies notwithstanding, they also had to maintain political order among Africans eager to advance their political and economic interests. On occasion, this latter role often forced them to shield Africans from extreme forms of European exploitation.[6]

---

[5] In parallel with these African councils were systems of "Native Authorities," legal regimes, and field administrations under British indirect rule. French direct rule (after 1904) relied on the *indigénat* system that permitted administrators to render draconian punishments against Africans without recourse to a court of law (whether European or "customary"). Portugal's *Regime do Indigénat* was similarly racist, and denied Africans equal protection before the law. It is worth noting that even under direct French rule, precolonial chiefs and authorities retained their powers or were incorporated into the field administration system. For example, the Mossi Kingdom in Upper Volta (Burkina Faso) retained its king, the Moro Naba. For the most part, colonial administrative systems sought to graft European hegemony onto African "Customary Law" as a means of governing on the cheap (Mann and Roberts, 1991; Berry, 1992; Spear, 2003). The British Colonial Service was staffed mainly by Oxbridge graduates. The French colonial service recruited among graduates of the École Coloniale in Paris (Dresang, 1975).

[6] While the racial cleavage was the most dominant under colonialism, it is important to note that political development in colonial Africa also revealed significant differences among Africans and Europeans. Mosley (1983), for example, documents divisions among European immigrants in colonial Kenya. Similarly, Wight (1947) documents intra-Africa divisions in the Gold Coast (colonial Ghana). And, in Senegal Jones (2013) documents the divisions that emerged between European trading interests, *métis* and *évolué* Africans in the urban communes, and rural Africans. Indeed, colonial governors also played an important role of protecting Africans from the excesses of the many "native"

Table 2.1 *The founding of legislatures and African membership*

County	Founded	African Membership	County	Founded	African Membership
Angola	1955	1955	Malawi	1932	1949
Benin	1904	1946	Mali	1904	1946
Botswana	1920	1920	Mauritania	1920	1920
Burkina Faso	1921	1921	Mauritius	1831	1926
Burundi	1961	1961	Mozambique	1967	1974
Cameroon	1946	1946	Namibia	1920	1978
Cape Verde	1961	1975	Niger	1922	1959
CAR	1908	1948	Nigeria	1922	1922
Chad	1910	1946	Rwanda	1960	1960
Congo-Brazzaville	1908	1946	Sao Tome and Principe	1951	1951
Cote d'Ivoire	1893	1960	Senegal	1848	1914
Djibouti	1946	1946	Seychelles	1790	1790
Equatorial Guinea	1959	1959	Sierra Leone	1807	1924
Eritrea	1991	1991	Somalia	1957	1957
Ethiopia	1931	1931	South Africa	1854	1854
Gabon	1908	1946	South Sudan	1948	1948
Gambia	1901	1901	Sudan	1948	1948
Ghana	1925	1925	Swaziland	1921	1964
Guinea	1895	1895	Tanganyika	1926	1958
Guinea-Bissau	1974	1974	Togo	1955	1955
Kenya	1907	1944	Uganda	1920	1945
Lesotho	1884	1884	Zambia	1924	1948
Liberia	1838	1951	Zanzibar	1926	1926
Madagascar	1946	1946	Zimbabwe	1899	1968

Notes: Liberia and Ethiopia were never colonized. Ethiopia was an absolutist empire until the 1931 constitution created a legislature. Liberia, founded by freed slaves in 1822, first admitted indigenous elites to its legislature in 1951, 104 years after it declared independence in 1847. Before the founding of the national legislatures, councils with limited coastal jurisdiction in Ghana and Nigeria were established in 1850 and 1862, respectively. For countries that had multiple colonial powers (e.g., Cameroon, Somalia, and Tanganyika), the dates indicated correspond to legislative development under the last dominant colonial power before independence. African membership is determined by indigeneity of individual legislators. In South Africa, ethnic Afrikaaners meet the autochthony test. I am grateful to James Fearon and David Laitin for their generosity in sharing data on colonial legislatures. Any errors herein are my own.

In order for governors to retain their ultimate authority, the early
colonial legislatures lacked ends independence. As Ojwang (1980)
observes, "the legislator was the Governor himself, rather than the
council, the latter's role being purely advisory" (p. 300).[7] Having
lost their relatively autonomous colonies in the Americas, European powers resorted to closer control of their African colonies
via absolutist governors. The lack of ends independence stunted
the institutional development of colonial legislatures in much of
Africa. However, in a number of cases – most among British settler
colonies – colonial legislatures had means independence that allowed
for their internal organizational development. In order to effectively
manage the emerging conflicts among the increasingly differentiated
classes of colonial immigrants (farmers, commercial interests, missionaries, and administrators) and the majority African populations
they governed, these institutions developed rules, norms, and habits
of parliamentary practice that were suited to their respective political
economies. As noted above, the duty of colonial administrators was
to cater to European immigrants' economic interests and exploitation
of Africans, subject to the constraint of maintaining political order.
The extent to which this happened through colonial legislatures
conditioned these institutions' organizational development.

On average, British colonies in Africa saw the establishment of
territorial legislatures much earlier than their French counterparts
(see Table 2.1). There were virtually no legislatures in Portuguese
and Spanish colonies. At independence nearly all French colonies had
experienced territorial assemblies for only 14 years. The average for
British colonies was 58.6 years. Informed by its experience in the
Americas, the British Colonial Office (Whitehall) promptly created
LegCos in its Crown Colonies and Protectorates in Africa. The French
policy of direct representation of colonies in Paris obviated the need
for territorial legislatures in the early colonial period.

administrations that were created and empowered under colonialism and
whose leadership quickly shook off most of the sociocultural constraints on
authority that existed before the arrival of European colonization.

[7] This fusion of the executive, judicial, and legislative powers extended
throughout the colonial administration. Colonial district administrative officers
were governments unto themselves. For example, under the indigénat system,
French administrators were at once the "police, magistrate, prosecutor, and
jailer" (Mann and Roberts, 1991, p. 17).

There was also significant variation in the age of legislatures across different colonies of the same European powers. For example, among British colonies the experience with legislatures ranged from 157 years in Sierra Leone to a mere 8 years in Sudan. Among French colonies, the first elective colonial assembly was established in St. Louis, Senegal, in 1840 (Idowu, 1968, p. 265). By contrast, other French possessions in both French West Africa (AOF) and French Equatorial Africa (AEF) saw the establishment of territorial legislatures (*conseils généraux*) for the first time after 1946, more than a century later.[8] In general, the institutionalization of French colonial rule in AEF lagged AOF.[9] Indeed, as late as 1929 much of AEF was still run by private concessionaires with the support of a skeletal public administrative structure (Thomson and Adloff, 1960; Manning, 1998). Even within AOF French hegemony was constantly challenged. For instance, full conquest of Upper Volta (Burkina Faso) was only achieved after the suppression of a tax revolt in 1934 (Morgenthau, 1964). Furthermore, after the

---

[8] The four communes of Dakar, Saint-Louis, Goree, and Rufisque in Senegal had appointed local officials and a representative in the French National Assembly as early as 1848. All of them were either European or mixed-race residents of Senegal's four communes. It would take until 1914 for the first African Senegalese – Blaise Diagne – to be elected to the French National Assembly (Johnson, 1966). A colony-wide *conseil général* was established in 1879. Accompanying the establishment of the *conseil général* in St. Louis was the creation of the *conseil d'arrondissement* in Goree. Both assemblies were abolished in the aftermath of the 1848 revolutionary upheavals in metropolitan France. Advisory administrative councils (that included appointed nominal African representation) were formed in 1920. After World War II, the French constitution of 1946 granted French colonies in Africa a complex tapestry of representative institutions, including at the territorial level, the federation level (in Saint-Louis and Brazzaville), as well as representatives in the metropolitan National Assembly in Paris. See Thomson and Adloff (1960), Hodgkin and Schachter (1961), Idowu (1968), and Chafer (2002).

[9] French colonial possessions in Africa were divided into two federations. AOF was created in 1895 and included Cote d'Ivoire, Dahomey (Benin), French Sudan (Mali), Guinea, Mauritania, Niger, Senegal, and Upper Volta (Burkina Faso). Togo became part of AOF after World War I. AEF was created in 1910 and included Chad, Congo (Congo-Brazzaville), Gabon, and Ubangi-Shari (Central African Republic). Each territory within the AOF and AEF had a lieutenant governor, with Governors-General stationed at the federation capitals in Dakar and Brazzaville, respectively. After 1934 AEF became a unitary state with the different territories governed as regions. Cameroon became part of AEF after World War I.

establishment of territorial assemblies in 1946, the French legislature in Paris retained nearly all lawmaking authority. This reality made the metropolitan legislature in Paris, and not the territorial assemblies, the focus of francophone West Africa's emerging African political elites.[10]

British colonies in Africa had a different experience. They were typically not considered to be integral parts of the United Kingdom and had local (albeit European-dominated) representative governments anchored in LegCos. These LegCos initially comprised a mix of elected (unofficial) and appointed (official) European members and had relatively more lawmaking authority compared to their French counterparts (albeit without ends independence). Official members of the LegCos were typically colonial civil servants while the unofficials were elected by European immigrants. To ensure executive control over LegCos, the official members invariably outnumbered the unofficial members (whether nominated by the governor, African chiefs or councils, or directly elected). For example, in 1922 only 4 of the 45 founding members of the Nigerian national legislative council were elected (Okafor, 1981).[11] Similarly, as late as 1951 only 38 of 81 members of the Gold Coast (Ghana) assembly were elected (Willis, Cheeseman, and Lynch, 2018). Furthermore, Whitehall reserved the right to override resolutions emanating from LegCos or issue decrees without the consent of the members of the same institutions. The typical legislative council in British colonies was "a mere voting machine for registering the decisions of the Executive"

---

[10] Voting rights in both AEF and AOF were restricted in order to dilute the political power of the territories vis-à-vis the metropole. For example, to protest against its limited powers, members of Senegal's territorial assembly boycotted sessions for a whole month in 1947 (Fink, 2015, p. 41).

[11] The Nigerian Legislative Council was founded in 1922. The oldest legislature in the colony was the Lagos Colony Legislative Council – founded in 1862, dissolved in 1874 upon the union of Lagos and Gold Coast colonies, and then reestablished in 1886 following the separation of the two colonies. The first African to serve in the council was Capt. James Lobulo Davies, nominated in 1872. Created in 1914, the Nigeria Council was the first attempt at an assembly that included representatives from both northern and southern Nigeria. However, it was largely advisory and lacked jurisdiction with respect to the northern region of Nigeria. And, even after the Legislative Council was created in 1922, ethnic and regional divisions within the colony limited the council's ability to serve as a unifying institution (Okafor, 1981).

(Greary, 1927, p. 18).[12] But, despite these limitations, the lack of direct representation focused emerging African elites' political efforts on their territorial LegCos. These institutions, and not the metropolitan parliament in London, became the main arenas of political contestation.

As shown in Table 2.1, direct African representation in colonial legislatures only became commonplace after World War II. Before then, colonial legislatures in the region were invariably majority European (with appointed indirect representatives of Africans) or had a few appointed African representatives (often from the precolonial elite class). But despite the lack of direct representation, the mere existence of legislatures exposed African political elites to norms governing executive-legislative relations and rules of parliamentary practice – as outlined in Standing Orders and *Réglement Intérieur*. Over time, these same elites internalized the norms and rules as models of *how legislatures work*. Some of these influences were positive while others were negative. Positive influences included the enduring importance of legislatures as constitutionally protected branches of government and loci for organizing intra-elite politics, procedural involvement of legislatures in the budgeting process, parliamentary immunity for legislators, and the direct election of the majority of legislators. Negative influences included constitutional engineering to limit legislative powers, a limit on the budgetary, calendar, and agenda autonomy of legislatures, and the maintenance of executive authority to appoint some legislators. Overall, the essence of the colonial legislative inheritance in Africa tilted executive-legislative relations in favor of the region's postcolonial presidents.

Figure 2.2 shows the persistent effects of the colonial experience with legislatures. The graphs demonstrate that the duration of the

---

[12] Subordination of LegCos to governors was by design. According to Wight (1947), "subordination [of the Legislative Council] to the executive [was] its primary feature, its composition only secondary; and the organization of a party system [was] as improper as it [was] unnecessary" (p. 77). The limited powers of LegCos was a direct result of Whitehall's experience with older colonies in the Caribbean and the Americas. There, experimentation with elected and quasi-autonomous legislatures resulted in the loss of control by London – either through demands for responsible government or outright rebellion and independence. Thereafter, all new territories acquired by Britain had powerful colonial governors serving as direct representatives of the British government and with significant control over LegCos in order to forestall agency loss (see Burns, 1966, p. 34).

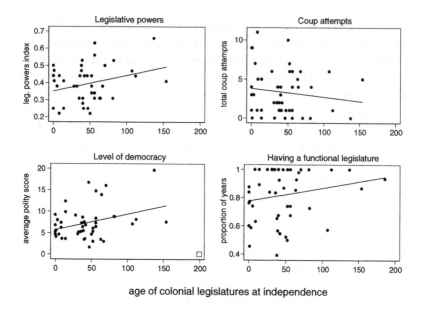

Figure 2.2 Age matters: colonial legislative experience and political development

Notes: Fitted correlations between age of legislatures and various measures of political development. Data on legislative powers from Fish and Kroenig (2009), level of democracy and coup attempts from Marshall and Jagger (2009), and existence of functional legislatures from Cheibub, Gandhi, and Vreeland (2010).

colonial legislative experience is positively correlated with indicators of political development. The age of African legislatures at independence is positively correlated with legislative powers, the average level of democratization after independence, and the number of postindependence years with a functional legislature.[13] Colonial legislative age

---

[13] The coefficients of the correlations between age at independence and legislative powers, total coups, average level of democracy, and proportion of country-years in which legislatures were functional are 0.3027 (0.0514), −0.1314 (0.0.3840), 0.3389 (0.0212), and 0.2016 (0.1742), respectively. I measure the age of colonial legislatures at independence in years starting from the year in which the first colonial legislative institution (whether national or subnational) was established. The indicator of legislative powers is from the parliamentary powers index created by Fish and Kroenig (2009). Data on the total number of coup attempts and levels of democratic consolidation (averaged between independence and 2015) are from Marshall and Jagger (2009). I calculated the proportion of postindependence years for which national legislatures were functional using data from Cheibub, Gandhi, and Vreeland (2010).

is also negatively correlated with the number of postindependence coup attempts. These findings reinforce the need to historicize legislative development in postcolonial states. Recall that for much of the colonial period, Africans lacked direct legislative representation. Yet, through elite socialization the functions and habits of these legislatures, *over time*, lasted into the postcolonial era. For example, writing about African members of the Gold Coast (Ghana) Legislative Council, Wight (1947, p. 58) observes:

The formalities of debate; the sense of contact with government and sharing in political decisions; the right of declaiming their opinions on policy openly and at length before a conscript audience of the highest government officers; the multifarious activities that attend a Council session – the meetings of the Select Finance Committee, perhaps of other select committees ... give them a sense of pride in their part in a Council session.

In addition to structuring elites' mental models of *how legislatures work*, colonial legislatures impacted the contours of political contestation among Africans. Intra-elite cleavages that emerged during the colonial period informed the patterns of political contestation after independence. Due to the nature of French colonialism, political development in French colonial Africa acquired a distinctly territorial-level flavor with an inclination to corporatist aggregation of competing economic and political interests (Robinson, 1991; Chafer, 2002). These colonies even had a supra-colony political party – the Rassemblement Démocratique Africain (RDA), and a student organization – the Comités d'Etudes Franco-Africaines (CEFA).[14] In general, representation in Paris and the existence of federation-level assemblies attenuated intra-territorial political divisions, especially during the immediate preindependence period. Indeed, many independence leaders in West Africa – such as Mali's Modibo Keita, Guinea's Sekou Toure, Cote d'Ivoire's Felix Houphouet Boigny, Benin's Hubert Maga, Cameroon's Ahmadou Ahidjo, Central African Republic's Barthélemy Boganda, Niger's Diori Hamani, and Senegal's Leopold Senghor – rose to prominence as deputies representing the two federations (AOF and AEF) and individual territories

---

[14] The pan-territorial orientation of elites in AOF was reinforced by their shared identity as graduates of the École Normale William-Ponty in Senegal. This made it possible, for example, for the Guinea RDA to field a Senegalese candidate in local elections in 1957 (Hodgkin and Schachter, 1961).

(future independent states) in the imperial French legislature in Paris.

In British colonies, the existence of territorial LegCos and indirect rule increased the salience of ethnic or subnational political machines and cleavages.[15] For example, Mozaffar (1998) notes the greater prevalence of local-level associational life (e.g., trade unions and political parties) in British colonies relative to their French counterparts. In French colonies, much of associational life took place at the territorial or federation levels. The primary focus of political elites was the National Assembly of the French Union in Paris. The governors-general in Dakar and Brazzaville were insulated from local politics, and received their marching orders from Paris. Emerging African elites therefore had strong incentives to focus their energies on the National Assembly in Paris rather than the grand assemblies in the federation capitals. As Fink (2015) observes, "[i]t took the *loi-cadre* reforms of 1956 and the establishment of semiautonomous territorial governments to establish the primacy of the territory in West African political divisions" (p. 148). The *loi-cadre* occasioned the balkanization of AEF and AOF into their respective constituent parts, and granted constituent assemblies powers over their governments. This effectively ended the rule of governments-general based in Dakar and Brazzaville.

Legislative politics under colonial rule also influenced intra-elite politics and the kinds of political parties that emerged as the vanguards of independence movements across Africa. Countries where independence leaders participated in colonial institutions (legislatures and administrations) were likely to see the emergence of moderate political parties and integrative political development. In contrast, populist and radical political parties were likely to arise in countries where leading political elites were excluded from colonial political institutions. These countries also saw precipitous institutional discontinuities after independence. In addition, the nature of intra-elite politics in the late colonial period structured party formation in Africa. Countries

---

[15] The only instance of a British supra-colony political institution was the short-lived Central African Federation that brought together present-day Malawi, Zambia, and Zimbabwe (1953–1963). Another prominent British attempt at regionalization was the largely economic East African Common Services Organization (EACSO), an outfit designed to create a common market for colonial Kenya, Tanganyika, and Uganda.

that experienced integrative politics were likely to have elite parties, while their counterparts with radical politics had mass parties. This pattern was driven either by the absence of strong African precolonial institutions or the existence of a conflictual relationship between new elites on the one hand and the old elite and colonial administrations on the other hand. Examples of countries that achieved independence on the back of mass parties include Ghana, Guinea, Tanzania, and Zambia. Countries that had elite parties include Benin, Cote d'Ivoire, Kenya, Niger, and Sierra Leone.[16] In summary, mass parties had direct membership among the masses and emphasized centralized party control. Power was concentrated in the hands of national leaders. Elite parties on the other hand relied on the support of local high status individuals (like cultural notables) and official colonial chiefs.

The types of parties that emerged in the late colonial period influenced the distribution of power among elites and executive-legislative relations in postcolonial Africa. Mass parties – due to their enabling of party leaders' direct access to individual party members – invariably produced unconstrained founding presidents

---

[16] For a summary of political party development during the colonial period, see Hodgkin (1961), Hodgkin and Schachter (1961), and Schachter (1961). The differences highlighted here were often layered onto contested relationships between "old" precolonial elites and the "new" educated elites. The decline of the old cultural elites (chiefs) was most stark in the French colonies. French direct rule coupled with the merit-based recruitment and training of a new cadre of elites at the École Normale William Ponty upended the power of the old elite. Chiefs were only able to dominate colonial territorial assemblies "where the new middle class had not yet succeeded in neutralizing the authority of precolonial ruling class" (Hodgkin and Schachter, 1961, p. 30). In colonial British Africa, the extent of elite inversion due to formal education and upward mobility was somewhat attenuated due to indirect rule. But, even in these contexts conflict between old and new elites drove the process of party formation. For example, in Ghana, a case of stark anti-Ashanti status inversion, out of the 104 members of the Ghanaian parliament on the eve of independence only 3 were chiefs. Among the remaining 95 whose professions were known, there were farmers (4), school teachers (30), members of liberal professions (18), petty professions (18), business people (18), and professional politicians (7) (Allman, 1993). The sparse representation of chiefs (or the old traditional elite more generally) in Ghana's founding legislature denied the institution the sociopolitical infrastructure it needed to be able to keep President Kwame Nkrumah in check. It also caused incessant political conflicts between Nkrumah and the Ashanti cultural and political elite class up until he was deposed in a coup in 1966.

(relative to fellow elites). These included Ghana's Kwame Nkrumah atop the Convention People's Party (CPP), Sekou Toure, head of the Democratic Party of Guinea (PDG), and Kenneth Kaunda, head of United National Independence Party (UNIP). Intra-elite relations under elite parties were different. Under elite parties, different elites served as intermediaries between presidents and the masses by autonomously mobilizing their bases of political support. These conditions were likely to produce relatively constrained party leaders (and presidents). Examples include Kenya's Jomo Kenyatta, head of the Kenya National African Union (KANU), Benin's Hubert Maga, head of the Dahomean Democratic Movement (MDD), and Sierra Leone's Albert Margai who headed the Sierra Leone People's Party (SLPP). On account of the power of elites (legislators) vis-à-vis presidents, countries with elite parties were likely to have stronger legislatures relative to their counterparts with mass parties.

2.3 Making Imported Legislatures Work

The process of adapting inherited legislative institutions to the realities of newly independent African states was marked by intra-elite contes-tation and eventual triumph of chief executives. After independence African legislatures served five main functions: (i) representation and the integration of specific populations and their interests to the center; (ii) aggregation of the policy preferences of masses and elites alike; (iii) linkage between the center and the periphery, distribution of governance rents, and facilitation of community development; (iv) oversight over the executive branch; and (v) debating and passing legislation. The first three functions addressed the demands of state building. If African states were to cohere, presidents had to find ways of integrating elites and their respective constituents to the center (Boone, 2003). To this end legislatures provided a ready-made arena through which largely autocratic presidents could credibly commit to share power and governance rents (through patronage) with fellow elites from different ethnic groups. In addition, the salience of clientelistic politics and popular demand for "development" resulted in legislators' material reliance on chief executives. As noted above, nearly all postindependence African chief executives enjoyed unchecked powers over their countries' finances. Legislators thus served as links between governments and the public and lobbyists for public projects for their respective constituents.[17]

The focus on elite integration, patronage, and clientelistic politics meant that the fourth and fifth legislative functions remained largely underdeveloped in most of postcolonial Africa. The primary challenge facing postcolonial African chief executives was how to organize developmentalist politics in a context of weakly institutionalized states and in the face of demands from fellow elites to share power and governance rents (access to public resources for private benefit). This created a strategic dilemma. On the one hand, they needed elite cooperation and political stability, outcomes that could only be credibly achieved by having legislatures with meaningful elite participation. But, on the other hand, they feared that strong legislatures would limit their powers at best and oust them at worst. Despite inheriting relatively "overdeveloped" executive branches, postcolonial African chief executives found themselves atop states that had for nearly six decades been governed via a largely extractive but skeletal colonial administration. They were powerful relative to other state institutions but lacked the ability to effectively project power and regulate elite political action (Herbst, 2000).[18] Under these conditions, ceding full powers to legislatures eager to assert their constitutional powers would have been akin to political suicide.

2.3.1 Contested Interbranch Relations Presidential Triumph

Take the example of Senegal. Barely two years after independence the legislature censured Prime Minister Mamadou Dia over alleged misuse of power. The parliamentary motion stated that the legislature "was

---

[17] In the euphoric postindependence moment many Africans internalized the optimism of Kwame Nkrumah's famous promise that "seek ye first the political kingdom, and all else shall be added unto you" (Nkrumah, 1957, pp. 162–163). For example, Barkan (1976) and Ollawa (1977) document the emergence of targeted clientelistic benefits and developmentalist constituency service as the currencies of legislative electoral politics in much of Africa.

[18] Like their postcolonial successors, European colonial administrations were at once skeletal and autocratic. In the terminology of Mann (1984), these administrations were endowed with despotic power and not infrastructural power. For this reason, scholars have characterized European colonial administrations as "the thin white line" (Kirk-Greene, 1980) and "hegemony on a shoestring" (Berry, 1992). The thin white line relied on a "circle of iron" composed of African employees that buttressed colonial administration and helped project imperial power in everyday lives of Africans (Osborn, 2003).

withdrawing the constant and unconditional support" rendered to the executive branch (Filipovich, 1980, p. 108). Dia's overreaction to the motion (including calling in *gendarmes* to arrest defiant legislators) occasioned a split with President Leopold Senghor, a constitutional crisis, a coup attempt, and Senegal's accelerated descent into authoritarianism under de facto single-party rule and centralization of power in Senghor's hands (Ademolekun, 1971, p. 544). It is noteworthy that the Senegalese legislature's assertiveness came in the face of repeated reminders by Senghor that the ruling party had "primacy over other organs," including the National Assembly (Sissokho and Thomas, 2005, p. 100).

Comparable dynamics were at play in Tanzania. While it is true that the Tanzania African National Union (TANU) and later Chama Cha Mapinduzi (CCM) eventually completely dominated the legislature, the institution did not go down without a fight. For example, in 1966 backbenchers forced the government to withdraw the controversial Gratuities Bill after it faced unprecedented criticism in parliament. In 1972 the government suffered its first defeat when the legislature failed to pass a constitutional amendment to allow executive administrators (Regional Commissioners) to also serve as legislators (Kjekshus, 1974). It also lost the Income Tax Bill of 1973. Nyerere only succeeded in completely subordinating the institution through the strategic selection of pliant legislators under single-party rule. Those who showed streaks of being institutionalist – like Modestus Chogga (MP, Iringa South), who dared to declare that "It is parliament that is supreme" – were simply expelled from the party and the legislature (Tordoff, 1977a, p. 239).

The processes of adapting inherited legislative institutional forms and practices to specific local contexts across Africa were invariably fraught with uncertainty and inter-elite conflicts. While some presidents succeeded in swiftly defanging postcolonial legislatures, some lost the interbranch contest against legislators and were swept out of office. In a number of cases, the contests between legislators and presidents led to a total breakdown of executive-legislative relations and the closure of legislatures. This is shown in the precipitous decline in the proportion of African states with functional legislatures shown in Figure 1.1.

In this regard the early postcolonial histories of Gabon, Sierra Leone, and Uganda are instructive. In all three cases interbranch contestations for power resulted in democratic collapse. On January 21, 1964 President Leon M'Ba of Gabon abruptly dissolved the National Assembly following disagreements with legislators, including those from his own party, over the formation of a single-party regime (Gardinier, 1982; Reed, 1987). M'Ba then scheduled fresh elections a month later, with a view of installing a more pliable legislature. This decision was met by an organized elite rebellion. The opposition boycotted the snap election. And, the ensuing political crisis resulted in a military coup that was supported by a section of legislators that were opposed to the president's proposal. It took the intervention of the French government to reinstall M'Ba in power and put the country on an autocratic path from which it has never departed.

Sierra Leonean democracy also collapsed in the face of executive centralization of power at the expense of legislatures. When Sierra Leone gained independence in 1961, the ruling party, the Sierra Leone People's Party (SLPP), was largely an elite party that "relied on the preexisting institution of chieftaincy" to mobilize voters (Minikin, 1973, p. 130). Following independence, the country's first two prime ministers had to balance the need for elite support among chiefs (to maintain power) and popular support (to legitimize their governments and keep elites in check). This balancing act collapsed after 1965 when Prime Minister Albert Margai began to openly consolidate power in his own hands by sidelining chiefs and appealing directly to the public. His end goal was to adopt a presidential system with a powerful executive. The chiefs reacted to this threat to their political authority by handing Margai a loss in the 1967 elections. Margai lost power because he wanted "to break the SLPP away from its dependence on the chiefs as its main local intermediaries" (Cartwright, 1978, p. 77).

Similarly in Uganda, a prime minister's resolve to shift to a presidential system led to democratic collapse and elite political instability. Following independence, the country's Prime Minister Milton Obote began the process of consolidating power in his own hands at the expense of the ceremonial president (Edward Muteesa) and the legislature. But, the legislature fought back. On February 15, 1966 the Ugandan National Assembly voted to set up a committee of inquiry to investigate Obote, Felix Onama (Defense Minister), and Idi Amin (Deputy Army Commander). The trio were accused of smuggling coffee, gold, and ivory from Congo-Kinshasa (the Democratic Republic of

Congo). The resolution passed in parliament with only one dissenting vote, signaling broad intra-elite consensus over the matter. It was not lost on Obote that members of his own party, the Uganda People's Congress, supported the resolution. Obote reacted to this open rebuke by suspending the legislature, abolishing Uganda's parliamentary system, and declaring himself executive president (in place of Muteesa). Obote's power grab ushered in an era of dictatorship and elite political instability that culminated in Amin's murderous dictatorship (1971–1979).[19]

More recent examples of off-the-equilibrium-path outcomes generated by conflicts between African presidents and legislatures include bargaining failures over presidential term limits in Burkina Faso, Burundi, Malawi, Niger, Nigeria, and Zambia. In all six cases presidents faced insurmountable opposition from their respective legislatures. Some of the presidents (in Malawi, Nigeria, and Zambia) accepted defeat and bowed out of office. But, others (in Burkina Faso, Burundi, and Niger) challenged the revealed intra-elite consensus, with disastrous consequences. In Burundi and Niger the choice by presidents to violate term limits despite opposition from legislators resulted in protracted street protests that precipitated coups. The Burkinabe president's intransigence resulted in his ouster via a popular revolt.[20]

The postcolonial interbranch contests between African presidents and legislators would eventually be resolved in favor of strong executive presidents. Thereafter, presidents came to view legislators not as members of coequal branches of government but as political subordinates whose primary job was to serve as a link between governments and the wider public. Addressing parliament in 1964 Kenya's Kenyatta reminded legislators that "theirs is a two-way obligation: to represent fairly to the Government the views of their constituents and then to interpret fairly to their people the policies and decisions of

---

[19] The first casualties of Obote's autocracy were Uganda's precolonial kingdoms. He attacked the Buganda palace with tanks in May 1966 and abolished all other kingdoms in September 1967. The collapse of constitutional order and politicization of the security forces thereafter led to Idi Amin's coup in 1971. See Mazrui (1970) and Uzoigwe (1983).

[20] See Dulani (2011) for a discussion of the politics of term limits in Africa. Baudais and Chauzal (2011) and Opalo (2016) provide analyses of the political crises in Niger and Burundi, respectively.

the Government" adding that "Members of Parliament must serve as a bridge between Government and the people."[21] Similarly, Kwameh Nkrumah of Ghana and Tanzania's Julius Nyerere considered MPs "out-of-school" (read non-parliamentary) functions of linking the executive branch with the wider public and explaining government policy to their respective constituents to be their most important role (Stultz, 1968, p. 491). In Zambia, legislators "largely abdicated their role as communicators of demands from constituents to government [and] tended to become agents of communicating government policies to the country."[22]

Single-party rule reinforced presidential power by vertically integrating legislatures with executive branches. Presidential monopoly over origination of legislation and the powers to call, prorogue, and dissolve legislatures served to limit legislative strength and independence. In Tanzania, for example, legislative sessions were "determined by the amount of Government business on hand, and not by the work-load created by members themselves" (Kjekshus, 1974, p. 21). The country's second parliament (1965–1970) passed an average of 54 bills a year while only meeting for an average of 48 days a year. The throughput of more than a bill per session was designed to limit legislative input in the lawmaking process. In addition to setting the agenda and controlling legislative calendars, African presidents also retained the power to co-opt legislators through appointments to their cabinets, the bureaucracy, or ambassadorships.[23]

2.3.2 *Balancing Legislatures under Autocratic Rule*

Presidential triumph over African legislatures did not render these institutions epiphenomenal. As noted above, legislatures still served

---

[21] Republic of Kenya, Official Record of the National Assembly, December 14, 1964, Col. 5.

[22] See Hakes and Helgerson (1973) as cited by Alderfer (1997), p. 91. Executive dominance over legislators in Zambia was achieved, in part, due to the strength of the ruling party UNIP. The party "went so far as to select, and impose, parliamentary candidates for Assembly elections" (Alderfer, 1997, p. 94).

[23] The clear intentions of these presidential actions were not lost on the African public. For example, Tanzanians questioned a constitutional dispensation that permitted "the M.P. for Bukoba to reside in Bonn, and the M.P. for Kisarawe to represent his constituency from Peking" (Kjekshus, 1974, p. 34).

important political roles of organizing elite cooperation, aggregating policy preferences, and providing links between governments and the wider public. Knowing this, presidents across the region went to great lengths to give their actions a veneer of procedural constitutionalism and legislative approval. Even in Mobutu's Zaire the legislature went through the motions of passing a budget even though corruption gobbled up 60–70 percent of the budget (Gould and Mukendi, 1989).

It is worth highlighting that these seemingly inconsequential instances of procedural constitutionalism created opportunities for African legislators to extract concessions from chief executives. Even as merely reactive institutions, African legislatures still had constitutional protections and powers that, in theory, posed real threats to presidents. This fact was not lost on African presidents. Before introducing any legislative proposals, they had to consider their likelihood of being passed in legislatures without generating open intra-elite disagreements. For this reason, whenever there was the possibility of irreconcilable intra-elite disagreements within legislatures, presidents often sought extra-legislative settlements – typically within political parties. Bargaining within political parties was cheaper. Being private institutions, intra-party deliberations and resolutions could be kept private and lacked the constitutional protections enjoyed by legislatures. For instance, in 1984 President Julius Nyerere's budget faced opposition in the legislature over the amount of funds allocated to the ruling party (CCM). Rather than suffer a humiliating public loss, Nyerere decided to call a party caucus to discuss the matter (van Donge and Liviga, 1986). Similarly in Kenya, President Kenyatta routinely called KANU Parliamentary Group meetings to resolve contentious matters before debate in the National Assembly (Hakes, 1970). These examples illustrate the fact that despite their subordination to relatively "overdeveloped" chief executives, postcolonial African legislatures still influenced the behavior of presidents. Presidents either had to propose legislation that they knew could pass without generating intra-elite conflict or spend material resources lobbying or coercing legislators.

Due to the important political functions of legislatures, African presidents had to worry about their composition. The imposition of single-party rule was a first step in establishing a screening mechanism to ensure party discipline within legislatures. The next step was to conduct autocratic elections that elicited the cooperation of elites and masses alike, but without producing hostile legislatures. In some countries, these elections were little more than state-managed "political rites performed to grant periodic legitimation" to the regimes in power (Chazan, 1979, p. 138).[24] But, in others they were more than mere legitimation exercises, and provided opportunities for genuine competition between individual candidates, albeit without posing any serious challenge to the position of the president or the single party regime. From the perspective of presidents, competitive elections were sometimes incentive compatible because "open competitive elections would give constituents a chance to remove unpopular officials without direct presidential intrusion into the removal process" (Dumbuya and Hayward, 1985, p. 65).[25]

The willingness of presidents to tolerate relatively competitive legislative elections was correlated with their perceived security of tenure and ability to effectively monitor and regulate elite political activity. Insecure presidents were more likely to meddle in legislative elections and deny fellow elites the ability to cultivate a personal vote and independent bases of political support. In doing so these presidents were able to control legislators' political futures thereby rendering legislatures into mere rubber-stamp institutions. More secure presidents

[24] In the extreme cases – like Nkrumah's Ghana (1965) and Houphouet-Boigny's Cote d'Ivoire (before 1980) – the ruling parties nominated candidates that were then automatically elected "unopposed." In other words, presidents selected legislators (Welch, 1972; Crook, 1989). The same logic obtained in states that had closed-list proportional representation electoral systems (most of them in francophone Africa). African legislatures also varied in the number of their members that were popularly elected. In most cases, the rules allowed for a handful of members to be appointed. In others, like Tanzania, the split was almost even – after 1965, 48 percent of Tanzanian legislators were unelected (Kjekshus, 1974). Politically dependent legislatures thus composed were destined to serve as rubber-stamp institutions. For instance, it is not surprising that in 1984 only 42 percent of Tanzanian legislators, all of them elected, asked 80 percent of the questions (van Donge and Liviga, 1986). In the Tanzanian legislature, appointed legislators were effectively part of the executive branch.

[25] Examples of countries that held competitive legislative elections include Botswana, The Gambia, Kenya, Mauritius, and Zambia. See Hyden and Leys (1972); Baylies and Szeftel (1984); Barkan (1987); Throup (1993), and Posner (2005) on autocratic elections in Africa. See also Gandhi and Lust-Okar (2009) for a general review of the utility of elections under authoritarianism.

were likely to tolerate relatively competitive legislative elections. In these states, individual candidates could compete by making personalistic appeals to voters and cultivate a personal vote. Legislatures in these states were also more likely to enjoy means independence and considerable influence over policy.

In the main, postcolonial African presidents' quest to control intra-legislative activities and elections negatively impacted legislative institutional development. Legislatures' lack of budgetary, calendar, and fiscal autonomy stunted their organizational development. The tendency to settle contentious intra-elite conflicts within parties denied legislatures the chance to develop the requisite institutional mechanisms of handling intra-elite bargains. In many countries parties, and not legislatures, emerged as the focal arena of intra-elite politics. The result was that legislatures became mere constitutional conveyor belts of resolutions passed by parties dominated by presidents. Presidential meddling in elections further served to reinforce legislative weakness. Legislative candidates' dependence on presidents for patronage and the resources needed for success under clientelistic politics meant that once elected they were in no position to check presidential power. By rationing access to patronage, African presidents could make and unmake the political careers of individual legislators. This resulted in persistently high turnover rates in African legislative elections that inhibited the accumulation of legislative institutional memory and careerism among legislators (Opalo, 2017).

By the late 1980s nearly all of Africa's presidents atop single-party regimes faced increasing pressure to liberalize politics. Economic decline for much of the 1980s and the structural adjustment programs (SAPs) that followed generated significant demand for the "structural adjustment of politics" (Herbst, 1990). The adjustment of politics meant the introduction of multiparty electoral competition. Popular protests across the region demanded political reforms (Bratton and van de Walle, 1992; Lebas, 2011). The tipping point was the end of the Cold War. The loss of economic and military aid from the Soviet Union and Western pressure for political liberalization forced one African president after another to adopt multiparty electoral politics (Atieno-Odhiambo, 2002; Posner, 2005). This is shown in Figure 2.3. Between 1989 and 1995 the proportion of African countries under single-party rule dramatically shrank from over 70 percent to under 15 percent.

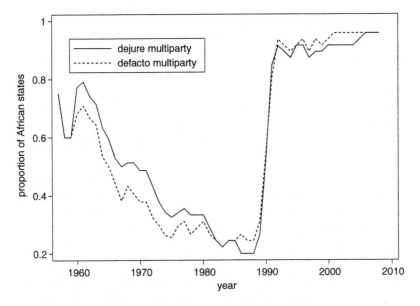

Figure 2.3 The fight for multiparty electoral competition
Notes: Graph based on author's calculations using data from Cheibub, Gandhi, and Vreeland (2010). Note the steady increase in the share of African states under single-party rule following independence; followed by the precipitous decline after 1990 following the end of the Cold War.

2.4 Contemporary African Legislatures

The reintroduction of multiparty electoral politics in the early 1990s ushered in a new era of legislative development in Africa. After nearly three decades of presidential domination via single-party rule, the sudden adoption of multiparty electoral politics across the region opened up opportunities for a rebalancing of executive-legislative relations. African presidents could no longer regulate entry and participation in legislatures via monopolistic single-party rule. Yet, as illustrated by the examples of Kenya and Zambia in the introduction, not all of Africa's legislatures took advantage of their new-found constitutional powers. Across the region presidents retained control over legislative budgets, calendars, and material resources needed for individual legislators' electoral success. In addition, the continued dominance of ruling parties – even under multiparty politics – provided African presidents with dependable majorities in their respective legislatures.

However, despite the persistence of executive dominance over legislatures, it is also true that the end of single-party rule catalyzed the process of institutionalization of politics in Africa (Posner and Young, 2007). For this reason it is worth documenting the diverse legislative institutional terrain that emerged in the region after the early 1990s. These institutional differences included the electoral systems, the number of legislative chambers, the intensity of representation (legislative seats), and specific legislative powers.

A majority of postcolonial African states adopted either proportional representation (PR) or Mixed electoral systems (see Table 2.2). The adoption of a system of Single Member Districts (SMDs) appears to have been concentrated among former British colonies in the region.[26] Interestingly, the type of electoral system does not appear to have a strong bearing on the effective number of legislative parties (ENLP) in Africa. Despite the region's high levels of ethnolinguistic fractionalization, the ENLP in Africa (regardless of electoral system) is lower than what has been observed in advanced democracies with PR systems (Taagepera and Grofman, 1985, p. 347). This is a surprising finding. Conventional wisdom holds that permissive electoral systems (i.e., PR systems) coupled with ethnic diversity ought to result in a relatively high number of viable legislative political parties (Grumm, 1958; Bormann and Golder, 2013). Yet, in Africa there is very little difference between states with permissive electoral systems (PR or Mixed) and those with restrictive systems (SMD). This is consistent with the findings by Elischer (2013) showing the ubiquity of interethnic political parties in the region.

Table 2.3 shows the distribution of the number of legislative chambers across Africa. Two patterns emerge from the data. First, slightly under two-thirds of African states have unicameral legislatures. Second, in states with bicameral legislatures, the upper houses have very limited powers and in most cases the majority of their membership is constituted through either indirect elections (by elected officials and councils at the subnational level) or presidential appointment

---

[26] It is important to note that the choice of electoral system is not exogenous to African political realities. For instance, Opalo (2012) documents the case of Cameroon where Paul Biya systematically engineered the country's Mixed system to maximize his party's seats in the legislature.

Table 2.2 *Electoral systems and effective number of legislative parties*

Electoral System	Country	Mean Effective Number of Legislative Parties
SMD	Botswana (1.9), Central African Republic (25.9), Republic of Congo (2.2), Ethiopia (1.2), The Gambia (1.1), Ghana (2.0), Kenya (5.1), Liberia (5.8), Malawi (4.4), Nigeria (2.0), Sierra Leone (1.9), Swaziland (1.0), Tanzania (1.9), Uganda (1.9), Zambia (3.1), Zimbabwe (3.0)	2.6 (4.0)
PR	Angola (1.5), Benin (4.7), Burundi (1.6), Cape Verde (2.1), Comoros (4.3), Djibouti (1.4), Equatorial Guinea (1.0), Gabon (1.1), Guinea-Bissau (2.1), Mali (4.3), Mauritania (3.4), Mozambique (2.2), Namibia (1.5), Niger (4.5), Rwanda (1.6), Sao Tome and Principe (2.2), South Africa (2.3), Sudan (1.7), Togo (1.9)	2.4
Mixed	Burkina Faso (3.6), Cameroon (1.5), Chad (2.5), Cote d'Ivoire (2.8), Democratic Republic of Congo (22.3), Guinea (3.2), Lesotho (1.6), Madagascar (3.3), Mauritius (1.7), Senegal (1.6), Seychelles (1.1), South Sudan	2.3 (4.1)

Notes: Figures based on author's calculations of the effective number of legislative parties (ENLP=$\frac{1}{\sum (s_i)^2}$) using data from the last election before January 2017. Data on African electoral systems are from the Inter-Parliamentary Union database, available here: www.ipu.org/parline-e/parlinesearch.asp. I categorize electoral systems into the broad categories of Single-Member Districts (SMD); proportional representation (PR), and Mixed (both SMD and PR). The third column represents ENP averages by electoral system. SMD average ENP excludes CAR, and that for Mixed systems excludes the DRC, respectively. The means with figures for the two countries are shown in parentheses.

(indicated by asterisks). In other words, these chambers seem to exist with the express purpose of protecting subnational elite power configurations or executive mandates. Only in a minority (five states)

Table 2.3 *The number of chambers and seats in African legislatures*

No. of Chambers	Country (No. of Seats)
Unicameral	Angola (220), Benin (83), Botswana (63), Burkina Faso (127), Cape Verde (72), Central African Republic (105), Chad (188), Comoros (33), Cote d'Ivoire (255), Djibouti (65), Eritrea (150), The Gambia (53), Ghana (275), Guinea (114), Guinea-Bisau (102), Madagascar (151), Malawi (193), Mali (147), Mauritius (69), Mozambique (250), Niger (113), Sao Tome and Principe (55), Senegal (150), Seychelles (34), Sierra Leone (124), Tanzania (357), Togo (91), Uganda (386), Zambia (167)
Bicameral	Burundi (106, 43*), Cameroon (180, 100*), Republic of Congo (139, 72*), Democratic Republic of Congo (500, 108*), Equatorial Guinea (100, 76), Ethiopia (547, 153*), Gabon (120, 102*), Kenya (350, 68), Lesotho (120, 33*), Liberia (73, 30), Mauritania (147, 56*), Namibia (104, 42*), Nigeria (360, 109), Rwanda (80, 26), Somalia (275, 54*), South Africa (400, 90*), South Sudan (170, 50*), Sudan (450, 56*), Swaziland (65, 31*), Zimbabwe (270, 80)

Notes: *More than two-thirds of Senators are either indirectly elected or appointed by the head of state. Data on the numerical size of legislatures are from the Inter-Parliamentary Union database, available here: www.ipu.org/parline-e/parlinesearch.asp (as of January 1, 2017).

are more than two-thirds of legislators in the upper chambers directly elected. In addition, in a number of states the upper chambers partly comprise representatives of cultural groups and precolonial authorities (mostly chiefs or their representatives).

The intensity of legislative representation in most African states appears to be suboptimal. While the number of seats in the region's legislatures generally conform to the *Taagepera Formula*, there is evidence of slight underrepresentation in a majority of cases. The formula stipulates that the size of the legislature tends to approximate the cube root of a country's population (Taagepera, 1972). As seen in Figure 2.4, only seven African lower chambers have representation that is larger than predicted by the formula. A majority of African

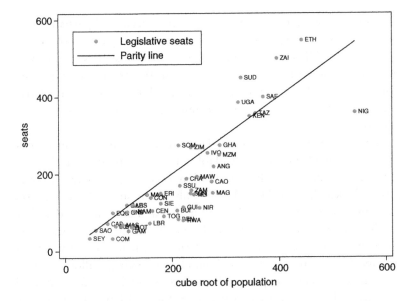

Figure 2.4 Intensity of legislative representation in Africa

Notes: The solid line represents the hypothetical legislature size based on the cube root of the population. Countries above the line have bigger than predicted legislatures. Those at the bottom have relatively underrepresented populations. Data are from author's calculations based on the number of seats in the National Assembly (or lower house in bicameral systems) and population size in 2015. Data obtained from the Inter-Parliamentary Union database, available here: www.ipu.org/parline-e/ parlinesearch.asp. Population sizes obtained from the World Bank.

countries have a lower number of seats than would be predicted by their population sizes.[27]

There is significant variation in the organizational features of African legislatures – including in the degree of calendar control, budgetary allocations, the remuneration of legislators, and political independence from chief executives. Calendar control and financial resources are critical for legislative operational independence. In order to effectively legislate and conduct oversight, legislators must assemble. The effectiveness of legislators once in session, in turn, depends on legislators' levels of professionalization and the availability

---

[27] Examining the determinants of the size of African legislatures is beyond the scope of this book. But, several factors could be driving this outcome – including the size of the economy, population, geographic area, and the number of subnational administrative and cultural units.

of resources for support staff, research, and specialized parliamentary committee work. Legislators' remuneration is a key driver of professionalization. All else equal, well-remunerated legislators are likely to be careerist in orientation and to invest in the organizational development of legislatures. For these reasons, limitations on legislative sittings and fiscal resources may curtail legislative institutionalization and strength.

The vast majority of African legislators have little control over the supply of plenary time available in their respective legislatures. Table 2.4 summarizes the distribution of calendar control powers across Africa. It is striking that in only seven states do legislatures have unlimited control over the maximum number of sittings that they can have in a given calendar year. In the rest of the states, presidents either have direct control over legislative calendars, or constitutions provide hard caps on the total number of sittings allowed. As I show in subsequent chapters, African presidents have often rationed legislative plenary time as a means of limiting legislative independence and institutionalization. As with the rationing of plenary time, African legislators are also starved of resources for legislative operations and constituency service. Table 2.5 shows the remuneration of legislators from a number of countries in the region.[28] While the nominal levels of remuneration may seem high, African legislators incur significant costs as part of constituency service. For example, a survey of 17 countries revealed that legislators spend, on average, between $823 and $1,207 in donations and between $948 and $3,492 on development projects every month (Barkan and Mattes, 2014). Under these conditions, legislators face strong incentives to supplement their salaries with other sources of income. The need for other sources of income diminishes the likelihood of legislative specialization and careerism – thereby contributing to the endemic lack of professionalization among African legislators. As I show in Chapter 7, the lack of resources

---

[28] These data are from varied sources including the Inter-Parliamentary Union (PIU); James Macharia, "Kenyan MPs Take First Pay Cut, but Allowances Mount," *Reuters,* June 12, 2013; Republic of Kenya, Salaries and Remuneration Commission (on Kenya); "MPs and their Benefits: What's the Way Forward?" *Lusaka Times,* August 18, 2014 (Zambia); Thom Chiuma, "Malawi President, VP Suspend Salary Hike: MPs Get 367% Pay Rise," *Nyasa Times,* December 6, 2014 (Malawi); and Clemans Miyanicwe, "MPs Want Better Pay and Status," *The Namibian,* April 19, 2013 (Namibia).

Table 2.4 *Control over legislative calendars in Africa*

Calendar Control	Unlimited Sittings	Maximum Set	Minimum Set
Head of State	Angola, Botswana, The Gambia, Guinea Bissau, Lesotho, Malawi, Mauritius, Mozambique, Namibia, Seychelles, Sudan, Swaziland, Uganda, Zambia, Zimbabwe	Guinea (6), Mali (5.5), Mauritania (8), Niger (5), Senegal (8)	Somali (8), Sierra Leone (4)
Legislature	Cape Verde, Ghana, Liberia, Kenya, South Africa, South Sudan	Benin (6), Burkina Faso (6), Burundi (9), Cameroon (3), Chad (6), DRC (6), Congo (6), Cote d'Ivoire (5), Djibouti (8), Equatorial Guinea (4), Ethiopia (8), Gabon (8), Rwanda (6), Togo (6)	Nigeria (6)

Notes: Information is from the most recent constitutions available. A maximum limit exists if legislative sessions are restricted to a period less than one year. Constitution limits are in parentheses (months). Minimum limits exist if more than two sittings are required in the constitution. The legislature controls the calendar if timetable is expressly specified in the constitution or if the constitution grants it the power to do so. Data are from author's coding of constitutional regulations over legislative calendars. Data obtained from the Constitute Project, available here: www.constituteproject.org/.

Table 2.5 *Comparative legislative compensation in Africa*

Country	Compensation (US$)	Pop. per Seat	Per Capita Income	Earning Ratio
Nigeria	189,000	483,333	3,005.76	62.9
South Africa	104,000	135,000	6,886.76	15.1
Kenya	102,700	126,074	1,245.55	82.45
Uganda	72,500	98,446	657.26	110.3
Senegal	64,400	94,200	1,046.71	61.5
Namibia	45,300	22,115	5,692.57	8
Ghana	45,100	94,180	1,858.69	24.3
Zambia	44,500	96,933	1,844.57	24.1
Malawi	21,800	84,767	226.47	96.3
Benin	11,600	124,337	804.94	14.4

Notes: Author's compilation from various sources as of December 2015. For a comparison the average and median parliamentary salary (PPP) was $62,075 and $48,971, respectively, from 104 states surveyed by the Inter-Parliamentary Union in 2012. Over half of legislators earned less than $50,000 p.a. Figures in the second column are in US dollars at current exchange rates (rounded to the nearest 100). Population and income data are from the World Development Indicators (World Bank Group, 2013). The last column depicts the ration of legislator compensation to per capita income.

for constituency service partially explains the high turnover rates in African legislative elections.[29]

In the next section, I analyze the determinants of the variation in levels of legislative strength and institutionalization shown in Figure 2.1. My analyses rely on cross-sectional data on both de jure and de facto legislative strength. While not meant to illustrate causal relationships, the results in this section will serve to motivate analyses in the rest of the book.

2.5 Determinants of Legislative Development

To explore the determinants of legislative institutionalization and strength in Africa, I use both de jure and de facto indicators of the

---

[29] As a sign of the importance of resources for constituency service, Barkan and Mattes (2014) report that legislators with access to more resources (e.g., via constituency development funds, CDFs) in the 17 countries surveyed reported a higher subjective probability of reelection (33 percent vs. 58 percent).

outcome variable. The de jure indicators are from the parliamentary powers index (PPI) developed by Fish and Kroenig (2009). The PPI is a snapshot of indicators of legislative institutionalization and strength in 2008–2009. I augment these data with a de facto indicator of legislative strength derived from the Open Budget Surveys conducted by the International Budget Partnership (IBP). The IBP data capture legislatures' *power of the purse* and cover multiple years between 2006 and 2012. In my analyses I use the mean indicator for each country over the years covered by the data.[30] In addition to the composite PPI, in my analyses I disaggregate the legislative powers index into four indicators – autonomy, capacity, executive influence, and specific legislative powers as coded by Fish and Kroenig (2009).

My main independent variables are the intensity of exposure to colonial legislatures (legislative age) and the nature of intra-elite relations at independence (types of independence parties). I operationalize the intensity of exposure to colonial legislatures using the numerical age (measured in years) of legislatures in 1990 right before the transition to multiparty politics. Recall that the early 1990s was a period marked by the end of single-party rule and a recalibration of intra-elite relations across much of Africa. I capture the nature of intra-elite relations with indicators of the types of political parties at independence (elite vs. mass parties) and whether or not a country's decolonization process was marked by a rural insurgency. Recall that mass parties were likely to concentrate power in the hands of presidents, while elite parties, by construction, dispersed power among elites. I augment this indicator of intra-elite relations with a binary indicator of whether or not countries had preindependence rural insurgencies – as coded by Garcia-Ponce and Wantchekon (2015). Like mass parties, rural insurgencies were likely to concentrate power in the hands of founding

---

[30] To develop the PPI Fish and Kroenig (2009) surveyed country experts and analyzed constitutions. They then constructed the index based on responses to the Legislative Powers Survey (LPS) – a list of 32 equally weighted items that seeks to quantify four indicators: (i) legislatures' institutional autonomy (9/32); (ii) influence over the executive branch (9/32); (iii) specific constitutional powers (8/32); and (iv) overall institutional capacity (6/32). The LPS mainly captures formal (official) constitutional powers and roles of legislatures. The IBP surveys mainly capture the levels of participation by key stakeholders and institutions (including legislatures) and reporting procedures in the budget-making process. The surveys used in this book are from 2006, 2008, 2010, and 2012. These data are available here: www.internationalbudget.org/.

presidents. I run separate regressions with these two measures of intra-elite relations.

I include a number of control variables in my analyses. Since the PPI and IBP indices were captured in 2008–2009 and between 2006 and 2012, respectively, I control for average income (from independence to 2005), the level of ethnolinguistic fractionalization, the average levels of democracy (from independence to 2005), the total number of attempted and successful coups (between independence and 2005), and whether or not a country was colonized by Britain.[31] High levels of income, democratic consolidation, and a British colonial history ought to be positively correlated with legislative strength and institutionalization. As noted above, material resources are critical for legislative organizational development. Democratic consolidation entrenches the idea of separation of powers and mandate, as well as the institutional stature of legislatures as coequal branches of government. A Westminster inheritance boosts parliamentary supremacy, on account of the strong British tradition of creating colonial parliaments (unlike other European powers that had representatives of their colonies in the metropole). Finally, ethnolinguistic fractionalization ought to be negatively correlated with legislative institutionalization and strength. Ethnic fragmentation is likely to lead to polarized intra-elite politics and to reduce presidents' willingness to tolerate relatively autonomous legislatures with means independence.

I regress measures of legislative institutionalization and strength on legislative age, the type of party (or existence of rural insurgency), and a number of control variables. Table 2.6 shows the results. With the exception of specific legislative powers, all other measures of legislative strength and institutionalization are positively correlated with the intensity of exposure to colonial legislatures. This is consistent with the findings in Figure 2.2. Because institutional development takes time (Pierson, 2004), a longer experience with colonial legislatures is

---

[31] The data on party types are from the author. Data on colonial rural insurgencies are from Garcia-Ponce and Wantchekon (2015). Data on country-year status of legislatures are from Cheibub, Gandhi, and Vreeland (2010). Indicators of level of democracy and number of coups are from Marshall and Jagger (2009). The economic data are from Heston, Summers, and Aten (2002).

Table 2.6 Correlates of legislative strength I

	(1) Autonomy	(2) Capacity	(3) Exec. Influence	(4) Powers	(5) PPI	(6) Budget	(7) PPI	(8) Budget
Age (1990)	0.106** (0.0348)	0.0358 (0.0367)	0.154** (0.0540)	-0.0217 (0.0609)	0.0739** (0.0241)	9.887 (4.887)	0.0737** (0.0256)	10.24 (6.092)
Mass Party	-0.0613 (0.0570)	-0.00728 (0.0435)	0.0938 (0.0594)	0.0149 (0.0499)	0.0113 (0.0308)	3.067 (5.892)	-0.00697 (0.0297)	-1.748 (6.220)
Per Capita GDP	0.000334 (0.0304)	0.0530* (0.0238)	0.0227 (0.0451)	0.0110 (0.0368)	0.0203 (0.0209)	0.212 (4.890)	0.0196 (0.0199)	-2.144 (4.925)
ELF	-0.198* (0.0901)	0.0199 (0.101)	-0.243 (0.150)	-0.112 (0.105)	-0.150** (0.0538)	1.626 (18.72)	-0.132* (0.0561)	-5.163 (20.88)
Polity 2							0.00852 (0.00554)	-0.584 (1.592)
Coups							-0.00582 (0.00379)	-1.087 (0.636)
Colbrit							-0.0390 (0.0368)	9.030 (7.005)
Constant	0.160 (0.218)	0.00500 (0.183)	-0.404 (0.384)	0.409 (0.257)	0.0310 (0.187)	-8.532 (45.79)	0.106 (0.190)	13.12 (51.68)
N	40	40	40	40	40	27	40	26
R^2	0.160	0.152	0.253	0.040	0.242	0.156	0.325	0.271

Standard errors in parentheses.

* ($p < 0.05$), ** ($p < 0.01$), *** ($p < 0.001$).

Notes: The dependent variables in the first four columns are disaggregated measures of the parliamentary powers index (PPI) from Fish and Kroenig (2009). The dependent variable in the sixth and eight columns is the average of the annual indicators of legislative budget powers (2006–2012) from the International Budget Partnership (IBP) surveys. Column 7 replicates Column 5 with additional control variables. Legislative age in 1990 is logged. Per capita GDP and Polity 2 measures reflect averages from independence to 2005. ELF (ethnolinguistic fractionalization) captures the degree of ethnolinguistic variation. Coups include both attempted and successful coups between independence and 2005.

positively correlated with contemporary legislative institutionalization and strength in Africa. I find a negative correlation between having a mass independence party and legislative institutionalization and strength in the full models (columns 7 and 8), although the point estimates are not statistically significant. This is suggestive evidence that mass parties, by empowering leaders vis-à-vis elites, structured intra-elite relations in a manner that stunted legislative institutionalization and strength.

The different control variables largely conform to the expected direction of correlation with the outcome variables. Save for the model in column 8, the average per capita income is positively correlated with all measures of legislative institutionalization and strength, albeit without reaching statistical significance. Relatively high income avails resources to finance legislative operations and for the remuneration of legislators. I find that ethnolinguistic fractionalization is negatively correlated with all outcome variables. This is consistent with the robust literature documenting a negative correlation between ethnic diversity and interpersonal trust, economic development, and institutional stability (Horowitz, 1985; Easterly and Levine, 1999; Robinson, 2017). The mean levels of democratization are positively correlated with the PPI aggregate measure but not the IBP measure of legislative input in the budget process. Finally, I find that a Westminster inheritance (being a former British colony) is negatively correlated with the de jure measures of legislative institutionalization and strength (PPI) but positively correlated with the de facto measure of the same (IBP). This is partially because the PPI measure gives a low rating to legislatures that lack formal separation of powers. Despite having adopted presidential systems, most former British colonies still maintain hybrid systems in which cabinet members serve as legislators.

Next, I substitute for the same regressions as above, but with the existence of rural insurgency as the measure of intra-elite relations and balance of power. From Angola to Burundi to Zimbabwe, independence-era militant rural mobilization for independence created opportunities for the emergence of strong postindependence rulers unconstrained by fellow elites. The results in Table 2.7 are largely similar to those in Table 2.6. As expected, I find that rural insurgencies are negatively correlated with legislative institutionalization

Table 2.7 *Correlates of legislative strength II*

	(1) Autonomy	(2) Capacity	(3) Exec. Influence	(4) Powers	(5) PPI	(6) Budget	(7) PPI	(8) Budget
Age (1990)	0.0543	0.0470	0.178**	−0.0178	0.0684*	9.651	0.0686*	9.692
	(0.0468)	(0.0496)	(0.0646)	(0.0646)	(0.0298)	(6.102)	(0.0333)	(7.369)
Rural Insurgency	−0.108	0.0141	0.0518	0.0280	−0.00712	−5.405	−0.00585	−6.426
	(0.0725)	(0.0579)	(0.0560)	(0.0648)	(0.0369)	(5.462)	(0.0358)	(5.852)
Per Capita GDP	0.00463	0.0500	0.0433	0.0151	0.0278	−0.761	0.0232	−3.057
	(0.0338)	(0.0254)	(0.0501)	(0.0416)	(0.0225)	(4.768)	(0.0205)	(4.541)
ELF	−0.226*	0.0244	−0.239	−0.112	−0.157**	−2.034	−0.146*	−3.401
	(0.0961)	(0.0996)	(0.173)	(0.100)	(0.0568)	(21.22)	(0.0572)	(21.76)
Polity 2							0.00616	−0.712
							(0.00546)	(1.383)
Coups							−0.00550	−1.039
							(0.00388)	(0.657)
Colbrit							−0.0252	8.078
							(0.0410)	(6.926)
Constant	0.367	−0.0303	−0.639	0.358	0.00616	7.056	0.0910	23.27
	(0.285)	(0.226)	(0.444)	(0.324)	(0.210)	(45.83)	(0.197)	(46.92)
N	38	38	38	38	38	25	38	25
R^2	0.207	0.150	0.243	0.049	0.266	0.194	0.330	0.326

Standard errors in parentheses.

* ($p < 0.05$),** ($p < 0.01$),*** ($p < 0.001$).

Notes: The dependent variables in the first four columns are disaggregated measures of the parliamentary powers index (PPI) from Fish and Kroenig (2009). The dependent variable in the sixth and eight columns is the average of the annual indicators of legislative budget powers (2006–2012) from the International Budget Partnership (IBP) surveys. Column 7 replicates Column 5 with additional control variables. Legislative age in 1990 is logged. Per capita GDP and Polity 2 measures reflect averages from independence to 2005. ELF (ethnolinguistic fractionalization) captures the degree of ethnolinguistic variation. Coups include both attempted and successful coups between independence and 2005.

and strength in five of the eight model specifications. These results are suggestive evidence of the ways through which intra-elite relations (and concentration of power in presidents' hands) impact legislative development in postcolonial states. Most postcolonial states inherited "overdeveloped" executives with the power to determine trajectories of legislative development. The findings in this section suggest that variations in early postcolonial constraints on presidents partially explain contemporary variations in levels of legislative institutionalization and strength.

Despite the accuracy of measurement limitations inherent in the operationalization of both the dependent and independent variables in the analyses in this section, the results in Table 2.6 and Table 2.7 are nonetheless important pointers to the drivers of contemporary variation in legislative institutionalization and strength in Africa. With material evidence from Kenya, the remainder of this book focuses on the two main independent variables – legislative development under colonialism and intra-elite relations and balance of power – to explain the variation in legislative development under autocracy, and the conditions under which democratic legislatures can emerge from their autocratic foundations.

2.6 Alternative Explanations

2.6.1 Explaining Legislative Development

In summary, the cross-national correlations shown above suggest that the colonial experience and the dynamics of the decolonization process had a lasting effect on legislative development in Africa. The duration of colonial legislative experience is positively correlated with political development in general (e.g., fewer coups and higher levels of democratic consolidation), and legislative development in particular. This is for the simple reason that the evolution of the customs, habits, and mental models that underpin political development takes time. A longer experience with colonial legislatures therefore bestowed upon Africa's independent nations the materials needed for organizational development. It is true that these institutions needed to be, in a sense, domesticated to the African context in order to reflect the realities of local political economies. But, the material resources for doing so were a mix of local conditions and inherited institutional forms and functions. More generally, African colonies that were scarcely institutionalized under colonialism experienced stunting in their postcolonial political development. In addition, political development under colonial rule and contingencies of the decolonization process put different African legislatures on different trajectories of institutional development. Some countries inherited localized means of political organization, while others had peak associations. Some had elite parties, while others achieved independence with mass parties. Some had rural insurgencies, while others did not. These differences generated variation in patterns of legislative development after independence.

Upon independence, most African legislatures succumbed to the overwhelming dominance of the relatively "overdeveloped" executive branches. In other words, the region's legislatures lacked ends independence. The institutional expression of this reality was the rapid adoption of single-party rule in much of the region. And, throughout the autocratic single-party era, structural factors that concentrated political power in the hands of chief executives (like independence mass parties or anticolonial rural insurgencies) were negatively correlated with legislative development. Patterns of intra-elite power distribution that favored chief executives led to stunted legislative development. The obverse provided opportunities for the emergence of organizationally strong legislatures with means independence. The actual effects of the structural distribution of power were mediated by the historical experience with legislatures, going back to the colonial period and beyond.

The end of single-party rule in the early 1990s was an important critical juncture that created opportunities for further legislative development in Africa. With loyalty to the ruling party no longer a precondition for legislative membership, multiparty electoral politics provided outside options for incumbent and aspiring legislatures. This shift increased the bargaining power of legislative incumbents vis-à-vis chief executives – thereby opening new avenues for institutional rebalancing of executive-legislative relations.

However, not all African legislatures were in a position to take advantage of this political opening. The historical experience with legislatures and level of organizational development at the point of transition determined African legislatures' ability to exploit the end of single-party rule. Stated differently, the ability of African legislatures to take advantage of the political opening created by multiparty party politics was conditioned by their historical organizational develop- ment going back to the colonial period. Both history and the specific modes of elite control employed by autocrats to keep legislatures in check under single-party rule mattered. Organizationally developed autocratic legislatures on the eve of transition made for strong demo- cratic legislatures after transition to relatively more open multiparty electoral politics.

2.6.2 *Competing Explanations*

It is important to delineate the arguments I present in this book from leading explanations for the origins and development of strong institu- tions of horizontal accountability and limited democratic government. While I emphasize the role of historical political development, these other explanations principally focus on the joint effects of historical discontinuities and subsequent contractarian outcomes. Such instances of institutional development may include formal constitutional pacts after revolutions (North and Weingast, 1989) or transitions from autocracy to democracy (Acemoglu and Robinson, 2006). In the specific case of institutional development in Africa, Barkan (2009*a*) attributes legislative development to the actions of "coalition[s] for change" led by "reformers" that emerge following transitions to multiparty electoral politics (pp. 18–19). These explanations are important but insufficient for several reasons.

First, institutional development takes time (Pierson, 2004). Polit- ical transitions seldom introduce completely new mental models of "how politics works." More often than not, new ideas typically get layered on top of the old (Greif and Laitin, 2004; Thelen, 2004; Mahoney and Thelen, 2010). Therefore, the emphasis on transitional discontinuities as sources of institutional development obscures the pretransition factors that drive posttransition institutional trajectories. The study of institutions and institutional development ought to be firmly grounded in history, with a focus on the factors, and *specific mechanisms*, that drive political development *over time*. Institutional forms that emerge out of the rubble of political discontinuities are often incomplete contracts whose impact is often structured by preexisting common knowledge assumptions of "how politics works."

Second, the dynamics of institutional development in postcolonial states that emerged after World War II markedly differs from the experience of Early Modern Europe and its offshoots. In these states, legislatures organically emerged to reflect the realities of medieval political economies and established custom. Heads of state granted the establishment of legislatures as concessions to fellow elites who had financial and (in some instances) coercive capacity to enforce the resultant intra-elite pacts (Thompson, 1953; Holt, 1992; Maddicott, 2010). Indeed, in the United States the legislature was literally the first branch of government (Squire, 2012).

Postcolonial states in the Global South have had a different experience. In these states, legislatures were created as imports imposed by colonizing European powers, and were often incongruous to existing political economies, the social milieu, and the intra-elite balance of power. Importantly, postcolonial legislatures in these contexts had to develop under the shadow of "overdeveloped" executive branches with significantly more fiscal and coercive powers. This is especially true in the case of sub-Saharan Africa, where chief executives served as chief patrons orchestrating the sharing of governance rents (Joseph, 1987; Boone, 2003; Arriola, 2009). My contention in this book is that this reversal of the nature of intra-elite relations and balance of power calls for a new theory of legislative development that reflects political realities of the postcolonial states.

Third, the degree of inclusiveness of political systems is not the primary driver of institutional development. The political struggle for institutions of accountability and credible commitment is seldom a contest purely between elites and the masses as theorized by Acemoglu and Robinson (2006) and North, Wallis, and Weingast (2009). In most polities, political contestation often splits elites and the masses alike (Ansell and Samuels, 2014). As such, the advent of mass politics is neither a necessary nor sufficient condition for the emergence of credible and strong institutions of limited government. Institutional development can take place under autocracy (Magaloni, 2006; Gandhi, 2008; Myerson, 2008; Blaydes, 2011; Svolik, 2012); and democracy is not a guarantee for strong state institutions. This observation calls for a reconsideration of electoral democracy as the means to normatively preferred institutions. As I show throughout this book, many of the good aspects of institutions of accountability have autocratic foundations. An important lesson that runs throughout this book is that strong political institutions of accountability emerge not from mass politics of inclusion, but from historical contingencies of political development that generate mechanisms for intra-elite accountability predicated on the prevailing intra-elite balance of power. These mechanisms take time to develop and congeal, and can often be eroded, rather than reinforced, by the introduction of inclusive mass politics.

Fourth, the effect of European colonialism on institutions and institutional development in former colonies is more nuanced than depicted in extant studies. First, the quality of European institutions varied by colony – largely conditional on whether these institutions were "accompanied baggage" or "unaccompanied exports"; and by time period in which they were introduced (Fletcher-Cooke, 1966, p. 145). Settler colonies got relatively "better" European institutions because of the availability of human capital imbued with the customs, habits, and mental models of how the exported institutions worked. Second, older European colonies, established in the seventeenth and eighteenth centuries, got relatively higher quality institutions than their counterparts in the latter parts of the nineteenth and twentieth centuries. Having learned from the experience of the Americas and the Caribbean – where strong institutions provided the bases for colonial rebellions and eventual political separation from the metropole – European colonizers were much more keen to establish subordinate colonial institutions in their possessions in Africa and Asia. A theory of colonial origins of "good institutions" is thus incomplete without an account of the variance in the quality of the original institutions to begin with. In this book, I begin this exploration by looking at the differential effects of colonial administrative styles and policies on legislative development in Africa.

Yet, another possible explanation is that postcolonial legislative development can be explained by the intentional establishment (by African presidents) of strong autocratic institutions (including legislatures) in order to guarantee regime durability. This would be consistent with the arguments and findings in Gandhi and Przeworski (2007); Gandhi (2008); Svolik (2012). This book goes further and endogenizes the choice by autocrats to govern through institutions. A driving assumption in the literature on the autocratic institutions is that elites need credible commitment from the autocrat, on account of the latter's relative coercive and fiscal powers. My innovation is to point out that this commitment problem goes both ways. In young states grappling with the uncertainties of "how politics works" rulers also need credible commitment from fellow elites. Once established, institutions can be used as mechanisms of elite collusion against the autocrat. The implication here is that the durability of autocratic regimes that govern through strong institutions may not necessarily arise from the stabilizing effects of institutions. Rather, strong rulers capable of keeping elites in check are more likely to govern through institutions (like legislatures). In other words, that politically secure autocrats, who are likely to preside over durable regimes anyway, are more likely to govern through institutions. As a corollary, insecure autocrats lead to institutional decay.

Endogenizing the autocratic choice to govern through institutions (of varying strengths and levels of institutionalization) allows for a more nuanced understanding of autocratic institutions in general, and institutional development under autocracy in particular. One of the central claims in this book is that secure autocrats preside over relatively strong institutions that in turn create the foundation for strong democratic institutions should such transitions occur.

The next chapter outlines the general theoretical framework through which to understand the discussions in this and subsequent chapters. First, I situate my study of legislative development within the broader literature on autocratic institutions. Second, I outline a simple informal model of intra-elite relations in the context of an autocratic legislature under conditions of political uncertainty. Lastly, I derive clear empirically testable hypotheses from this model that I then evaluate in subsequent chapters with material evidence from Kenya and Zambia.

3 | *Intra-Elite Politics and Credible Commitment*

3.1 Introduction

As demonstrated in the previous chapter, there is significant variation in the institutional structures and strengths among African legislatures. The region's legislatures vary in their powers over national budgets and internal financing, political autonomy and control over legislative calendars, ability to constrain chief executives, and general organizational capacity. Some of this variation is driven by the persistent legacies of colonialism. But, some of it is also a result of intra-elite political contestations that characterized the postcolonial processes of adapting colonial legislative institutional forms and practices to local political economies. In addition, throughout much of their existence, African legislatures developed under the shadow of relatively more powerful chief executives with strong incentives to curtail legislative independence and strength.

This chapter provides a model that addresses the questions that emerge from the aggregate patterns among African legislatures: what explains the variation in legislative institutional independence and strength under autocracy? And under what conditions do independent democratic legislatures emerge from their autocratic institutions? To answer these questions, the chapter begins by outlining the mechanisms through which intra-elite contestations for power under autocracy structure the institutional development of legislatures. The second section presents a dynamic informal model of postcolonial legislative development under both democracy and autocracy. The chapter concludes with a discussion of the implications of the model for legislative development in postcolonial Africa, and an outline of the empirical strategy for the remainder of this book. The analytical scope of the model presented in this chapter is limited to legislatures in former European colonies – a category that encompasses nearly all African states. These legislatures can generally be viewed as "unaccompanied" European "exports," in contrast to their counterparts that developed in the European offshoots of North America and the Antipodes.[1]

I conceive of elites as belonging to two groups – the core elites (comprising the chief executive and close associates) and the peripheral elites (other elites not in the core group). I characterize intra-elite relationships as inherently conflictual and plagued by a two-way commitment problem. In order for political stability to obtain, chief executives must credibly commit to share power and governance rents with fellow elites. To this end, legislatures function as institutional forms of credible commitment (Gandhi, 2008; Myerson, 2008). At the same time, chief executives must have sufficient executive power: the ability to effectively monitor, regulate, and balance fellow elites acting collectively in legislatures. As the examples of Dia, Margai, M'ba, and Obote in the previous chapter demonstrate, weak chief executives face the risk of rebellion or ouster by fellow elites acting collectively in legislatures.[2] The manner in which elites negotiate this intricate balance of power largely determines the feasible scope of legislative institutionalization and strength.

The focus on intra-elite politics herein is informed by two empirical considerations. First, most state institutions are structurally elitist. Therefore, intra-elite divisions define much of politics since they are typically the best-placed group to influence the actual organizational

[1] Fletcher-Cooke (1966) distinguishes between legislatures in European offshoots with majority ethnic European immigrants and those in colonies with non-European ethnic majorities (p. 145). The former colonies imported European human capital and sociopolitical underpinnings of executive-legislative relations. In the latter colonies the introduction of legislative institutions was constrained by local political realities, including the need to maintain an autocratic colonial administration. Burns (1966) describes how different colonial legislatures were organizational manifestations of constitutional development in England, with older colonies (the majority of which were European offshoots) being endowed with relatively more autonomous legislative institutions (p. 13). See Wight (1947) for a discussion of the evolution of legislative councils in British colonies.

[2] This conceptualization of a two-way intra-elite commitment problem is not a new idea. For instance, elites in the United States republic were acutely aware of the risk of legislative tyranny. Having lived with powerful state legislatures for almost a decade, the framers of the American constitution were keen on creating a strong enough executive to keep an empowered legislature in check (Greene, 1994).

and operational characteristics of institutions or to determine the leadership.[3] For example, between 1946 and 2008, 68 percent of all authoritarian leaders were ousted via coups d'état, while only 11 percent left office following mass protests. "The predominant political conflict in dictatorships appears to be not between the ruling elite and the masses but rather one *among* regime insiders" (Svolik, 2012, p. 5). Mass revolutions are decidedly rare events. This sentiment is echoed by Ansell and Samuels (2014), who emphasize the focal importance of intra-elite politics in the process of democratization: "[i]ndividuals are far more likely to mobilize when they constitute smaller, wealthier groups with more homogenous and concrete interests" (p. 11). Second, even when the masses participate in institutional processes, they typically do so intermittently (usually every few years during elections) and indirectly (via representatives). Whether acting as delegates or trustees, elites dominate state institutions regardless of regime type.[4] Understanding the dynamics of intra-elite politics is therefore crucial for explaining the development and evolution of state institutions such as legislatures.

3.2 The Logic of Autocratic Legislatures

Stable and predictable intra-elite cooperation is crucial for the sharing of political power and governance rents (access to public resources for private benefit) between chief executives and fellow elites. However, such cooperation is often plagued by commitment problems on account of the uneven distribution of political and coercive powers. On the one hand, chief executives' command of

[3] This formulation differs from Boix (2003) and Acemoglu and Robinson (2006) who characterize political contestation as being primarily a struggle for power between wealthy elites and the poor masses.

[4] There is an old debate among students of representative government – going back to John Stuart Mill – over whether elected officials ought to act as delegates or trustees. The former definition posits that officials merely echo the demands of their constituents. In the latter case officials act in a manner that reflects the general will of the wider public. My goal here is not to wade into this debate, but rather to highlight the power of elites even under democratic representative government. For discussions on representative government see Madison (1788), Mill (1861), and Bagehot (1867). For more recent explorations of this subject see Manin (1997) and Stokes (2001). A related research agenda has included works that show that voters are "rationally ignorant" and often defer to elites whom they believe to be more informed (see, for example, Downs [1957], and Martinelli [2006]).

coercive powers (police and military), control over governance rents, and overall agenda-setting powers create incentives to renege on intra-elite cooperative arrangements with minimal cost. On the other hand, despite being individually weak, elites acting collectively in institutions – such as parties or legislatures – pose a serious political threat to chief executives.

Solving the first half of this two-way commitment problem often involves the institutionalization of political rule in order to credibly share power with fellow elites. Institutionalization of rule lowers the cost of intra-elite collective action and enables elites to punish chief executives that abrogate intra-elite cooperative arrangements.[5] To solve the second half of the commitment problem, chief executives must have sufficient powers to balance elites acting collectively in institutions such as legislatures with a view of maintaining constitutional order and enforcing intra-elite cooperative arrangements.[6] Unchecked elites acting collectively may have incentives to redistribute power and governance rents by replacing incumbent chief executives with weaker individuals. The specter of legislative tyranny or palace coups inform the behavior of autocratic chief executives eager to stay in office. Stable institutionalized rule only obtains in contexts where there is credible two-way interbranch balance of power between chief executives and fellow elites acting collectively in institutions.[7]

3.2.1 Checks against Executive Tyranny

The first half of the two-way credible commitment problem has been extensively explored by students of institutions, while the latter half has been largely ignored. This is partially due to the focal position and sheer visibility of the powers of chief executives. Human experience with governments under centralized authority – whose primary embodiment is the chief executive – has made it such that the quest for limited government has historically been defined as a struggle to constrain chief executives. Along these lines, a substantial literature

---

[5] See North and Weingast (1989), Stasavage (2003), Magaloni (2006), Gandhi (2008), Myerson (2008), Wright (2008), and Cox (2016).

[6] See Madison (1788), Carey (1978), Greene (1994).

[7] Notice that interbranch balance of power is not synonymous with equal distribution of power between chief executives and legislatures. Here "balance" simply means an equilibrium that is incentive-compatible for both chief executives and fellow elites.

exists on the emergence of legislatures as a means of constraining executive power in Early Modern Europe. Canonical theoretical and empirical works in this literature emphasize the importance of legislatures as credible means of checking the powers of chief executives and protecting democratic government (North and Weingast, 1989; Persson, Roland, and Tabellini, 1997; Stasavage, 2003; Myerson, 2008; Cox, 2016). The core argument in these works is that elites acting collectively in legislatures can credibly punish errant chief executives by withholding revenue (through the power of the purse) or coercive ouster (baronial rebellions and coups).

A related literature examines the logics of institutions under autocracy. These works argue that chief executives may willingly establish institutions that constrain their power in order to elicit elite cooperation, secure their tenure in office, and to attract private investment. The empirical evidence supports these claims. Under autocracy, institutionalized rule (such as through legislatures or parties) has the benefit of enhancing regime durability as well as the tenures of individual chief executives – either through routinized co-optation of the opposition or credible power sharing.[8] The existence of intra-elite credibility-enhancing institutions under autocracy is also correlated with positive economic outcomes, including property rights protections (Weymouth, 2011; Wilson and Wright, 2015) and relatively higher levels of private investment and economic growth (Wright, 2008; Gehlbach and Keefer, 2012; Jensen, Malesky, and Weymouth, 2014). Scholars have also highlighted additional benefits of institutionalized autocratic rule coupled with elections (Geddes, 1999; Gandhi and Lust-Okar, 2009). The evidence suggests that routinized intra-elite competition for popular support under autocracy serves to generate information on the popularity of the regime, individual politicians, and potential opposition (Magaloni, 2006). Elections also reveal the policy preferences of various segments of the society (Gandhi, 2008; Malesky and Schuler, 2011), and serve as a "fair" mechanism of recruiting elites and granting them access to governance rents (Lust-Okar, 2006; Blaydes, 2011). In the main, these works demonstrate that autocratic institutions, such as legislatures, are not epiphenomenal.

---

[8] See Haber (2006); Brownlee (2007); Gandhi and Przeworski (2007); Svolik (2012); Wright and Escriba-Folch (2012); Boix and Svolik (2013).

Institutionalized rule – including through legislatures – has clear benefits. Yet, looming over this literature is the question of how chief executives balance fellow elites acting collectively in legislatures. For example, Gandhi (2008) remarks that chief executives ultimately reserve "the power to close down these institutions" (p. 81) – implying that despite the many advantages of institutionalized rule, an autocratic chief executive that is keen on maximizing her authority and staying power only tolerates competing institutions up to a point. This point is determined by the continuing ability of the chief executive to balance the legislature, veto outcomes that are at variance with her preferences, or (in extreme cases) to abolish legislatures altogether. The corollary of this claim is that when faced with a chief executive lacking these powers, a collection of elites in a legislature have a strong incentive to establish a more equal form of government (at least among elites) either by stripping the chief executive of excessive powers or simply appointing a more favorable leader from among their ranks.

As a matter of fact, there is no empirical basis for assuming permanently omnipotent chief executives capable of balancing autocratic elite institutions. Just as chief executives may abrogate intra-elite cooperative arrangements in an effort to enhance their power, empowered elites acting collectively in autocratic legislatures can renege on intra-elite commitments by taking power and governance rents away from chief executives. Therefore, chief executives governing with autocratic legislative institutions must actively work to ensure a favorable executive-legislative balance of power. Relaxing the critical assumption of executive omnipotence raises important questions about the nature of institutional development under nondemocratic regimes, to which we now turn.

3.2.2 *The Risk of Legislative Tyranny*

The second half of the two-way intra-elite credible commitment problem is seldom explored in the literature but is just as important as the first. Politics does not end with the establishment of autocratic institutions. A weak autocrat who tolerates the existence of a relatively stronger elite institution – such as a legislature – stands little chance of lasting in office. England's Charles I and France's Louis XVI lost their heads.[9] The fiscal relationship between the King and the *Sejm* in the Polish-Lithuanian Republic was infamously dysfunctional – due to the very permissive legislative *liberum veto* that granted individual legislators immense powers relative to the chief executive. Legislative preponderance contributed to the Republic's military weakness and subsequent conquest and partition by rival states.[10]

More recently, a number of autocratic African presidents (temporarily) lost power to self-declared "sovereign" National Conferences (that acted as interim legislative bodies) in the democratic wave that swept the region in the early 1990s. In these cases, disaffected elites who had previously been excluded from intra-elite power-sharing arrangements mobilized around citizen protests and mass strikes to wrest power, albeit only briefly in some cases, from incumbent African presidents. The rapid shift in the balance of power between presidents and elites emboldened the latter group who proceeded to suspend constitutions and declare themselves sovereign.[11]

---

[9] The public trial and execution of the two kings marked a watershed in popular European understanding of the limited power of monarchs, and dealt a fatal blow to the notion of the divine right of monarchs. The rise of empowered elite institutions meant a decline in the power of monarchs. After the restoration of Charles II, Louis XIV, remarking on the ascendance of the English parliament, noted that the "subjugation, which forces the sovereign to take the law from his people, is the last calamity that can fall upon a man of our rank" (Walzer, 1992, p. 622). It was not lost on keen observers that the ascendance of legislatures necessarily implied the loss of power of chief executives.

[10] See Davies (2005); Rohac (2008).

[11] Benin (1990), Chad (1993), Comoros (1992), Republic of Congo (1991), Ethiopia (1991), Gabon (1990), Ghana (Consultative Assembly, 1991–1992), Guinea-Bissau (1990), Mali (1991), Niger (1991), South Africa (1991), Togo (1991), and Zaire (1991) all held National Conferences between 1990 and 1993. These conferences deposed chief executives in Benin, Republic of Congo, and Niger, after the respective presidents quickly lost control of resolutions emanating from the citizen fora. Although scarcely studied, Africa's National Conferences in the early 1990s should be viewed as a foreshadowing of what popular sovereignty could look like in the region. They are also proof of the relative weakness of African chief executives when faced with a united elite rebellion on the back of popular protests. The experience of the Beninois *Conférence Nationale* (CN) offers the best example of an elite revolution. After declaring itself sovereign, the CN established an interim legislature – the *Haut conseil de al républic* (HCR) – and elected Archbishop Isidore de Souza as its chairman, before electing Nicéphore Soglo as prime minister. This effectively stripped President Kérékou of all his formal powers. He no longer controlled parliament. And he was suddenly directly answerable to an independent group of elites that he had previously excluded from power. See Heilbrunn (1993), Nwajiaku (1994), and Lund and Santiso (1998) for discussions on the fight for multipartyism in West Africa.

Benin's National Conference is a paradigmatic example of the dangers faced by weak autocratic chief executives confronted by empowered elite institutions. In early 1990 (February 19–28), President Mathieu Kérékou, in power since 1972, was forced by a crippling general strike and a collapsing economy to convene a National Conference. Ahead of the conference, Kérékou had agreed to the creation of an interim elite institution composed of previously excluded elites as a way of easing tension in the country. However, as soon as the conference began matters spiraled out of his control. Robinson (1994, p. 575) offers a concise summary of the events that led to Kérékou's fall:

Benin's National Conference lasted ten days. The delegates' first official act was to declare the conference sovereign. By the time the deliberations ended, the delegates had suspended the constitution; dissolved the National Assembly; adopted plans for multiparty elections; and chosen Nicéphore Soglo ... as Interim Prime Minister. Although Kérékou was allowed to remain in office as head of state until the elections, he was stripped of most of his powers and executive authority. A year later when Benin held its first multiparty elections in over two decades, Kérékou came in second to Soglo in a three-way race.

The examples of Benin and other West African countries highlight the dangers posed by empowered elite institutions under autocracy. They are also a reminder that institutionalized rule is not solely about credibly constraining chief executives, but also about credible commitment by elites not to use their power to rewrite the rules governing intra-elite relations.[12] In short, for intra-elite stability to obtain, chief executives must have *sufficient capacity* to balance empowered elites acting collectively – such as in legislatures. This is the concern that motivates Madison (1788)'s warning against "the danger from legislative usurpations, which, by assembling all power in the same hands, must lead to the same tyranny as is threatened by executive usurpations." It is not a coincidence that these concerns surfaced in the first early modern Republic – the United States of America – with a strong legislature. Having lived with a sovereign national legislature for the better part of a decade, a section of American political elites wanted a president "strong enough" to

---

[12] For example, Saiegh (2011) documents cases – in Brazil, Kenya, Poland, and Thailand – of chief executives' initiatives that were defeated by autocratic legislatures (pp. 79–82).

balance a powerful Congress (Greene, 1994, p. 130). As Levi (1976) points out, "for considerable periods of time, the concern in the United States has been with the weakness of the executive, not with its strength" (p. 372).

These observations expose a lacuna in existing works on institutional development under autocracy in general and autocratic legislatures in particular. If indeed autocratic institutions are not epiphenomenal, and in fact to do constrain chief executives in nontrivial ways, then it follows that autocrats' continued stay in office is conditioned by their ability to balance fellow elites acting collectively in institutions. For this reason, executive power – the ability to effectively monitor, regulate, and balance elite political activity – is positively correlated with chief executives' willingness to tolerate independent institutions. Put differently, a weak chief executive has strong incentives to actively avoid institutionalizing her rule for fear of being deposed by fellow elites serving in an empowered institution. Factors limiting executive power may include a lack of legitimacy (as may happen if the leader is unelected or from a marginalized ethnic, religious, or cultural group); the relative novelty of the chief executive's position (as may be the case in new states); or the lack of coercive capacity to monitor and regulate political action among elites (as may be the case in relatively poor states). A number of factors may result in higher levels of executive power. Established political culture and norms of separation of powers can prevent unwarranted elite collusion against chief executives. A robust administrative capacity to monitor and regulate elite political activity (backed, for example, by competent intelligence and security apparatuses) can provide sufficient coercive deterrence against potentially subversive elites. Similarly, a strong political party that serves as a gatekeeper and screens out elites that may threaten the chief executive from within the legislature can strengthen the chief executive's position vis-à-vis fellow elites.

In general, a combination of history and the chief executive's specific strategic investments in tools of elite control may determine executive power and the risk of legislative tyranny, and by extension the chief executive's ability to tolerate the existence of a functional and independent legislature. This is especially true under autocracy. By collectively empowering elites, institutionalized autocratic rule increases the odds of public intra-elite disagreements. The historical records show that public intra-elite conflicts elevate the risk of regime collapse, palace coups, or mass uprisings and civil conflict.[13]

It follows that governing with an autocratic legislature requires a balance between conceding power and autonomy to legislators while at the same time retaining the ability to balance their collective actions in legislatures – for example, through monitoring, co-optation, and/or coercion. A direct implication of this observation is that only chief executives that are *strong enough* (i.e., have sufficient executive power) to effectively balance fellow elites will grant legislatures means independence. In the same vein, their relatively weaker counterparts will either deny their legislatures operational autonomy (means independence) or rule without legislatures. Simply stated, executive power and subjective security of tenure of autocrats determine the strength and degree of institutionalization of autocratic legislatures. This observation explains the empirical regularity of relative regime stability and longevity under institutionalized autocracy. Only relatively strong autocrats choose to credibly institutionalize their rule. The logical implications of this observation are consistent with findings in the literature. Geddes (1999), Gandhi and Przeworski (2007), and Wright and Escriba-Folch (2012) find a positive correlation between regime duration and institutionalized autocratic rule. Similarly, Wilson and Wright (2015) find that nonpersonalist autocrats grant legislatures more power to protect property rights relative to their personalist counterparts.

Most of these works demonstrate the utility of autocratic institutions, but largely avoid the question of why some autocrats institutionalize their rule while others do not; or why there is variation in the strength and scope of autocratic institutions. For example, Gandhi and Przeworski (2007) attribute the variation in autocratic institutionalization to error, noting that "[f]or whatever reason, some autocrats do err, and as a consequence have institutions weaker or stronger than the threat from the opposition would require" (p. 1289). A core claim in this book is that autocrats' choice to institutionalize their rule is endogenous to their subjective security of tenure and

---

[13] See O'Donnell and Schmitter (1986) on intra-elite splits and regime collapse. Roessler (2011) and Svolik (2012) document how fellow elites pose the biggest risk to chief executives' tenure. Finally, Martinez (2000) shows how the failure to honor elections (a form of intra-elite institution) led to civil war in Algeria.

capacity to effectively balance fellow elites. Strong autocrats are more likely to govern with strong institutions. Weak autocrats, on the other hand, are more likely to govern either with weak institutions or without institutions altogether.

3.2.3 Political Foundations of Legislative Power

Having explored the two-way intra-elite commitment problem at the heart of institutionalized autocracy, it is important to examine the specific political micro-foundations and logics of legislative power under autocracy. To this end, two important factors – the primary functions of legislatures and how they are constituted – deserve further consideration.

Legislatures derive their power from their role as institutional mechanisms for lowering the cost of intra-elite collective action. Elites may engage in collective action to promote their interests or punish chief executives that abrogate intra-elite agreements on power sharing and the distribution of governance rents (Myerson, 2008). Constitutional interbranch separation of powers reinforces this intra-elite distribution of power. Even in contexts where chief executives enjoy substantial powers, legislatures typically retain a formal constitutional monopoly over lawmaking. This power creates opportunities for legislators to reject executive legislative proposals or rewrite intra-elite pacts at significant cost to chief executives.

All else equal, legislators prefer intra-elite bargains that maximize their share of governance rents and influence over public policy. To this end, they have incentives to act collectively in order to boost their bargaining power vis-à-vis the chief executive. From the chief executive's perspective, it is costlier to renege on collective agreements than on bilateral deals with individual legislators. The desire to maximize power and governance rents means that at any time there exists an intra-elite bargaining outcome that is arbitrarily close to but better than the status quo and that can garner majority support among legislators.

From this micro-foundation, the possibility of disequilibria over the collective preferences of legislators due to cyclical majorities majorities becomes apparent (Arrow, 1951; Riker, 1980). Therefore, for stability over policy and the distribution of governance rents to obtain, autocratic legislatures must be guided by structure-induced equilibria. A key feature of such equilibria is the maintenance of legislative majorities loyal to chief executives. This is only possible under a chief executive that is strong enough to not only set the agenda, but also deter legislators from reneging on or constantly renegotiating prevailing intra-elite agreements.

Elections are also a source of legislative power. Individual legislators derive power from the loyalty of specific political constituencies, and can leverage their public support to improve their bargaining position vis-à-vis fellow elites. Legislators' political power increases with the ease with which they are identified with specific constituencies – such as cultural, ethnic, or religious groups.[14] Therefore, legislative elections provide an opportunity for individual elites to signal their popularity among the public.[15] For this reason, legislative elections create real problems of adverse selection and moral hazard for chief executives. They must ensure that the electoral process selects loyal legislators and that, once elected, the same legislators do not leverage their public support and the institutional power of legislatures to undermine executive authority.

These two important sources of legislative power map neatly onto the stylized functions of legislatures – representation, lawmaking, and provide checks and balances on chief executives. Elections are a mechanism for achieving representation. Constitutional separation of powers ensures legislative input (either directly or indirectly) in the lawmaking process. And, finally, the quest to ensure that chief executives honor intra-elite bargains over the distribution of power

---

[14] Legislators associated with specific cultural, ethnic, or religious groups are particularly powerful because they are not easily substitutable and can build bases of political support that are less dependent on political parties or the largesse of chief executives.

[15] It is common for legislators – even in autocratic states – to be elected in relatively competitive elections. Studies from regimes as varied as Hosni Mubarak's Egypt (Blaydes, 2011), Julius Nyerere's Tanzania (Hyden and Leys, 1972), Vietnam under the Communist Party (Malesky and Schuler, 2011), and the Jordanian monarchy (Lust-Okar, 2006), illustrate that it is possible for autocratic regimes to allow for credible intra-elite competition, as long as their own position is secure. Lust-Okar (2006) notes that "[c]andidates invest enormously in elections; even in the most seemingly repressive regimes, such as Syria and Saddam Hussein's Iraq, candidates spend large amounts of time and money" to campaign for votes (p. 457). Similarly, Throup (1993) contends that Kenya's elections under Kenyatta were "relatively free and democratic affairs" (p. 381) with no limit on the number of candidates that could run in any given constituency.

and governance rents provides a mechanism for achieving interbranch checks and balances.

It emerges that in order to remain in office, a chief executive must be able to: (i) screen candidates for legislative elections; and (ii) monitor incumbent legislators and deter them from engaging in regime-undermining activities. A common means of achieving this dual object is to govern through a hegemonic ruling party coupled with a strong coercive apparatus or to ban opposition parties. However, neither option sufficiently addresses the chief executive's electoral dilemma. Direct electoral interference attenuates the informational function of legislative elections – such as revealing the public's views on government performance or the popularity of specific elites. All else equal, the autocrat prefers legislative elections to be as competitive as possible, subject to the constraint that they do not generate results that pose a direct threat to the regime. Indeed, electoral competitiveness – that serves as a "fair" means of accessing governance rents – often serves as a core feature of intra-elite pacts (Blaydes, 2011). As such, excessive electoral interference can result in elite rebellion against the chief executive.[16]

This account of the political foundations of legislative power is not meant to refute the immense powers of (autocratic) chief executives. Rather, it is an acknowledgment that chief executives are often at once strong and insecure. Their power comes from their agenda-setting roles, coercive powers, and control over vast bureaucracies, economic resources, and access to governance rents. However, chief executives also constantly face the threat of elite rebellion should they fail to honor intra-elite bargains over the distribution of power

---

[16] The example of Algeria is instructive. In December 1991 the Front Islamique du Salut (FIS) won the first round of the Algerian election, gaining 81.3 percent of the seats in the National Assembly. Fearing an ineluctable FIS victory, the incumbent military regime canceled the second round election. The act plunged the country into civil war for much of the 1990s, costing more than 100,000 lives (Martinez, 2000). The cancellation of the election was an abrogation of commonly accepted facts about FIS' popularity and legitimacy. After the June 1989 elections, FIS controlled over half of Algeria's municipalities, thereby making their electoral popularity common knowledge. Their victory in the first round of the parliamentary elections in 1991 reinforced this fact in elites' and the public's minds. As a result, the nullification of the election was a transgression against an implicit electoral pact that provided a focal point around which opposition to the military dictatorship could be organized.

and governance rents. In constitutional democracies threats may come from veto-proof legislative super majorities or impeachment. Autocratic chief executives face constant threats of palace coups or civil conflict. In summary, chief executives that institutionalize their rule (including by tolerating legislatures) are only able to last in office or effectively exercise their power if they can credibly balance fellow elites acting collectively.

3.3 Toward a Model of Autocratic Legislative Development

Having outlined the foundations of legislative power, in this section I present a theoretical framework through which to understand legislative development *over time*. While developed primarily to explain postcolonial legislative development under autocracy in postcolonial Africa, this model applies more generally to legislative development in the shadow of relatively more powerful chief executives in both autocracies and democracies.

3.3.1 *Critical Assumptions*

I assume that autocratic legislatures serve two critical functions: (i) as a mechanism for credible commitment among elites; and (ii) as an instrument for generating critical information on policy and politics for the chief executive. Both functions require a nontrivial degree of legislative autonomy. A credible legislature is one that is *independent enough* to enable elites, acting collectively, to impose costs on the chief executive for reneging on intra-elite commitments. The informational function of legislatures is also important. The ability of the chief executive to get credible information from parliamentary processes – such as on the true state of public affairs and citizens' demands – is predicated on relatively competitive elections and open debate that allows legislators to reveal their opinions and preferences. Furthermore, the complexities of policymaking, sharing of governance rents, managing the specific interests of individual legislators, and the monitoring of subordinates via the state bureaucracy necessitate the creation of an open forum in which legislators can reveal crucial information to the autocrat about the general state of the regime.

I conceptualize executive-legislative relations as a bilateral veto arrangement – with the chief executive monopolizing proposal powers and a reactive legislature. Once presented with a legislative proposal (bill), legislators vote to either accept, reject, or amend the proposal. Executive bills require a simple majority to get passed. If a proposal is amended, it is renegotiated by the chief executive and legislators before being subjected to a vote. If rejected, the chief executive has the option of submitting an alternative proposal or may ignore the legislature and unilaterally implement the proposed policies. Unilateral executive action is costly. Open disagreements with legislators may signal executive weakness, inability to lobby legislators, or an abrogation of intra-elite commitment to share power and governance rents. This may result in elite rebellion or a coup. Coercing legislators also has the disadvantage of short-circuiting the legislature's informational function.

The chief executives seeks to maximize executive power and share of governance rents. Executive power is the capacity to effectively monitor, regulate, and balance political action among fellow elites. The chief executive boosts executive power by investing in the state's coercive apparatus and control over the distribution of governance rents. All else equal, the chief executive seeks to maximize the informational benefits of governing with a relatively autonomous legislature, subject to the constraint of being able to balance the institution. In dealing with legislators, the chief executive submits proposals that have a high likelihood of getting passed, or invests in lobbying or coercing pivotal legislators. Lobbying may be in the form of targeted patronage or promises of pork to pivotal legislators' constituencies. Coercion may include threats of arrest, imprisonment, or expulsion from the legislature. The chief executive's ability to balance the legislature is conditioned by exogenous or historically determined factors that are costly to change in the short term. These factors include established norms that govern executive-legislative relations, or the ability to monitor, persuade, and coerce legislators through the police and intelligence agencies, party cadre, the state administrative structure, or patronage.

Individual legislators serve in single-member districts under plurality voting, and are primarily concerned with reelection in order to maintain access to a share of governance rents. In addition, legislators have to signal loyalty to the chief executive. In other words, individual legislators are careerist and know that they operate in a political context dominated by the chief executive who can make or break their political careers. Therefore, incumbent legislators spend their time investing in localized political support – by performing constituency service and delivering targeted clientelistic benefits – subject to the constraint of remaining loyal to the chief executive and regime.

There is a separation of powers between the executive and legislative branches of government. The chief executive executes laws passed by the legislature and is head of the state bureaucracy and security services. In addition, the chief executive has decree authority, and can engage in unilateral action without the direct consent of the legislature. The legislature is empowered to pass laws (including those touching on fiscal matters) and to oversee executive functions.[17] Interbranch separation of powers is underpinned by a separation of mandate.[18] Legislators and the chief executive derive their electoral mandate from different constituencies. Legislators are elected by voters in Single-Member Districts. The chief executive is elected by a national electorate. Therefore, legislators seek to please pivotal voters in their respective constituencies while the chief executive targets pivotal voters among the national electorate. The policy preferences of these two sets of voters do not always coincide, making executive-legislative relations structurally conflictual. On occasion, even loyal legislators have incentives to oppose the chief executive's legislative proposals – thereby necessitating amendments, renegotiations, direct lobbying, or coercion.

More generally, individual legislators are cross-pressured on account of being multitask agents with multiple principals (see Figure 3.1). The electoral channel constitutes a vertical accountability relationship with voters (depicted by *a*). To this end their electoral success is contingent on being perceived to have done a good job of making policy, performing constituency service, and providing targeted clientelistic benefits to their constituents (*b* and *c*). Constituency service may include initiating local development projects, securing public sector jobs for constituents, or enabling easy access to government services. Targeted clientelistic

---

[17] There also exists a judicial branch, whose role is to adjudicate on legal matters. However, the powers and effectiveness of the judicial branch are endogenous to the prevailing executive-legislative balance of power.

[18] See Persson, Roland, and Tabellini (1997) for a formal discussion of separation of mandate as a basis for the realization of separation of powers.

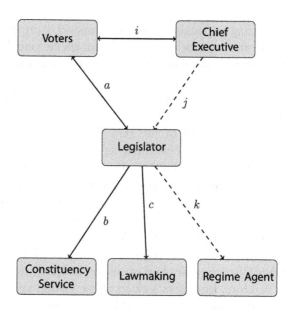

Figure 3.1 The cross-pressured legislator: multiple principals and tasks
Notes: The figure depicts the legislator as a multitask agent with multiple principals. The strength of the principal–agent relationships (*a* and *j*) and the effort the legislator applies (*b*, *c*, and *k*) determine observed levels of independence of individual legislators and legislative institutional strength. Legislatures are strongest when individual legislators act not as agents of the chief executive (weak *j* and *k*), but as agents of voters in their localized constituencies (strong *a*, *b*, and *c*).

benefits may include paying for funerals, hospital costs, or school fees.

At the same time, legislators are incentivized to signal support for the chief executive and the ruling regime (*j*). In this capacity, they serve as regime agents to their constituents and work to popularize the chief executive's policies and the regime in general (*k*). Catering to the demands of both principals requires a delicate balancing act. In anticipation of elections, legislators must work to please pivotal voters in their respective constituencies by differentiating themselves from challengers and exerting effort in constituency service and the provision of targeted clientelistic benefits. At the same time, legislators must carefully calibrate their investments in reelection in order to avoid being perceived to cultivate localized power bases that are independent of the chief executive and ruling party.

Determining the optimum levels of investment in a personal vote (localized support in a constituency) and being a regime agent constitute diurnal intra-elite politics. Legislators must balance their need to remain loyal to the regime with the need to boost their individual bargaining power by signaling strong local electoral support. The chief executive must also calibrate her demands for personal loyalty with the need to bolster public support for the regime through the cooptation of popular elites as legislators. These calculations are at the core of the realized distribution of power in executive-legislative relations.

3.3.2 The Lawmaking Process

Having outlined the specific parameters governing interbranch relations, this section delves into the specifics of lawmaking in autocratic legislatures. Under normal political conditions, the chief executive proposes pieces of legislation (bills) to guide public policy. Individual legislators debate the chief executive's policy proposals in order to ensure that their specific interests (both political and private) are taken care of. During such debates suitable amendments can be made on executive proposals within the legislature, subject to the approval of the chief executive. The chief executive signals a specific range of acceptable amendments and debate topics, and allows for intra-legislature coalition building in order to win majorities for specific policy proposals. The chief executive employs multiple tactics to ensure that statutes emerging from the legislature are not at variance with her preferences; and that intra-legislative coalitions do not become strong enough to challenge executive authority. In other words, the autocratic legislature has agency, but in a tight corner.

The legislature can react to the chief executive's proposed bills in one of three ways. It can reject the proposal by voting against it. It can pass the proposal without amendments. Or it can add amendments, renegotiate with the chief executive, and then vote on the amended proposal. An outright rejection of a chief executive's proposal would be a sign of an interbranch informational breakdown. Recall that the chief executive has an incentive to propose legislation with a high likelihood of getting passed. When a bill is rejected, the chief executive can either act unilaterally or submit a new proposal that is able to garner support from a legislative majority. Under conditions whereby the chief executive can accurately predict the policy preferences of pivotal legislatures, all bills introduced get passed.

Because the chief executive cannot anticipate every possible effect of a proposed piece of legislation, sometimes legislative debates reveal new information on a bill's distributional consequences. The new information is then incorporated into the original bill as amendments before renegotiation or passage. It is important to note that even when new information allows for amendments, the chief executive retains the right to kill a bill or to veto the eventual outcome. In other words, legislatures lack ends independence.

In order to maintain ultimate control over the legislature, the chief executive makes a clear distinction between what is considered legitimate versus subversive political action; and then monitors elite political activity both within and outside the legislature to ensure that it is restricted to the former. These objectives are achieved through both intra-legislative and extra-legislative means of elite control. Intra-legislative control includes monopoly over agenda setting, initiation of bills, and the threat of the veto. Extra-legislative control includes threats of expulsion from the ruling party, arrest or imprisonment, and the rationing of access to governance rents. Subversive political action may include openly criticizing the chief executive, investing in an independent localized political base, or building a majority legislative coalition with the intention of ousting the chief executive. Legitimate political action may include localized intra-elite contests in the quest to win over votes, or open debate in the legislature that seeks to generate more efficient policy outcomes for the benefit of the regime, chief executive, and the wider elite class.

Notice that constitutions, being incomplete contracts, cannot fully anticipate the full range of laws required to maintain executive-legislative balance of power. Even under autocracy, diurnal intra-elite politics determines the realized levels of interbranch separation of powers and executive-legislative relations. In the words of Madison, "a mere demarcation on parchment of the constitutional limits of these several departments, is not a sufficient guard against those encroachments which lead to a tyrannical concentration of all the powers of government in the same hands" (Madison, 1788).

In short, stability in executive-legislative relations is maintained through not only legislators' ability to check executive power, but also the chief executive's capacity to effectively balance legislatures. In the next section I examine executive-legislative relations further by injecting dynamic understanding of politics in the lawmaking process.

3.3.3 The Dynamic Politics of Lawmaking

The model legislative process proceeds as follows. At the beginning of each legislative session, the chief executive determines how much intra-legislative autonomy (means independence) to grant the legislature. This decision is informed by her ability to effectively monitor elite political activity within and outside of the legislature. The amount of autonomy granted to the legislature is increasing in the capacity of the chief executive to monitor and regulate elite political activity. After the executive makes clear the acceptable bounds of political action and policy debate, individual legislators respond by building coalitions that maximize their personal share of governance rents and chances of reelection.

In equilibrium the chief executive is able to predict, with reasonable accuracy, the preferences of the pivotal legislator. And, most, if not all, executive legislative proposals get passed. The preferences of pivotal legislators incorporate the preferences of their respective constituents, the distributional consequences of specific bills, and the chief executive's lobbying and tolerance for coercion. Thus, the law of anticipated reactions conditions the behavior of the chief executive and legislators alike, and the lawmaking process seems scripted.

Two factors may disturb this equilibrium. First, the chief executive may fail to fully anticipate specific bills' complexity and demands for open parliamentary debate. This reality may force her to allow for greater legislative autonomy than prescribed at the beginning of the legislative session. Second, unanticipated crises may alter the executive-legislative balance of power. Major scandals, sustained economic decline, or an unforeseen decline in the chief executive's popular support may cause an imbalance in executive-legislative relations by strengthening legislators' bargaining power. Under these conditions, entrepreneurial legislators may seek to expand legislative authority beyond the chief executive's stated bounds. And, a (temporarily) weakened chief executive may increase legislative operational autonomy, means independence, and legislators' share of governance rents as a concession to fellow elites.[19] Furthermore, an unanticipated shock in executive-legislative relations may embolden legislators during debates to reveal damaging information that could kill executive bills – thereby reducing the proportion of executive bills passed in any given legislative session.

The chief executive's subjective conception of security of tenure conditions her response to new information on bills, political crises, or unanticipated changes in executive-legislative balance of power. As shown in the previous chapter, a chief executive who is unsure of her ability to give concessions to fellow elites without losing power may react by abolishing the legislature altogether. A less drastic response may involve the use of threats and coercion to curtail legislative autonomy, or direct interference in the legislature to engineer outcomes that are consistent with the preferences of the chief executive. In short, a weak chief executive reacts to crises and unanticipated new information by hoarding power and curtailing the legislature's operational autonomy. By contrast, a stronger chief executive is more likely to give concessions to fellow elites – in no small part because of her ability to effectively monitor and regulate elite political activity and to balance the legislature. In this manner, the chief executive's capacity to balance fellow elites acting collectively within and outside the legislature determines the level of legislative means independence.

Over time, intra-elite contestations over legislative means independence with respect to specific bills and in reaction to unanticipated crises and changes in executive-legislative relations drive legislative development. The lack of means independence among legislatures under relatively weak chief executives disincentives legislators from

---

[19] Consider the example of the murder of Kenyan legislator Josiah M. Kariuki (MP, Nyandarua) in March 1975. In the preceding months, Kariuki had become increasingly critical of President Jomo Kenyatta. Therefore, his murder generated a crisis that severely eroded Kenyatta's legitimacy (Tamarkin, 1978; Ajulu, 2002). Amid the crisis, entrepreneurial legislators (led by Martin Shikuku and Jean-Marie Seroney) pushed for the establishment of an independent parliamentary commission of inquiry whose report implicated the president's allies in the murder. It is noteworthy that once the storm over the assassination blew over, Kenyatta reasserted his control by jailing Shikuku and Seroney at the earliest opportunity (Opalo, 2014).

investing in legislative organizational development – the overall outcome of which is stunted legislative development. Sustained means independence under stronger chief executives – even if restricted to specific types of bills – incentivizes legislators to develop and act within the stipulates of organizational mechanisms needed to manage intertemporal legislative bargaining processes and capacity to balance the chief executive. Specific investments may include factors that facilitate both effective policymaking and the development of the legislature's institutional authority. Thus, legislatures with means independence are likely to bargain for resources to boost policy research and legislative drafting expertise, creation of specialized legislative committees, development of internal procedural rules, and more plenary time through an increase in the frequency of legislative sittings.

It is worth noting that legislative development is not unidirectional. A legislature with means independence today may prove too powerful to veto tomorrow. Executive-legislative relations are therefore subject to revision depending on the prevailing intra-elite balance of power. In general, a chief executive intent on staying in office maintains agenda control by denying the legislature ends independence. In addition, the chief executive's subjective sense of security of tenure defines the upper bound of legislative means independence – and by extension, legislative development. In this manner, strong chief executives preside over relatively autonomous and organizationally developed legislatures. In the next section I apply this model to briefly explain legislative development in postcolonial Africa.

3.4 Postcolonial Legislative Development as Catch-Up

African legislatures were founded weak. And, at the core of legislative weakness in the region was a fundamental structural imbalance in executive-legislative relations. Having been created by fiat, these legislatures largely mimicked European institutions' forms and functions but without the backing of powerful elites (barons) with sufficient economic and coercive powers to balance chief executives. Founding presidents and prime ministers inherited colonial political systems with fused executive, legislative, and judicial functions almost intact (Mamdani, 1996). Therefore, at independence African executive branches of government were orders of magnitude more developed relative to the legislative and judicial branches. An indication of the preponderance of executive power in the region was the quick adoption of centralized presidential systems of government and single-party rule in the decade after independence. As a general matter, Africa's phenomenon of "Big Man Presidentialism" stunted legislative development in the region.

Postcolonial legislative development in Africa was therefore a decidedly catch-up process. Imbalanced executive-legislative relations in the region granted presidents significant control over legislative development. The problem of overdeveloped executive branches of government was compounded by the fact that Africa's founding legislators were, for the most part, individuals of limited economic and political power. For instance, a majority of the founding legislators in Kenya, Ghana, and Senegal were either teachers or petty businesspeople. Many of these legislators were also part of the newly educated class of politicians that lacked precolonial sociocultural bases of political power.[20] For these reasons, postcolonial African legislators were largely dependent on chief executives for patronage and the advancement of their political careers.

Executive dominance over legislatures found expression in the spread of single-party rule, control over legislative budgets and calendars, monopoly over the origination of legislation, and the maintenance of coercive powers to punish disloyal legislators. Single-party rule enabled African presidents to address the problems of averse selection and moral hazard associated with legislative elections. Sole ruling parties screened candidates (for loyalty) before legislative elections and enforced party discipline and loyalty among incumbent legislators. The threat of expulsion from the party and the legislature kept legislators in check. Exploiting the monopoly over the origination of legislation, African presidents invariably introduced bills that reinforced their power. The powers to call, prorogue, and dissolve legislatures enabled the same presidents to keep legislators in recess during crises and to engineer loyal legislative majorities. In order to

---

[20] Hornsby (1985) documents the case of Kenya's postcolonial legislators. See Allman (1993) for a description of Ghana's founding legislature. Hodgkin and Schachter (1961) provide a description of founding legislatures in former French colonies in West Africa. In all these cases the elites that comprised legislatures lacked sufficient political or economic power to balance founding presidents.

limit legislative oversight, presidents rationed legislatures' financial resources through the budget process. When these controls failed, presidents resorted to coercion. Disloyal legislators were denied access to patronage, jailed, or killed. In extreme cases some presidents simply abolished legislatures.

Through these mechanisms African presidents were able to monitor and regulate elite political activity within and outside of legislatures. However, intra-elite politics and unanticipated shocks often disturbed established equilibria of executive-legislative relations. In reaction, relatively secure presidents granted legislatures means independence. Their less secure counterparts hoarded even more power or abolished legislatures altogether. History also mattered. In an effort to balance executive power, legislators in states with relatively longer colonial experiences with legislatures appealed to established traditions governing executive-legislative relations and political culture. Such appeals increased the likelihood of achieving legislative means independence, in part due to the fact that established ideas of *how legislatures work* made such a concession less threatening to chief executives' power.

A number of factors moderated these presidential powers. First, presidents' informational needs created incentives for the conduct of relatively free legislative elections and the granting of legislative means independence. For example, Senegal, Kenya, Tanzania, and Zambia have all held competitive legislative elections throughout their postcolonial history. Second, the need to popularize their respective regimes forced African presidents to incorporate elites with established local bases of political support in legislatures. This was primarily driven by the high levels of ethnic fractionalization in African states. The imperatives of nation building necessitated ascriptive representation of specific ethnic groups in legislatures. And, in order to boost the regime's legitimacy, presidents were at times forced to tolerate legislators representing specific regions or ethnic groups whose political loyalties were not always guaranteed. And, once in office, such legislators typically leveraged their popularity to enhance their bargaining power vis-à-vis presidents.

Third, the mere existence of legislatures conditioned presidential action. The incentive to only propose bills with a high likelihood of getting passed defined the set of possible executive bills. As outlined above, this constitutional and procedural hurdle both conditioned executive action and created opportunities for bargaining over policy and renegotiation of established intra-elite pacts.

Finally, the end of single-party rule across Africa in the early 1990s loosened presidential control over legislatures. No longer was legislative incumbency conditional on being a member of the ruling party. The availability of outside options with regard to electoral vehicles strengthened legislators' bargaining power vis-à-vis presidents. This was particularly true for legislatures that had enjoyed means independence under single-party rule and therefore had higher levels of organizational capacity. In other words, the rate of legislative development at the dawn of multiparty politics was directly correlated with the level of means independence under single-party rule.

This formulation of legislative development as catch-up in the shadow of preponderant chief executives matches the postcolonial historical record. The model presented in this chapter explains variation in legislative development under relatively more powerful chief executives; and the conditions under which strong democratic legislatures were likely to emerge from their autocratic foundations. In short, strong chief executives are likely to govern with strong autocratic legislatures; and strong autocratic legislatures beget strong democratic legislatures.

3.5 The Empirics of Legislative Development

A core claim of this book is that legislative strength and institutionalization under a relatively more powerful chief executive is positively correlated with the chief executive's political strength and subjective security of tenure. Due to the risk of legislative tyranny, chief executives' ability to concede legislative independence to fellow elites is conditioned by their capacity to balance legislatures. In this section I provide a number of empirically testable hypotheses derived from this claim.

3.5.1 Hypotheses

Using material evidence from Kenya and Zambia, the empirical analyses in this book are driven by two simple hypotheses and their observable implications:

*H*1: Secure chief executives are more likely to govern with legislatures that have relatively high levels of means independence and operational autonomy.

> *H*1.1: The number of legislative sittings and the proportion of the budget allocated to legislatures are directly proportional to the chief executive's security of tenure. At the same time, the share of executive bills passed is inversely proportional to the chief executive's security of tenure.
>
> *H*1.2: Legislators' ability to cultivate a personal vote and local support is directly proportional to the chief executive's security of tenure. In other words, secure chief executives are less likely to directly interfere in legislative elections relative to their less secure counterparts.

*H*2: Following transition from autocracy to democracy, the process of legislative strengthening and institutionalization is likely to be faster under legislatures previously dominated by secure chief executives relative to those dominated by insecure chief executives.

3.5.2 Empirical Strategy

Kenya and Zambia are ideal cases for testing these hypotheses. The two countries share a number of similarities – including British settler colonial rule, a Westminster-style legislative institutional inheritance, postcolonial single-party rule, and politicized ethnicity. However, despite these similarities, the two countries have also had divergent trajectories of legislative development – with the Kenyan legislature emerging as relatively stronger and more institutionalized compared to its Zambian counterpart. To explain these differences, my qualitative analyses employ the Mills Method of Difference to explain the divergence in organizational strength and institutionalization between the Kenyan and Zambian legislatures.

To identify the effects of means independence on legislative strength and institutionalization in both Kenya and Zambia, I examine structural breaks in measures of legislative strength and institutionalization over time. I consider two important transition periods. The first transition is the end of colonial rule, which created national legislatures in both countries under the shadow of relatively more powerful presidents. The second transition is the end of single-party rule, which altered executive-legislative relations by increasing the bargaining power of legislators. I exploit the quasi-exogenous nature of these transitions to identify the causal relationship between means independence and legislative strength and institutionalizations. As I show in the next chapter, independence in both countries was achieved earlier than had been anticipated by British colonial authorities. As late as 1959 British authorities were still insisting that Africans were not yet ready for self-government (Willis, Cheeseman, and Lynch, 2018). Similarly, the end of single-party rule in both countries was forced on their respective presidents following the surprisingly swift collapse of the Soviet Union in 1990 (Kuran, 1991).

In Chapters 4 and 5 I focus on the first hypothesis. I begin by documenting the colonial origins of the Kenyan and Zambian legislatures, and show how contingencies of political development in the late colonial period endowed the two countries with different state administrative and party structures; and how these outcomes in turn impacted their respective trajectories of legislative development in the postcolonial period. In short, the decolonization process endowed Kenya with a relatively secure president compared to his counterpart in Zambia. The analyses in these chapters are primarily historical, and seek to interpret the political histories of Kenya and Zambia using the model outlined in this chapter. In both chapters, my goal is to highlight the political nature of executive-legislative relations as well as the importance of conceptualizing intra-elite relations as two-way commitment problems.

Chapters 6 and 7 address both the first and second hypotheses. In Chapter 6 I explain the variation in longitudinal data on measures of legislative strength and institutionalization conditional on the security of tenure of presidents in Kenya and Zambia. These measures include the number of legislative sittings, proportion of executive bills passed, legislative budget allocation and remuneration of legislators, and instances of unilateral executive rule-making. Chapter 7 focuses on the electoral connection. Using data on postcolonial legislative elections in Kenya and Zambia I explore how presidents' perceived security of tenure impacted their willingness to tolerate free legislative elections and legislators' cultivation of local bases of power. My primary outcome of interest in the chapter is the existence (or absence) of legislative incumbency advantage across time. Combined, these chapters present a rich array of material evidence that support the claims derived from the model of legislative development presented in this chapter.

4 | Colonial Origins of Parliaments in Kenya and Zambia

4.1 Explaining Institutional Divergence

To the casual observer, the Kenyan and Zambian legislatures would have looked very similar in 1990 right before the end of single-party rule. Both legislatures were exports of the British Westminster Model of Parliamentary Sovereignty, but that struggled for relevance in the shadow of autocratic presidents atop single-party regimes. Both had very limited influence on public policy and were relatively poorly resourced – in terms of both their organizational budget and the remuneration of legislatures. And, due to single-party rule, both were populated by legislators whose political careers and material well-being depended on remaining in the good graces of their respective presidents. In short, the two legislatures fit the general profile of African legislatures that had for three decades been variously described as "residual" or "rubber-stamp" institutions that were peripheral to the policymaking process on account of their complete subservience to chief executives.

Yet, these outward similarities masked very important underlying differences. Kenya's first five parliaments had met for a total of 2,355 legislative sittings and passed 615 bills, at an average annual rate of 80.48 percent of executive bills introduced. Over the same period Zambia's parliaments had 42 percent fewer sittings (1,371) but passed 50 percent more bills (934), at a rate of 90.1 percent of executive bills introduced. For every bill passed, the Kenyan legislature held 4.6 sittings, while its Zambian counterpart only averaged 1.7 sittings. Lastly, in its first 25 years of existence the postindependence Kenyan parliament got, on average, a higher proportion of the annual national budget to finance its activities (0.53 percent) compared to the Zambian legislature (0.3 percent).[1]

---

[1] Between independence and 1991 the introduction of legislation in both Kenya and Zambia was monopolized by the executive. According to the Standing Orders, Members of Parliament had to seek permission from the whole House

What these underlying statistics and organizational characteristics reveal is that while on the surface the Kenyan and Zambian legislatures may have looked uniformly weak, in reality they were different. In particular, it is clear that during the single-party era the Kenyan legislature was organizationally more developed than its Zambian counterpart. It held relatively more legislative sessions per year, was better resourced, and passed executive bills at relatively lower rates. Both legislatures existed under the shadow of autocratic presidents and lacked ends independence. But, the Kenyan legislature enjoyed higher levels of means independence relative to its Zambian counterpart. Kenyan chief executives allowed for intra-legislative debates and bargains, a fact that created demand for more sittings and exposed the lawmaking process to occasional bargaining failures and the consequent abandonment of specific bills. In Zambia, executive control over the lawmaking process limited intra-legislative bargains and debates. Lacking the ability to influence legislation, the Zambian legislature had relatively few sittings and passed nearly all executive bills introduced.

In this chapter I explore the colonial origins of the divergence in legislative development in Kenya and Zambia. My objectives are twofold. First, I highlight the similar colonial origins of the two legislatures under British rule. Kenya and Zambia are former settler-dominated British colonies that had Legislative Councils founded on the Westminster Model, underpinned by the doctrine of Parliamentary Sovereignty. Second, I analyze the processes of political developments under colonial rule, and especially in the late colonial period, and their lasting impact on institutional development in the two countries. Both countries experienced critical junctures on the eve of independence. After decades of European rule, local political elites were charged with the task of adapting inherited legislative structures and practices to their respective political economies. The core finding in this chapter is that the contingencies of political development in the late colonial period

before submitting Private Members' Bills. These requests were disincentivized through restrictions on drafting facilities (for which members had to pay for out of pocket) and the threat of the Speaker's pen. Only two Private Members' Bills ever made it to the floor of the Kenyan National Assembly (1968 and 1969). One got passed and got presidential assent (Josiah M. Kariuki's Hire Purchase Bill, 1968). The second was hijacked and reformulated by the executive (Jean-Marie Seroney's National Assembly and Presidential Elections Bill, 1969). Zambia did not have any Private Members' Bills over the same period.

put Kenya and Zambia on separate paths of legislative development. Kenya inherited a much stronger administrative state, a weak elite party, and a political culture that elevated the legislature to be the focal locus of intra-elite bargaining over power and governance rents. All these factors enabled Kenya's founding president to tolerate legislative means independence in the postcolonial period. In Zambia, independence was achieved on the back of a strong mass party and followed by the dismantling of the country's administrative apparatus. Unable to credibly monitor and regulate political action by fellow elites, Zambia's founding president curtailed legislative means independence.

4.2 Legislative Councils under Colonial Rule

The Kenyan and Zambian legislatures have deep colonial roots. For much of the interwar period both territories were settler colonies destined to become dominions in the mold of Southern Rhodesia and South Africa (see Table 4.1).[2] The governor in either colony headed the Executive Council (proto Cabinet) and the Legislative Council (LegCo), and was the embodiment of metropolitan authority. Power was concentrated in the hands of the governor, supported by an executive council and an autocratic provincial administration. The governor also served as both the President (proto Speaker) and official government spokesperson in the LegCo. In 1948 both colonies' LegCos saw the appointment of substantive Speakers. The Northern Rhodesian LegCo also saw its term extended from three to five years. In Kenya, the LegCo retained its four-year term.[3] However, this institutional change had little impact on executive-legislative relations. The Colonial Office (Whitehall) could still veto any piece of legislation emerging from either LegCo. And, the metropolitan parliament in London retained the ultimate legislative authority in either colony. Simply stated, the colonial LegCos in Kenya and Zambia lacked ends independence.

---

[2] Mosley (1983) defines settler colonies as British possessions where "European [farmers] owned land and were dependent on the labour of indigenous people" (p. 9). This definition makes the list of African settler colonies include Algeria, Angola, Botswana, Kenya, Mozambique, South Africa, Swaziland, Zambia, and Zimbabwe.

[3] Kenya's LegCo Speakers included William K. Horne (1948–1955), Ferdinand W. Cavendish-Bentinck (1955–1960), and Humphrey Slade (1960–1970). Northern Rhodesia's LegCo Speakers included Thomas S. Page (1948–1956) and Thomas Williams (1956–1964).

Table 4.1 *Colonial administration in Kenya and Zambia*

Country	Population (m)	Settlers (%)	Indirect Rule	Administration	Service
Kenya	7.65	0.5	58.8	350	1,362
Zambia	2.73	3.0	59.6	210	654
British Colonies			58.9	179	548

Notes: The second column shows European settlers as a share of the total population. Colonial administration figures are from 1957. The population estimates are from 1958 for Kenya and 1955 for Zambia. The colonial service (European) figures are from 1939. Settler population and the index of the extent of indirect rule are from 1955. The last row presents averages for all British colonies in Africa with available data. Zambia had the highest administrators to population ratio of all British colonies in Africa. Data are from Jeffries (1972), Kirk-Greene (1980), and Lange (2004).

4.2.1 Balancing Competing Interests

Both colonies' LegCos had mixed membership comprising "officials" appointed from among senior executive officers and "unofficials" from the civilian population. Officials represented Whitehall's interests. Typically, this involved ensuring that the LegCo internalized the political costs of legislative outputs – especially with regard to their impact on Africans. Unofficials represented the interests of European immigrants. Official majority effectively made both LegCos subordinate to Whitehall, an arrangement that was supported by officials and opposed by unofficials. For example, in 1924 Governor Stanley of Northern Rhodesia argued that "a council like ours is not a parliament in the generally accepted sense," adding that the LegCo's composition "obviously places the government in a position to exercise effective control" (Davidson 1974, p. 99). Whitehall also extended its control over LegCos through the publication of Model Ordinances with a view of standardizing legislative outputs in the colonies (Pike, 1951).

Governors' delicate task of balancing African and European interests occasionally resulted in clashes with extremist European Members of the Legislative Councils (MLCs). For instance, in 1908 Governor Sadler of Kenya suspended two MLCs for protesting against the administration's labor policy (Hakes, 1970, p. 5). In Northern Rhodesia, where after 1935 there was greater cooperation between officials and unofficials, the need to openly debate sensitive matters resulted in the odd LegCo procedure of holding private sessions for which the only records kept were notes from the council's Clerk (Davidson, 1974). Governors in both colonies served relatively short tenures.[4] In general, governors in Kenya displayed greater independence from unofficial influence relative to their counterparts in Northern Rhodesia.

Kenya's colonial Legislative Council (LegCo) was founded in October 1906. At its first meeting in August 1907 it was entirely composed of appointed European immigrants. The election of unofficials became a reality in 1919 with the passage of the Electoral Representation Bill (Hakes, 1970). The first elections were held in 1920 (Amutabi, 2010). The dominant group among unofficial MLCs consisted of representatives of agriculturalist rural settlers. Political development among European immigrants began in 1911 with the formation of the Convention of Associations, a hardline political outfit that represented rural agricultural interests and advocated for policies that protected Europeans from African competition and flirted with forced labor among Africans. Through its political influence, this group was able to capture important aspects of state policymaking in the service of its economic interests (Mosley, 1983). The Convention effectively functioned as "The Settlers' Parliament" that discussed bills "clause by clause before they received similar treatment in the Legislative Council" (Bennett, 1957, p. 114). Until 1927, governors and official MLCs attended these sessions.

However, "narrow factionalism and sterile personal squabbling" prevented the emergence of a strong European political movement as existed in the settler colonies of Southern African

---

[4] Colonial governors served for an average of 4 years in Kenya and 3.3 years in Zambia. In Kenya they included James H. Sadler (1906–1909), Percey Giround (1909–1912), Henry Belfield (1912–1917), Charles Bowring in an acting capacity (1917–1919), Edward Northey (1919–1922), Robert Coryndon (1922–1925), Edward Grigg (1925–1930), Joseph Bayrne (1931–1937), Robert Brooke-Popham (1937–1939), Henry M. Moore (1940–1944), Philip Mitchell (1944–1952), Evelyne Baring (1952–1959), Patrick Renison (1959–1962), and Malcom J. MacDonald (1963). In Zambia, they included Herbert Stanley (1924–1927), Richard A. J. Goode in an acting capacity (1927), James Maxwell (1927–1932), Ronald Storrs (1932–1935), Hubert W. Young (1935–1938), John Maybin (1938–1941), William M. Logan in an acting capacity (1941), John Waddington (1941–1947), Robert C. S. Stanley (1948), Gilbert Rennie (1948–1954), Alexander T. Williams (1954), Arthur Benson (1954–1959), and Evelyn D. Hone (1959–1964).

(Clough, 1990, p. 32). In the 1930s, the Elected Members Organization emerged as a moderating European influence within the LegCo.
However, the Convention remained to be the dominant European
voice in the LegCo until the 1940s when its members' economic
power was eclipsed by a moderate urban European industrial and
commercial class. Increasing reliance on African markets and trained
labor forced this latter group to moderate its politics. Thereafter,
the more liberal European voices – led by Michael Blundell – gained
ascendance at the expense of hardline agriculturalists (Wasserman,
1976, p. 26). It was not until November 1944 that the first
African, Eliud Wambu Mathu, was appointed to the LegCo.[5] Beneah
Apolo Ohanga was the second African MLC, appointed in 1947.
Before then various appointed European members – many of them
missionaries – represented African interests in the council.[6] Substantive African representation through elections became a reality in 1957.

In Northern Rhodesia (colonial Zambia), the legislature was
founded in February 1924 after Whitehall's takeover of the colony
from the British South African Company (BSAC). Like in Kenya,
initially African representation in the LegCo was through appointed
Europeans. It was not until 1948 that Rev. Henry Kasokolo and
Nelson Nalumango sat in the Northern Rhodesian LegCo following
nomination by the African Representative Council (ARP) and
appointment by the governor. Substantive African representation
through elections was achieved in 1954. Before the discovery of
copper in the early 1930s, European farming and small business
interests dominated the Northern Rhodesian LegCo. But, after 1938,

---

[5] Demands for African MLCs were first voiced in 1924 and persisted for the two
decades preceding Mathu's appointment. The appointment was in anticipation
of postwar politics led by returning soldiers (Roelker, 1976, p. 72). Mathu was
chosen from a list of three nominees selected on advisement by African Local
Native Councils (LNCs) on the strength of his moderate political and social
views. The other two were Peter Mbiyu Koinange and Chief Paul Mboya Snr.
Appointed African MLCs (recommended by LNCs) increased to two in 1947,
four in 1948, and six in 1952, and eight after the 1957 elections.

[6] The appointment of missionaries was driven by the fact that they were
perceived to be sympathetic to African interests. This was not always true. For
the most part, missionaries operated as complements to the general colonial
project and received significant state assistance (Berman, 1974, p. 182). Over
time, the political influence of European missionaries in the colony declined
with the emergence of African independent churches and schools in the 1930s.
Thereafter, politicians (Europeans and later Africans) were appointed to
represent African interests in the LegCo.

hardline trade unionists, most of them linked to the burgeoning mining and (rail) transportation sectors, rose to prominence in the institution. In 1941 this faction of European immigrants founded the Northern Rhodesia Labor Party (NRLP) under the leadership of Roland "Roy" Welensky, an engine driver first elected to the council in 1938.

Under Welensky's leadership the NRLP took an overtly racist path, and pushed for greater pay and working conditions for European industrial and mineworkers at the expense of Africans. The party also adopted calls for European-dominated responsible government, as had existed in Southern Rhodesia since 1923.[7] All these moves naturally followed from the fact that the NRLP's "political ideas were largely derived from the European labour organizations of Southern Rhodesia and the Union of South Africa" (Davidson, 1974, p. 43). A constitutional amendment in 1945 further strengthened the position of European immigrants by providing for an unofficial majority in the LegCo. As I demonstrate below, the NRLP's singular hostility to African interests irreparably poisoned interracial politics in the colony.

Both colonies had subcolony assemblies that were designed to co-opt African elites and to preserve the "tribal" or "traditional" orientation of African peoples (Mamdani, 1996, p. 24).[8] In the words of the Chief Native Commissioner in Kenya, Africans were "to get some sort of assembly which will attract the younger and more

---

[7] The Southern Rhodesian LegCo had unofficial majorities beginning in 1907. In October 1922 the colony held a referendum that approved the establishment of responsible government (as opposed to incorporation into the Union of South Africa). Thus, 1923 saw the advent of racialist (white supremacist) government in Southern Rhodesia that only ended with Zimbabwean independence in 1980 (Bowman, 1971).

[8] The definition of "tradition" was, of course, a Janus-faced political move that served the specific goal of European domination and control on a shoestring budget. European administrators empowered African elites through the invention or reinforcement of African "customary law" and structures of "traditional authority" in moves that reified previously fluid and contested notions of law and ethnic differences (Tignor, 1971; Ranger, 1983). The cost of the protection of African "tradition" was economic exploitation in the context of highly racialized economies and political systems that largely benefited European immigrants at the expense of Africans (Rodney, 1982). A direct consequence of this approach to colonial administration of African societies was the evolution of parallel sociopolitical systems that produced the postcolonial African "bifurcated state" characterized by the moral-legal dualism of "two publics" comprising the "civil" (Europeanized) and "traditional" (African). By creating opportunities for moral, political, and economic arbitrage, this dualism severely stunted political (and economic) development in much of Africa (Ekeh, 1975).

vigorous brains among the natives and leave them to take an active part in their own administration, and thus to ensure that they are for the Government, not against it" (Lonsdale, 1968, p. 128). In short, membership to these councils was limited to collaborationist African elites – largely chiefs and public workers.

Kenya's Local Native Councils (LNCs) were established in 1924, largely modeled on British notions of Kikuyu councils of elders (they were renamed African District Councils in 1946).[9] The LNCs were partly elected and only dealt with African issues - including tax collection, labor mobilization, and enforcement of colonial policies emanating from Nairobi. Coterminous with district-level administrative boundaries, the LNCs were primarily created for specific ethnic groups. This was the beginning of ethnicized local administration in Kenya.[10] These councils were in turn supported by a prefectural system of African chiefs directly accountable to the Provincial Administration. Supervising the LNCs were District Commissioners with broad discretionary powers that fused police, judicial, and administrative functions. In the words of Joseph Murumbi, Kenya's second Vice President, "[t]hey were little demigods in their little empires, their District Empires" (Thurston and Donovan, 2015, p. 46). Unlike in other British colonies, the lack of strong precolonial chieftaincies in Kenya foreclosed on the possibility of a strong system of indirect rule (Tignor, 1971).[11] Undeterred, the colonial government invented chiefs and vested them with local administrative and "traditional" powers (Clough, 1990, p. 13). Kenyan chiefs were effectively government bureaucrats "appointed, paid, and controlled by the Provincial Administration" (Berman, 1974, p. 231).

[9] The process of inventing chieftaincies and grafting administrative authorities onto African societies came with its challenges. For example, Anderson (1993) documents how British elevation of Nandi and Kipsigis *Orkoiik* into administrative positions created tensions between them and traditional elders within these communities (p. 860).

[10] The only truly multiethnic councils in Kenya under colonialism were the African Advisory Councils created in Nairobi and Mombasa after 1939.

[11] The Wanga Kingdom in Western Kenya was the sole society with a strong and centralized kingdom in precolonial Kenya (Dealing, 1974). However, because the formative stages of the creation of the Kenya Colony were focused on the highlands, colonial administration evolved with the demands of having to pacify and then control the lands occupied largely by the decentralized Kikuyu and Maasai societies. Before 1920 the region between the present Kenya–Uganda border and Naivasha was part of the Eastern Province of the Uganda Protectorate.

In Zambia, African participation in colonial institutions co-evolved with its system of indirect rule. The "Native Administration" and "Native Courts" became a reality after 1929 under a system of indirect rule anchored on local chieftaincies (and modeled on the British experience in West Africa). Unlike in Kenya, the existence of strong precolonial centralized chieftaincies among the Lozi (Barotseland), Bemba, Lunda, and Ngoni made possible the establishment of indirect rule in Zambia (Baldwin, 2010, p. 52). By 1936 nearly all parts of the colony had recognized chiefs who headed local governments comprised of Native Administrations and Councils, and who were in turn supervised by District Commissioners (Meebelo, 1971; Davidson, 1974; Bond, 1975). Where chiefs did not exist, the colonial government simply created them *ex nihilo*. A number of subterritorial multiethnic councils were also created around this time – the African Urban Advisory Councils (AUACs) in the Copperbelt and African Provincial Councils (APCs) in Zambia's provinces. The latter were dominated by local chiefs. In 1946 the colony-wide 29-member African Representative Council (ARC) was created (with members nominated from APCs) and two years later granted the power to nominate two Africans to the LegCo.

Despite their institutional impotence, the subterritorial African councils defined early political development in both colonies (Ogot, 1963; Chuunga, 1968). In particular, their membership and organizational scope defined the contours of political mobilization. Zambia's African institutional structure comprising AUACs, APCs, and the ARC favored political mobilization across ethnic lines in the urban Copperbelt and at the provincial and national levels in the rest of the country. Kenya's LNCs incentivized political mobilization along ethnic lines at the district level.[12]

---

[12] Despite repeated official discussions beginning in the early 1920s, the idea of provincial and colony-wide African councils never took hold in Kenya. Beginning with the Kavirondo Tax Welfare Association (KTWA) in the southwest, African elites had demanded for African Provincial Councils and a national African Central Consultative Council. Similar calls also came from the African leadership in the LNCs in central Kenya – led by leaders in Murang'a District (Fort Hall). These calls were met with opposition from the colonial administration. In 1940 the administration informally established provincial advisory councils in Central and Nyanza provinces. Further calls for provincial and national African legislative institutions faded with the appointed of the first Kenya African to the Legislative Council in 1944. Thereafter, the political objective of nationalist politicians became to expand African representation in

Outside of established colonial institutional frameworks, African reactions to colonialism in the two colonies can be broken up into three phases. The first phase was characterized by resistance to colonial violence and land expropriation. This was met by a mix of "punitive expeditions" and British perfidy in dealing with African elites (Berman, 1974; Phiri, 1991).[13] Violent "pacification" campaigns were punctuated by treaties with African leaders that the British had no intention of honoring. Having lost the resistance struggle, in the second phase Africans resorted to channeling their grievances through institutional means. These grievances included the loss of land, exploitative taxation and labor laws, the color bar, the lack of public goods, and general violations of Africans' rights to assembly and free movement. The lack of direct representation in LegCos forced African elites to appeal directly to Whitehall by invoking stated British policy to "protect" African interests.

4.2.2 Institutionalization of Minority Rule

The institutional subordination of African interests to European demands was a core feature of colonialism in both Kenya and Zambia. In both colonies, European domination of institutions enabled extra-market operations designed to give European immigrants an upper

---

the LegCo – a process that was significantly dependent on district-cum-ethnic political machines and associations (Omosule, 1974).

[13] An infamous example is the October 19, 1905 murder of Koitalel arap Samoei, a Nandi leader in Kenya. Samoei was scheduled to meet Col. Richard Meinertzhagen for peace negotiations. But, Meinertzhagen, who came armed and backed by over 80 armed soldiers (75 of whom hid in the bush) shot the unarmed Samoei at point-blank range as the Nandi leader stretched his hand to greet him (Anderson, 1993, p. 858). In general, British "pacification" came with the destruction of farmland, seizure of livestock, and indiscriminate murder. Writing about the "Conquest State of Kenya," Lonsdale (1992) notes that the "British employed violence on a locally unprecedented scale, and with unprecedented singleness of mind" (p. 13). As late as 1911 the British were still fighting pacification wars against the Marakwet, Turkana, and Tharaka of Kenya. The Giriama Uprising (1913–1920) – inspired by Mekatilili wa Menza – was evidence of the shakiness of *Pax Britannica* in the early decades of colonial administration. Such rebellions among previously "pacified" regions point to the inherent precariousness of early colonial administrations. British conquest in Northern Rhodesia was equally bloodyConflict with the Ngoni marked the end of the *chamtendere* (a time of peace) period under Chief Mpezeni. In the same vein, violent clashes often punctuated the process of procuring treaties from the Bemba and Lunda (Macpherson, 1976).

hand in agriculture and trade (Mosley, 1983; Vickery, 1985). For example, the Northern Rhodesian LegCo unanimously passed the Maize Control Ordinance (1935) that allotted European farmers three-quarters of the market (Davidson, 1974, p. 64). Similarly, in 1937 the Cattle Control Board was established to "protect Europeans from African competition" (Dresang, 1975, p. 78). Kanogo (1987) notes that as early as 1929 Africans squatting on alienated land complained about *kifagio* – forced de-stocking that robbed households of hundreds of livestock (a common store of wealth). European immigrants in Kenya also successfully lobbied for a ban on cash crop production by Africans in the interwar period, in part to forestall low-cost competition for both markets and African labor (Wasserman, 1976, p. 24). In general, European immigrants in both colonies wanted land and labor at below-market rates (i.e., through coercion), guaranteed domestic and international markets, better working conditions, and public goods such as security and transportation infrastructure. They channeled these demands to Whitehall either through the LegCo or direct lobbying in London.

In Kenya the settlers initially organized around the Convention of Associations (that brought together district-based political groups). In Zambia, initial political action among settlers took place via the North-Western Rhodesia Farmers' Association and the North-Eastern Rhodesia Agricultural and Commercial Association, before they were eclipsed by mining and commercial interests in the Copperbelt. Thereafter, the Northern Rhodesian economy became heavily reliant on copper and its LegCo saw the ascendance of the NRLP. In Kenya, European immigrants were politically relevant on account of the size and economic importance of their landholdings. Northern Rhodesian European immigrants found voice through sheer (relative) numbers (see Table 4.1) and proximity to the charged racialist politics of South Africa and Southern Rhodesia.

In both Kenya and Zambia, governors – together with their Executive Councils (proto Cabinets), Secretariats (Civil Services), and field officers (Provincial Administrations) – served as prefectural apparatuses accountable directly to Whitehall. The delicate balance between the governors and European immigrants defined the "Dual Mandate" (Lugard, 1922). European exploitation of Africans was to be tolerated, indeed even encouraged, but only to the extent that it did not lead to (administratively costly) open rebellion by Africans. To this end colonial administrations worked to ensure that European intrusions into Africans' lands and social life did not completely exhaust African tolerance. In the words of the Northern Rhodesian Chief Secretary (1932), "we [are] here primarily to exploit the tropical belt in the interests of the Empire while at the same time taking care to protect the legitimate interests of the autochthonous peoples" (Davidson, 1974, p. 37).

Denied institutional representation, Africans resorted to extra-institutional forms of political action. In Kenya, Nairobi was rocked by protests in March 1922. Protesters demanded the release of Harry Thuku, a leading organizer against the Native Registration Ordinance (1921) that established the *kipande* labor registration system (Furedi, 1973).[14] In reaction, police killed 22 protesters. Thuku was later deported to Kismayu, Somalia for a decade and became a loyalist upon his return to Kenya. Similarly, Africans in the Northern Rhodesian Copperbelt resorted to strikes to demand for better governance and working conditions. The first African mineworkers' strike (against a poll tax increase) took place in 1935 in Nkana, Mufulira, and Luanshya (where police killed six protesters). European mineworkers responded to these strikes by forming the Northern Rhodesia Mineworkers' Union (NRMU) that successfully pushed for wage increases after a 1940 strike. But, when Africans struck to demand similar terms they were met by lethal force, with police killing 17 protesters in Nkana (Henderson, 1975). It was not until 1949 that the colonial administration acquiesced and registered the African Mineworkers' Union (AMWU/AMU) under the leadership of Lawrence Katilungu. In 1950 the mineworkers' union joined other sectoral unions to form the United Trade Union Congress (UTUC), also headed by Katilungu.[15]

---

[14] The *kipande* registration system required all male Africans to get registered, finger printed, and carry with them at all times a certificate (*kipande*) that contained their employment history. Africans opposed the system on the grounds that it limited their labor mobility. Europeans favored the system because it stabilized labor supply below market rates. The 1922 ordinance built upon the Registration of Natives Ordinance (1915) and the Resident Native Laborers Ordinance (1919) that had severely limited African labor mobility.

[15] In 1964 the AMWU/AMU changed its name to the Zambia Mineworkers' Union (ZMU). From the beginning, the AMWU was wary of being seen as an arm of the political nationalist movement, instead choosing to focus on the advancement of mineworkers' interests in the Copperbelt. In 1967 the ZMU became the Mineworkers' Union of Zambia (MUZ) and was subsumed within

Maintaining political stability in the early colonial period was not an easy task. The shortage of European colonial administrators – what Kirk-Greene (1980) calls "the thin white line" – meant that European immigrants often took the law in their own hands, both in conflicts among each other and with African populations. To address this concern, Colonial District Commissioners were laws unto themselves, with fused administrative, judicial, and rule-making powers within their respective jurisdictions. Whitehall reinforced "the thin white line" with "Native Administrations."

On occasion, European MLCs nominated to represent Africans succeeded in moderating LegCo resolutions. For example, during the debate on the Native Lands Trust (Amendment) Bill (1934) Rev. George Burns, MLC for African interests in the Kenyan LegCo, defended Africans' rights to land and consultation before land alienation for settler commercial interests.[16] In Northern Rhodesia, Steward Gore-Browne (MLC for African interests) advocated for the expansion of public goods and services available to Africans. In addition, his position as the senior unofficial MLC (even after the rise of the NRLP) enabled him to have a moderating influence on European politics. Sometimes the views of MLCs representing African interests conflicted with their mandate. This was the case in Kenya in 1929 when Rev. John Arthur resigned from the LegCo in opposition to the administration's tolerance of female circumcision.[17] On this matter the Department of Native Affairs had sided with the Kikuyu-speaking elite in favor of the practice (Kenyatta, 1965; Clough, 1990). Similarly, in Northern Rhodesia, in 1948 Gore-Browne proposed the establishment of responsible government under minority white rule despite African opposition (Rotberg, 1977).

In many ways, colonial administrators' balancing act in carrying out the dual mandate was self-undermining. In both colonies, the color bar, exclusion of Africans from key institutions, and overtly

---

the wider Zambia Congress of Trade Unions (ZCTU) created in 1965 through an Act of Parliament. Katilungu's coziness with the colonial administration unsettled rank and file AMWU members. This resulted in his dismissal as UTUC head and the creation of a rival umbrella union, the Reformed Trade Union Congress (RTUC) that declared support for the United National Independence Party (UNIP) in 1961 (Larmer, 2005).

[16] Kenya Legislative Council, August 1, 1934, Col. 441.

[17] Kenya Legislative Council, November 9, 1929, Col. 620.

racist policies laid bare colonial hypocrisy and lack of legitimacy. As European exploitation of African land and labor intensified, so did extra-institutional political mobilization among Africans. In Kenya, Harry Thuku founded the East African Association in 1921 to protest the *kipande* system, land alienation, and unfair taxes. In Zambia labor-related political mobilization began in the early 1930s in the urban Copperbelt. These early movements focused on highlighting the gaps between Whitehall's stated commitments to Africans and their lived realities (Lonsdale, 2006).

An important example in this regard is the Devonshire Declaration of July 1923, which proclaimed British commitment to the paramountcy of African interests in Kenya and whose influence reverberated into other colonial possessions. Despite the lofty declaration, the norm in colonial Kenya and Zambia was the paramountcy of European interests (Sindab, 1984; Phiri, 1991; Kanogo, 1987). In fact, the Devonshire Declaration was a political gimmick designed to sidestep the question of the political rights of Indian immigrants in Kenya (vis-à-vis Europeans). The end goal was to give credence to Whitehall' vacuous argument that immigrants's interests, Indians included, could not override African interests in all of British Africa (Atieno-Odhiambo, 1974).

The Devonshire Declaration was also unenforceable. Settlers in both Kenya and Northern Rhodesia remained openly hostile to the principles of the declaration; and increasingly sought to establish responsible government under minority European rule. In Kenya, the "fundamental conflict between the settlers and the bureaucracy concerned whether the Legislative Council would have majority unofficials" (Hakes, 1970, p. 6). Indeed, Commissioner Charles Eliot (1900–1904) had "predicted that Kenya could become a new Australia or New Zealand" (Clough, 1990, p. 19). Many Europeans saw unofficial majority as a shortcut route to greater influence on administration policy or outright responsible minority government. Both outcomes were inimical to African interests in the colony.

Similar struggles obtained in Northern Rhodesia, where politics was dominated by "European demands first for amalgamation with Southern Rhodesia [creation of unitary state] and later for a federation of the two Rhodesias and Nyasaland; and African responses to these initiatives" (Phiri, 1991, p. 17). Harry Nkumbula, who would later found the African National Congress (ANC), captured African opinion on federation in December 1943 when he reminded members of the Western Province regional council that the "Prime Minister of Southern Rhodesia has made it clear to everybody that his country is a white man's country and that the black man shall always remain a servant of the white man, if not a slave" (Davidson, 1974, p. 114). Under the circumstances, Whitehall stood as the only institutional barrier to racialist minority European rule in Kenya and Northern Rhodesia.

Whitehall prevailed in Kenya but capitulated in Northern Rhodesia. And, the outcomes in both cases were consequential for postcolonial political development. In Kenya, the Executive Council (a proto Cabinet) was only opened to European unofficials in 1945, and unofficials did not acquire a majority until 1948. But, by then it was already too late since half of the unofficials were non-European following successive enfranchisement of Africans, Arabs, and Indians (Hakes, 1970). Furthermore, the Kenyan settler community had by this time undergone significant differentiation that produced two dominant interest groups representing on the one hand farmers (most of whom were extremists), and on the other commercial and industrial interests (most of whom were moderates). The latter group were increasingly more profitable and less dependent on state subsidies, which increased their value in the eyes of a fiscally conscious colonial government. Due to its declining dependence on agriculturalists, the colonial administration (through official members) routinely voted with non-European and moderate European MLCs to stymie extremist settler ambitions. Perhaps the most important sign of the erosion of the political power of agriculturalist setters was the election in 1945 of Alfred Vincent (a Nairobi businessman) in place of Lord Alfred Scott (a farmer) as the public voice of European immigrants (Wasserman, 1976, p. 26).[18]

In Northern Rhodesia, the initial dominant cleavage among European settlers was around the question of amalgamation with Southern Rhodesia (to create a unitary state). This cleavage emerged well before BSAC's departure in 1924 and was largely characterized by

---

[18] The curtain fell on agriculturalist settler dominance in Kenya on March 4, 1960 with the resignation of William Cavendish-Bentinck as Speaker of the LegCo. Cavendish-Bentinck accused Whitehall of "abandoning their past pledges to the settlers" (Wasserman, 1976, p. 29).

a north–south divide (with the south in favor of amalgamation). After the discovery of vast deposits of copper in the 1920s, Governor Hubert Young (1934–1938) and a sizable section of settlers wanted mineral revenue to remain in Northern Rhodesia. But, with time Northern Rhodesian interests coalesced around federation with Southern Rhodesia (Zimbabwe) and Nyasaland (Malawi) as a means of achieving responsible government under European minority rule. In the eyes of many European immigrants, "federation was a means whereby they might rid themselves of further supervision by the British Colonial Office" (Rotberg, 1965, p. 222). Their calculus was that, if need be, it was easier to break free from Salisbury (Harare) than London.[19] The federal constitution retained Southern Rhodesia's autonomy from London (attained in 1923), and opened the door to European minority rule in Northern Rhodesia (Dresang, 1975).

Whitehall's institutional surrender in Northern Rhodesia was long coming. It started with the granting of unofficials numerical parity with officials in the LegCo in 1932, the appointment of unofficials to the Executive Council in 1939, and the realization of unofficial majority in the LegCo in 1945.[20] These moves limited the governor's (and Whitehall's) ability to balance the extreme elements in the settler community. On September 3, 1953 Europeans realized their lifelong dream of federation with the establishment of the Central African Federation of Rhodesia and Nyasaland (1953–1963). The Federal Constitution came into full effect on October 23, 1953.

The Federal Constitution created a 35-member Federal Assembly composed of six Africans (two from each territory) and 29 Euro-

[19] It is worth noting that Northern Rhodesia had, in addition to the hardline European immigrants, a less powerful and more liberal grouping of immigrants – the Capricorn African Society. The Society advocated for a racially desegregated colony marked by partnership across races (Phiri, 1991). However, it never gained traction within the mainstream European community and, more importantly, lacked the institutional means of influencing the colonial administration.

[20] Whitehall's capitulation can be explained by the persistent influence of BSAC on the colonial administration. Even after 1924 Northern Rhodesian governors and official MLCs continued to be BSAC alumni and were therefore more partial to settler interests than to Whitehall's political mandate (Davidson, 1974, p. 37). After 1945 there were 13 unofficial European members of the LegCo (3 of whom represented African interests) and only 9 official members. Settler extremism in Northern Rhodesia in the immediate postwar period was only tempered by the victory of the UK Labour Party (Mulford, 1967).

pean members.[21] Northern Rhodesia's two African representatives – Mateyo Kakumbi and Dauti L. Yamba – were elected by the African Representative Council. The incumbent Southern Rhodesian United Party became the ruling party under federation (and was renamed the Federal Party). The Southern Rhodesian premier, Godfrey Huggins, became the first prime minister of the federation. But, even as Whitehall was losing control over the minority European immigrant population, it remained keen on giving the impression of trying to accommodate African interests. In order to protect Northern Rhodesians from the harsher realities of the color bar in Southern Rhodesia, the handling of "Native Affairs" was excluded from the domain of the federal government. Whitehall also insisted, against settler opinion, on the token six-member African representation in the federal legislature. Lastly, an African Affairs Board comprising African members of the Federal Assembly was created to scrutinize federal legislation. However, it lacked powers to stop any such legislation from passing in the European-dominated assembly.[22]

Federation stunted legislative development by forcing the ANC's leadership to engage in extra-institutionalist politics. The party decided to boycott colonial institutions. Elections in August 1953 yielded a "more militant group of officer-bearers" (Mulford, 1967, p. 37). In addition, the decision by some of its leaders to end the boycott only served to split the party and empower the extra-institutionalist wing. Due to divisions between the ANC and the ARC, the two Africans elected to the Federal Assembly were independents. European politics was affected, too. For European immigrants, federation increased the possibility of independence from the Colonial Office. Thus, their focus shifted to federal politics, with Welensky succeeding Higgins as premier in 1956.

---

[21] In addition to 2 African members, each territory returned 1 European to represent African interests. The European elected members included 8 from Northern Rhodesia, 4 from Nyasaland, and 14 from Southern Rhodesia.

[22] See Hyam (1987) for a detailed account of the politics of amalgamation/federation in Central Africa. Whitehall's motivation to allow for federation was partly driven by the fear of South African demographic annexation of Southern Rhodesia through immigration. However, in implementing federation, Whitehall proved powerless against Southern Rhodesian racialist institutional designs. As a result, federation was achieved with very weak safeguards for African interests.

Federation under Southern Rhodesian dominance would prove to be a pyrrhic victory for European immigrants in Northern Rhodesia. The sense of British betrayal unleashed a reinvigorated nationalist fervor, leading to Zambian independence on October 24, 1964. Before federation Africans had primarily challenged the economic and social aspects of colonialism. But, the harsh reality of federation created a focal point for political agitation against the very legitimacy of colonialism. In the eyes of Africans, federation irrevocably destroyed the implicit "trusteeship" pact under Whitehall's dual mandate and rhetorical commitment to the paramountcy of African interests. Furthermore, Southern Rhodesian racialist rule made a mockery of the stated policy of multiracial "Partnership" across the three territories. It did not help matters that following the emergency of March 1959 (in Malawi) and the *Cha Cha Cha* disturbances of July 1961 (in Zambia), European Southern Rhodesian troops were deployed in Northern Rhodesia and Nyasaland to quell protests (Bratton, 1980). In a desperate attempt at mending fences, and against federal policy, the Northern Rhodesian government started to legislate against racial discrimination in 1960. But, this proved to be too little too late. By then no respectable African leaders would align themselves with either the federal or constituent colonial governments (King, 2008). For the first time a sense of the ineluctability of African independence permeated political discourse throughout Northern Rhodesia.

At this juncture it is important to briefly outline the economic origins of interracial political conflict in colonial Kenya and Zambia. Both colonies had racialist policies in open contradiction to Whitehall's stated commitment to the paramountcy of African interests. But, geography conspired to make this situation worse in Zambia. First, proximity to South Africa and Southern Rhodesia provided strong demonstration effects on race relations. Europeans in Northern Rhodesia – many of whom had come from these two territories – sought to replicate the racialist policies of their neighbors to the south. Second, the discovery of copper and the emergence of a mining industry attracted a class of European immigrants (mineworkers) that was in direct conflict with African workers. Combined, these two factors irredeemably poisoned interracial political relations in Northern Rhodesia. In Kenya, colonial immigration primarily resulted in large-scale land alienation in rural areas for the benefit of British aristocrats, wealthy economic adventurers, and ex-soldiers. This set the stage for future conflicts over a largely divisible resource, a fact that generated opportunities for interracial compromise during the decolonization process.

For these reasons the interracial incompatibility proved soluble in Kenya but not in colonial Zambia. Forcefully alienated land (by European immigrants) in Kenya could be bought and redistributed to landless African subsistence farmers and elites (Wasserman, 1976, p. 36). But, in Northern Rhodesia there was virtually no mutually beneficial and politically feasible way of compensating African and European mineworkers for the loss of their jobs, or the abolition (or maintenance) of the color bar (Mijere, 1985, p. 83). To please the African Mineworkers' Union would have meant displeasing the European Mineworkers' Union, and vice versa (Zelniker, 1971, p. 85). Welensky fully understood this reality. Speaking in the LegCo in 1945, he noted that "[i]f the only distinction between the African and ourselves [European immigrants] is this question of education ... then it is a difference that will disappear, and if it disappears then the African gradually takes over ... The African takes over post after post from Europeans in the country ..."[23] These differences facilitated a positive-sum politics in Kenya, and zero-sum politics in Northern Rhodesia. Stated differently, political realities favored moderation in Kenya and extremism in Zambia.

4.3 Political Developments in the Late Colonial Period

4.3.1 Gradualist vs. Radical Nationalists

To understand legislative development in Kenya and Zambia is to also understand how divergent processes of political development in the late colonial period structured postcolonial executive-legislative relations in the two countries. As late as 1950 both colonies were on course to remain under minority European rule in the mold of South Africa and Southern Rhodesia (Izuakor, 1983).[24] Then came the Mau Mau insurgency in Kenya and "wind of change"

---

[23] Official Report, Northern Rhodesia Legislative Council, August 28, 1946, 60–62. As quoted in Davidson (1974).

[24] In March 1956 Gov. Arthur Benson of Northern Rhodesia gave a speech outlining the intention to transfer power to a locally elected settler government (Rotberg, 1965, p. 276).

speech by Prime Minister Harold Macmillan in South Africa in 1960. The sudden change in Whitehall's willingness to cling to its colonial territories meant that independence would be achieved under different political and institutional formations in Kenya and Zambia. In Northern Rhodesia, the independence movement was pan-ethnic, mass-based, and primarily extra-legislative. It was also led by what was considered to be the radical wing of the nationalist elites who had been largely excluded from colonial institutions. In contrast, Kenya's independence movement had a distinctively ethnic orientation, was largely elite-based, and co-evolved with African participation in the LegCo. The situation in Kenya favored politics of moderation. In Zambia, European extremism in the LegCo encouraged the emergence of a radical nationalist movement. The triumph of gradualists in Kenya ensured institutional continuity from the LegCo to the House of Representatives (later National Assembly) at independence. In Zambia, the exclusion of leading nationalists from both the federal and territorial LegCo put the country on a path of institutional discontinuity between the LegCo and the postindependence National Assembly.

Political mobilization among Zambia Africans began in the form of urban cultural welfare organizations in various towns along the "line of rail" from Livingstone to the Copperbelt. One of the first such organizations was the Mwenzo Welfare Association, cofounded in 1923 by Hezekiah Kawosa and David Kaunda (Kenneth Kaunda's father). The typical welfare association had localized urban membership and focused on specific issue domains. They also served as alternatives to the various African councils set up by the colonial administration (Rotberg, 1965, p. 203). At first the associations styled themselves as apolitical advocates for the welfare of urban Africans. For example, the Mbeni Dance Society, a cultural organization, was critical in organizing the 1935 mineworkers' strikes in the Copperbelt. The first welfare organization with pretensions of colony-wide membership was the Northern Rhodesia Native Welfare Association (NRNWA), founded in 1929 in Livingstone (Lusaka became the capital in 1935). NRNWA petitioned for recognition by the colonial government in 1932 and 1933 but was denied on both occasions. In 1946, 14 different welfare associations merged to form the Federation of African Welfare Societies in Northern Rhodesia (FAWSNR). The leadership of FAWSNR included G. Mbikusita Mukubesa (chairman),

Dauti Yamba (vice chairman), and Robinson Nabulatyo (secretary-general). The first national political party in Zambia, the Northern Rhodesia African Congress (NRAC), grew out of FAWSNR in 1948 and eventually became the African National Congress (ANC) in 1951 led by Harry Nkumbula.[25]

But, no sooner had the ANC gained a stronghold in national politics (around 1951) than it began to be buffeted by internal divisions. At issue was how to deal with European designs for federation with Southern Rhodesia and Nyasaland. The ANC's initial response reflected its leadership's failure to grasp the political zeitgeist.[26] Led by Nkumbula, a section of the ANC leadership preferred using existing institutional channels (including the federal legislature) to address the problem of federation. But, other leaders understood full well the extent of African opposition to federation. Led by Kenneth Kaunda, Simon Kapwepwe, Munukayumbwa Sipalo, and Reuben Kamanga, these leaders rode the wave of African populism and extra-institutional political action (including boycotts, strikes, and demonstrations) to reject the entire colonial institutional apparatus.[27]

To foreshadow Kaunda's future struggles with the Copperbelt's mineworkers in the 1980s, AMU's leader, Lawrence Katilungu, was partial to Nkumbula's gradualist/institutionalist style. As a trade

---

[25] Nkumbula began his political career as the founding secretary of the African Teachers' Association of the Copperbelt (ATAC) under the chairmanship of Dauti L. Yamba in 1942. His rise in Northern Rhodesian politics was, in part, driven by his staunch opposition to the Central African Federation of Rhodesia and Nyasaland (Macola, 2010). However, despite his initial opposition to amalgamation, Nkumbula's perceived moderation later on during the decolonization struggle (under federation) cost him the leadership of the African nationalist movement. See Henderson (1975), Sindab (1984), and Musambachime (1991) for discussions on political mobilization in late colonial Northern Rhodesia.

[26] According to Scott (1976), initial success at turning "congress from an elite to a mass party" floundered on account of its leadership's continued participation in colonial institutions even after the Central African Federation became a reality in 1953. Furthermore, the "increase in the level of rural discontent ... was not matched by an increase in organizational efficiency" (p. 44).

[27] These differences in strategies were also overlaid with ethnoregional and socioeconomic differences. Nkumbula represented largely Bantu Botatwe interests reliant on rural peasant agriculture. The radicals' political base was in the multiethnic, Bemba-speaking, and urban Copperbelt and the rural Northern and Luapula Provinces (Gewald, Hinfelaar, and Chiozza, 2011).

unionist, Katilungu was generally wary of Kaunda's radicalism and inclination to subordinate workers' interests to the nationalist cause. The AMU advocated for higher wages and decent living conditions in the Copperbelt's company towns. To this end it had incentives to channel its grievances through the colonial institutional structure.[28] Kaunda, Kapwepwe, and Sipalo wanted to politicize labor relations as a way of improving the ANC's bargaining position vis-à-vis the colonial administration. This was the origin of the incompatibility between the party and the union (Bates, 1971, pp. 136–140).

The ANC's "increasing accommodation of the colonial order," including the refusal to boycott the 1959 territorial LegCo election, led to a significant erosion of public confidence in its leadership (Bates, 1971, p. 10). The overtly racist European politics in the LegCo and federal legislature did not help the fortunes of the institutionalist/moderate wing of the African nationalist movement. Unable to dissuade the ANC leadership from its institutionalist moderation, Kaunda and his allies formed the Zambia African National Congress (ZANC) in 1958.[29] The ZANC was founded on strong grassroots foundations, in no small part because "Kaunda himself was reputedly responsible for the formation of about one hundred ANC branches" (Scott, 1976, p. 48). The colonial government swiftly banned the ZANC in 1959 and detained its leaders, including Kaunda. Following the ban ZANC members split into the African National Independence Party (ANIP) and the United National Freedom Party (UNFP), before regrouping to form UNIP in the latter part of 1959 (Mulford, 1967). UNIP's core base was in the multiethnic urban Copperbelt and

---

[28] Katilungu went as far as serving in the Monckton Commission in 1960 (formed to review the constitution of the Federation of Rhodesia and Nyasaland) despite widespread boycott from Northern Rhodesia's African nationalists.

[29] Macola (2010) slightly amends this depiction of the ANC/ZANC split, arguing that it was not Nkumbula's (short-lived) institutionalist moderation that led to the split. He argues that the split was due to the insurmountable contradictions between the interests of Nkumbula's base in Southern Province and the demands of the urban Copperbelt. The Southern Province's "well-to-do, self-improving peasant farmers were much less likely to be led down the costly road of potentially violent political agitation than such wage-earning, unionized labour migrants as gravitated around the Copperbelt" (p. 72). It's unclear, however, why southern farmers would not support an increase in the purchase power of the Copperbelt's residents. A possible explanation is that southern farmers feared a loss of markets due to instability in the Copperbelt.

northern Zambia. Its ideology was populist and socialist, in opposition to both African and European conservative/gradualist political
elements. On January 31, 1960 Kaunda emerged from detention to
lead UNIP. This marked the beginning of the end of the ANC as a
viable independence party.

The last straw was the ANC's handling of the *Cha Cha Cha*
revolts in 1961–1962. To oppose federation, UNIP campaigned to
make the colony ungovernable through civil disobedience. Some of
these campaigns turned violent (Bratton, 1980, p. 61). Instead of
backing the antifederation protests, the ANC used this opportunity
to burnish its reputation as a moderate party and distanced itself from
the campaigns (Macola, 2008). The public interpreted this as apologia
for federation. The association of UNIP with the *Cha Cha Cha*
disturbances catapulted Kaunda to become the leading spokesman
for the Zambian independence movement. Having outflanked the
gradualist nationalists, UNIP was now in a position to neutralize the
conservative elements among chiefs who underpinned the system of
indirect rule. By 1962 the party was strong enough to simply "pay
their respects to the chiefs and ignore them" (Scott, 1976, p. 54).
UNIP's extra-institutional tactics paid off, and placed Zambia on a
path to precipitous institutional discontinuity at independence.[30]

The decolonization process played out differently in Kenya. The
colony's nationalist movements were largely rural and catered to
local interests in the respective LNCs. The dominant organizations
also tended to have settler connections, and were relatively

[30] This is not to say that chiefs were politically irrelevant in the independence
movement and in postcolonial Zambia. Indeed, their influence is evident in
postcolonial Zambia's House of Chiefs – established to co-opt "traditional"
authorities into Kaunda's regime and advise the government on "traditional"
matters (van Binsbergen, 1987). To shore up his authority amid an economic
crisis, in 1983 Kaunda appointed the Lozi and Bemba chiefs onto the UNIP
Central Committee. Baldwin (2015) also documents the continued influence of
chiefs in contemporary electoral politics. Besides the ANC and the
conservative chiefs Kaunda and UNIP also faced competition from the Lumpa
Church headed by Alice Mulenga Lenshina. Begun in the mid-1950s to protest
federation and colonialism, the Church's millenarian doctrine forbade
members from participating in politics. This position created conflict with
UNIP, whose cadres were intent on recruiting new members in Chinsali
District (Northern Zambia). The standoff precipitated the "Lumpa uprising"
that was met by brutal state-led operation against the church, resulting in
hundreds of deaths. The church was banned in 1964 (Gordon, 2008).

conservative in nature.[31] Earlier access to missionary education put Kikuyu- and Luo-speaking Kenyans at the forefront of political development (Ogot, 1963). Kiambu chiefs Koinange wa Mbiyu, Philip Karanja, Josiah Njonjo wa Mugane, and Waruhiu wa Kungu founded the Kikuyu Association (KA) in 1919 with the support of the colonial administration and Harry Leakey, a missionary (Roelker, 1976, p. 23). Among Luo speakers, Jonathan Okwiri, Benjamin Owuor, and Simeon Nyende founded the Kavirondo Taxpayers Welfare Association (KTWA) in 1921 with the help of W. E. Owen, a missionary (Atieno-Odhiambo, 2002). KTWA's platform focused on opposition to forced labor and high taxes. In June 1921 Harry Thuku founded the Young Kikuyu Association (YKA). A month later, the organization changed its name to the East African Association (EAA) to broaden its appeal beyond Kikuyu speakers. Unlike the KA, the YKA/EAA was perceived as radical and in direct conflict with the colonial establishment over the *kipande* system, forced labor (especially of women), and land alienation. On March 14, 1922 Thuku was arrested. The following day throngs of his supporters marched to the police station in Nairobi to demand his release in vain. When the crowd grew restive the police opened fire, killing at least 21. Among those killed was the leader of the protest, Mary Muthoni Nyanjiru (Clough, 1990, p. 60). The colonial government promptly banned the EAA thereafter.[32] In 1924 the EAA reemerged as the Kikuyu Central Association (KCA) to advance Kikuyu interests. Unlike the YKA/EEA, the KCA and KTWA adopted a strategy of working through the Local Native Councils (LNCs) created in 1925. This, in effect, meant collaboration with conservative and loyalist African elites (Lonsdale, 1968, p. 129). As I show below, the localization of politics within LNCs had the effect of ethnicizing political development in Kenya.

[31] Political mobilization among Kenyan Indians began a little earlier. The India Association of Mombasa was formed in 1900. In 1914, Alibhai M. Jeevanjee led the formation of the East Africa Indian National Congress (EAINC) that brought together various associations to defend Indian interests. However, the EAINC was quickly eclipsed with the rise of African politics, especially after the Devonshire Declaration of 1923.
[32] Thuku's speeches following the founding of EAA became increasingly "anti-chiefs, anti-missionaries, and anti-government" (Wipper, 1989, p. 303). The banning of the EAA marked the collapse of pan-ethnic politics in Kenya that would persist well after independence.

After the banning of EEA, it was not until 1944 that Kenya saw another interethnic political association. Mathu's appointment to the LegCo precipitated the creation of the Kenya African Study Union (KASU). The colonial government formed KASU to aggregate African interests and to advise Mathu (Ajulu, 2002, p. 255). In 1946 KASU morphed into the Kenya African Union (KAU) with a leadership that was loyalist and sought to advance African interests within colonial institutional structures. Lacking a strong national presence, "much of [KAU's] work was done through local branches in the districts" (Hakes, 1970, p. 32). This only strengthened the localized ethnic political machines organized around the LNC system. Jomo Kenyatta took over the leadership of KAU in 1947, having returned to Kenya the previous year after a 15-year stint in Europe. Being a loyalist, Kenyatta found himself outflanked by radical elements in the nationalist movement – including Mau Mau supporters. Ironically, his political career would be saved by Mau Mau's 1949 insurgency and the Emergency Declaration of 1952 (Spencer, 1985; Ajulu, 2002). On October 20, 1952 KAU was banned and its leaders – including Kenyatta, Achieng' Oneko, Bildad Kaggia, Kung'u Karumba, Fred Kubai, and Paul Ngei – detained for suspected links to Mau Mau. The Kapenguria Six, as they became known, became instant political martyrs. Like in the case of the EEA, the banning of KAU meant a return to ethnic-based politics within the LNCs.

The full effects of the ethnic basis of political development in Kenya was evident when the ban on political parties was partially lifted in 1955. A proliferation of ethnic-based district parties with powerful local political machines emerged ahead of the 1957 elections. According to Mboya (1965), the ban on colony-wide political mobilization had "harmed national unity immeasurably" (p. 75).[33]

---

[33] The ban continued in Kikuyu districts that were hardest hit by the Mau Mau insurgency until 1959. Localized ethnic parties included the Abagusii Association of South Nyanza, the Abaluhya People's Association, the African People's Party (formerly the Akamba People's Party), the Baringo District Independence Party, the Coast African People's Union, the Federal Independent Party, the Kalenjin Alliance, the Kenya Asian Party, the Kenya Coalition, Kenya India Congress, the Kilifi African People's Union, the Maasai United Front Alliance, the Mombasa African Democratic Union, the Nairobi District African Congress, the Nakuru African Progressive Party, the New Kenya Group, the North Nyanza District Congress, the Progressive Local Government Party, the Rift Valley People's Congress, the Somali National Association, the Taita African Democratic Union, and the West Kalenjin

The March 1957 elections brought into the LegCo 8 African MLCs (increased to 14 in 1958) representing different district/ethnic parties. For coordination purposes they formed the African Elected Members Organization (AEMO).[34] In 1959 the colonial government unbanned national parties, and in January 1960 unexpectedly announced an accelerated decolonization plan. But, by then splits had already emerged within AEMO that in 1960 produced two parties – the Kenya African National Union (KANU) and the Kenya African Democratic Union (KADU). Though national in character, KADU and KANU were little more than confederations of different district-cum-ethnic parties.[35]

Kenya's fragmented political development generated cross-cutting cleavages among both Africans and Europeans. KANU represented the larger ethnic groups, mainly the Kikuyu, Luo, and sections of the Kamba and Luhya. In the words of Oginga Odinga, KANU cofounder and Kenya's first Vice President, "KANU was never a strongly centralized party but an amalgam of many diverse tendencies and policies" (Odinga, 1967, p. 247). The KADU leadership was composed of district representatives of minority ethnic groups – mainly the Kalenjin, Mijikenda, Somali, and a section of the Luhya – that feared domination by the more numerous and better-organized Kikuyu and Luo speakers. Kenyan Europeans were

Political Congress. These were all ethnic parties rooted in the politics and patronage of the Emergency years (Ajulu, 2002, pp. 257–259). Many of these parties were supported by the colonial administration in a bid to blunt support for the Mau Mau insurgency (Ogot, 1995).

[34] The 1957–1958 elections were conducted under a restricted franchise. Only about 60 percent of male Africans qualified to vote. In Central Province – the hotbed of the Mau Mau insurgency – only individuals with loyalty certificates issued by the District Commissioner could vote (Branch, 2006). Out of a population of 1.75 million, only 35,644 successfully registered to vote (Roelker, 1976, p. 139).

[35] KANU and KADU grew out of a 1959 split among the 14 AEMO members that created the Kenya Independence Movement (KIM) and the Kenya National Party (KNP), respectively. Oginga Odinga, Julius Kiano, D. N. Mumo, Bernard Mate, Lawrence Oguda, and Thomas Mboya were in KIM. Daniel arap Moi, Taita Towett, Justus ole Tipis, Masinde Muliro, Jeremiah Nyagah, James Nzau Muimi, Francis Khamisi, and Ronald Ngala were in KNP. KNP's leadership was conservative in orientation and had a loose alliance with rural landowning European immigrants. KIM brought together centrist and left-leaning leaders of the independence movement (Anderson, 2005, p. 551).

also divided between the conservatives (United Party) and the moderates (New Kenya Party). Others – like Shirley Cooke and Derek Erskine – openly caucused with Africans within the LegCo (Wasserman, 1976; Berman, 1990). European conservatives (mostly rural farmers) demanded continued government restrictions on African labor (the *kipande* system) and access to land (especially in the so-called "White Highlands"). Moderates (mostly urban commercial and industrial interests) favored market-based approaches to allocating both land and labor as a way of increasing productivity. After 1945, economic changes in the colony in favor of the urban sector increased the moderates' bargaining power from the perspective of Whitehall.

Unlike in Northern Rhodesia, the existence of the cross-cutting cleavages (within and across race) described above moderated political action among African nationalists as well as European immigrants in Kenya. In addition, Kenya's independence elites were primarily institutionalist, on account of their membership in the LegCo. Remarkably, in the twilight of colonial rule in Kenya even conservative European immigrants were willing to work with KADU in order to preserve local control over land. Both KADU and the United Party supported a regionalist *Majimbo* system of government with semiautonomous subnational units and a strong Senate backed by robust constitutional protections for minority groups (Anderson, 2005; Opalo, 2012). On their part, European moderates championed KANU's calls for land reforms in fear that absent any changes "the pressures of 1948 [pre Mau Mau] will begin to build again."[36] The divisions among Europeans and Africans enabled the colonial administration to invest in "wooing away the moderate nationalists from their more militant cohorts, thus weakening the remaining opposition (Wasserman, 1976, p. 168).

4.3.2 Divergent Political Development in Kenya and Zambia

Despite their shared institutional inheritance, political development in the late colonial period put Kenya and Zambia on divergent trajectories of legislative development. Three important factors

---

[36] See Official Record, Kenya Legislative Council, Friday June 16, 1960, Col. 1624.

drove this divergence: (i) the types and ethnic composition of the political parties that emerged out of the independence movements, (ii) the degree of preindependence institutional inclusion of African elites, and (iii) race relations and its impact on institutional (dis)continuity after independence. I summarize these differences in Table 4.2.

These differences had profound effects on legislative development in Kenya and Zambia. Kenya's history of district-cum-ethnic political parties spawned a fragmented nationalist movement and an elite independence party (KANU) anchored in rural districts. Kenyatta's inability to control KANU and use it to organize intra-elite politics was a boon for Kenya's legislature. Thus, parliament, and not KANU, became the focal arena for intra-elite politics. This reality afforded the legislature considerable means independence. In Zambia, the proliferation of urban-based multiethnic welfare associations, the existence of multiethnic African institutions (AUACs, APCs, and ARC), and polarized interracial relations facilitated the emergence of a territory-wide pan-ethnic nationalist movement. Under these conditions, UNIP emerged as a mass-based party, thereby enabling Kaunda to bypass fellow elites (including legislators) in dealings with Zambians. But, UNIP's dominance came at parliament's cost. In postcolonial Zambia, the focal arena for organizing intra-elite politics was UNIP and not the legislature. Lacking means independence, the Zambian legislature was relegated to serve as a mere constitutional rubber stamp of UNIP's (Kaunda's) policies.

The two colonies also differed in the levels of institutional inclusion of nationalist political elites. In Northern Rhodesia, the boycott of colonial institutions under federation (1953–1963) put Zambia on a path of institutional discontinuity at independence. Zambia was the only former British colony to attain independence under a presidential system. In addition, in a desire to have a clean break with the colonial era, Kaunda disbanded the colonial Provincial Administration at independence, thereby limiting his ability to effectively monitor, regulate, and balance elite political activity. Kaunda's resulting insecurity forced him to deny the legislature means independence, thereby contributing to the stunting of legislative development in Zambia.

The reverse was true in Kenya. There, African nationalism co-evolved with African institutional inclusion in the LegCo. This

Table 4.2 *The impacts of political development in the late colonial period*

Country	Important Late Colonial Political Characteristics	Type of Nationalist Independence Movements	Immediate Postcolonial Consequences
Kenya	District-based African Councils (LNCs)	Fragmented district-focused mobilization in the interwar period	Weak elite ruling party that preserved parliament's stature as key arena of policy debates
	Rural ethnic-based district political parties	Nationalist independence movements as confederations of ethnic parties	Institutional continuity and conservatism in the postcolonial period
	Strengthening of administrative structures due to Mau Mau insurgency	Moderate nationalist politics within the confines of colonial institutions	
	Both interracial and intra-racial differences within the LegCo		
Zambia	Provincial and territory-wide African Legislative Councils	Interethnic mobilization in the interwar period	Strong mass-based ruling party that usurped parliament's role as key arena of policy debates
	Multiethnic and urban-based political organizations	Mass-based national parties after World War II	Institutional discontinuity and radical politics in the postcolonial period
	Preponderance of interracial differences on the question of the Central African Federation	The triumph of radical extra-institutional and urban-based politics	

Notes: This table summarizes the ways in which colonial institutions and policies structured political development in Kenya and Northern Rhodesia. District-based LNCs and the ban on interethnic parties produced Kenya's ethnic parties. In Zambia, Provincial Councils, the African Representative Council, and the strength of the African Urban Advisory Councils in the Copperbelt enabled mass-based interethnic politics. Cross-cutting cleavages and institutional inclusion of Africans moderated nationalist politics in Kenya. In Zambia, interracial strife over amalgamation/federation and the exclusion of the leading nationalist figures provided a fertile ground for radical extra-institutional politics.

created incentives for the colonial administration to invest in moderate nationalist political elites. Due to the salience of land, the colonial administration decided that land ownership would have "a stabilizing even conservative influence on the political arena" (Wasserman, 1976, p. 160). The linchpin of this strategy was the Swynnerton Plan (1955–1962), which sought to commercialize African agriculture through land consolidation and secure titling, credit facilities for Africans, provision of extension services, and the opening of cash crop farming to Africans (Berman, 1974, p. 466). This plan – together with others such as the Yeoman Scheme, Assisted-Owner Scheme, Million-Acre Scheme, Stamp Program, "Z" Plots, and the Land Bank – "had twin political and economic objectives: to ensure political stability by creating a class of yeomen African farmers whose prosperity would not only lead to allegiance and support of the status quo, but also absorb potentially rebellious or radical landless Africans as wage laborers" (Ochieng', 2007, p. 459).

In general, colonial Kenya's cross-cutting cleavages favored institutional and administrative continuity and strong constraints on the chief executive. Kenya maintained a parliamentary system of government for the first year after independence. The independence constitution created a regionalist system of government and a bicameral legislature.[37] Given that the regionalist system was favored by the minority (Kenya's smaller ethnic groups and rural European immigrants), the Senate was granted significant powers to check presidential authority on matters that touched on the regions (Stultz, 1969; Opalo, 2012).

In addition, the House of Representatives (National Assembly) retained the LegCo Speaker, Humphrey Slade, until 1970. This was unlike in Zambia where Wesley P. Nyirenda, the first Speaker in the independent parliament (1964–1968), was a party man affiliated with the UNIP branch from Eastern Province. Upon his retirement as

---

[37] The country was divided into the Nairobi area and seven regions. Each region had a Regional Assembly and a president (speaker) elected from among its members. The Senate comprised 41 representatives from the country's districts. The House of Representatives had 117 elected and 12 nominated members. The Senate was abolished in December 1966 and its members absorbed in the new National Assembly.

Speaker he joined Kaunda's cabinet as Education Minister.[38] Similarly, Kenyatta retained the Provincial Administration intact, a factor that enabled him to grant legislators means independence without fear of losing power. As Dresang (1975) observes, "the weak provincial administration of Zambia contrast[ed] sharply with that of Kenya" (p. 120). In sum, the combination of institutional continuity in the legislature, KANU's organizational weakness, and Kenyatta's ability to rely on the Provincial Administration to monitor and balance fellow elites enhanced the stature of the postcolonial legislature in Kenya.[39]

4.4 Implications for Studying Imported Western Institutions

The causes of the variation in the local institutional expressions of imported Western institutions in former colonies are seldom explored. Yet, as I show above, political development under colonialism structured the adaptation of Western institutions' former colonies. In addition, the quality of Western institutions introduced in the colonies

---

[38] Kenya's Speakers of the National Assembly have included Humphrey Slade (1960–1970), Frederick M. Mate (1970–1988), Moses arap Keino (1988–1991), Jonathan K. arap Ng'eno (1991–1992), Francis X. ole Kaparo (1993–2007), Kenneth O. Marende (2008–2013), and Justin Muturi (2013–). Senate Speakers include Chitasi M. Chokwe (1963–1966), Ekwe Ethuro (2013–2017), and Ken Lusaka (2017–). Northern Rhodesia's last LegCo Speaker, Thomas Williams (1956–1964), retired at independence in 1964. Postindependence Zambian Speakers include Wesley P. Nyirenda (1964–1968), Robinson M. Nabulyato (1968–1988), Fwanyanga M. Mulikita (1988–1991), Robinson M. Nabulyato (1991–1998), Amusaa K. Mwanamwambwa (1998–2011), and Patrick Matibini (2011–).

[39] These differences in late colonial political development were also reflected in Kenyan and Zambian approaches to economic Africanization following independence. In Kenya, the transition away from a European-dominated economy was gradual, and was marked by a policy of Kenyanization as opposed to Africanization. This created a loophole for non-Africans (Europeans and Asians) to maintain their jobs and economic influence, if they chose to acquire Kenyan citizenship (Vinnai, 1974; Chege, 1998). In Zambia, racial discord increased the political pressure on UNIP to Africanize the economy as part of Zambianization. The fact that Zambia only had 109 African graduates and 1,200 holders of secondary school certificates at independence forced important sectors of the economy to absorb relatively low human capital than they would have otherwise (Tordoff, 1977b). The wave of nationalizations of the economy that began with the Mlungushi Declaration of April 19, 1968 were therefore almost inevitable. Zambia's highly racialized politics in the late colonial period thus influenced its postcolonial government's approach to economic empowerment of the majority African population (Sindab, 1984; Mumeka, 1987).

varied over time. For example, Burns (1966) documents the variation in institutional forms of British colonial legislatures across time; and attributes this to sets of colonies having constitutions that were "modeled on that of England of that period" (p. 13). British colonies in the Americas, the Old Dominions (Canada, New Zealand, Australia, and South Africa), the Indian subcontinent, and the newer colonies in Africa, the Middle East and elsewhere had legislatures with varied institutional forms because of the timing of their colonization. Even among legislatures established in the same time period, local demographic and economic realities further inflected their realized institutional form. In some colonies the Westminster Model went as "accompanied baggage" (with European immigrants), while in others it was an (unaccompanied) "export" (Fletcher-Cooke, 1966, p. 145).

These observations call for detailed studies of the varied histories of imported Western institutions in former European colonies. Building on existing works on the legacies of colonialism (Engerman and Sokoloff, 2000; Acemoglu, Johnson and Robinson, 2001; Easterly and Levine, 2016), such scholarship ought to focus on specific institutions (e.g., legislatures and judiciaries) while at the same time highlighting the nuances of the colonial institutional experiences of colonized populations and elites. In addition to documenting the actual realities of the colonial experience with institutions, new works should unpack the bundles that were "colonial institutions" and examine their constituent parts (legislatures, administrations, land tenure systems, trade policies, etc.). Similar approaches should inform studies of persistent contemporary effects of the colonial experience. Rather than analyzing aggregated outcomes such as protection of property rights or economic growth, analyses of the colonial origins and persistence of specific institutions and policies would go a long way in increasing our knowledge of the legacies of colonialism.

As this books shows, while postcolonial African elites adopted the institutional forms and functions of European legislatures, it was not a case of simple isomorphic mimicry. The realities of colonial rule and contingencies of local politics structured the institutional expression of inherited colonial legislatures. First, the colonial experience with legislatures was far from the imagined ideal of institutionalized horizontal checks and balances. At the core of colonialism was autocratic and arbitrary rule. Colonial governors were accountable to the metropole and served a system designed to propagate the hegemony of European immigrants. To the modal African, colonialism was the epitome of unchecked and unaccountable power. This understanding of colonial administration was adopted by postcolonial elites intent on consolidating power. Thus, in addition to colonial legislatures, the postcolonial milieu was characterized by vestiges of the autocratic powers of colonial governors.

Second, the specific expressed functions of inherited colonial institutions depended on context. For example, while European legislatures were intended to provide checks and balances, pass budgets, and legislate, the dominant functions of postcolonial African legislatures were ascriptive representation of different ethnic groups in the center and the distribution of patronage and targeted benefits (variously described as "development"). Postcolonial legislators were expected to function as agents of development and were judged by voters on this basis. Thus, clientelism became the fuel of legislative electoral politics and the dominant form of constituency service. This reality enabled African presidents to control the electoral careers of legislators through the rationing of access to patronage and development resources. The end result was a reversal in the fiscal relationship between African legislative and executive branches of government. Instead of possessing the power of the purse, African legislators found themselves dependent on presidents for patronage.

In the main, this chapter provides a nuanced understanding of the colonial origins of the Kenyan and Zambian legislatures, and how political development in the late colonial period structured postcolonial legislative development in the two countries. Both countries had a common legislative origin under British rule. And, in both countries political development – characterized by competing moderates and radicals – emerged as a reaction to European immigrants' quest for minority rule. However, despite these common origins, the colonial administrations' efforts to engender politics of moderation among African and European politicians succeeded in Kenya but failed in Zambia. As a result, Kenya was set on a path to postcolonial institutional continuity. In Zambia, African elites tied their hands by engaging in radical extra-institutional politics through which they committed to postcolonial institutional discontinuity. Thus, these two legislatures from the same region of the world, with similar colonial origins (as Westminster exports), and that were established around roughly the same time period, diverged after independence.

5 | *Elite Control and Legislative Development*

5.1 The Politics of Executive-Legislative Relations

A two-way commitment problem underpins executive-legislative relations. Legislatures enable chief executives to credibly commit to share political power and governance rents with fellow elites. This arrangement necessarily requires chief executives to cede certain powers to legislatures. The former's credibility hinges on legislators' ability (acting collectively) to punish chief executives that renege on their commitments. However, chief executives' willingness to cede power to legislatures is predicated on executive power – their ability to effectively balance fellow elites acting collectively in legislatures. In other words, a tension exists between the twin needs to avert tyranny from both the executive and legislative branches of government. The manner in which elites negotiate this balancing act and the organizational structures that they rely upon to do so determine the realized nature of executive-legislative relations and legislative means independence. An implication of this two-way commitment problem is that legislative means independence is positively correlated with executive power. And, *over time*, sustained legislative means independence leads to legislative organizational development and institutionalization.

Therefore, to understand legislative development is to also understand the specific ways in which chief executives balance fellow elites. In this chapter I extend the analysis in the previous chapter by examining the impact of postcolonial intra-elite politics and balance of power on legislative development in Kenya and Zambia over the first 30 years of independence. In particular, I focus on how presidents' ability to effectively monitor, regulate, and balance elite political action – through ruling parties and administrative structures – conditioned both their executive power and willingness to tolerate legislative means independence.

To identify the causal relationship between executive power and legislative means independence, I contend that the decolonization process in Kenya and Zambia quasi-exogenously limited the menu of strategic options available to the two countries' postcolonial presidents in their quest to balance fellow elites acting collectively in legislatures. This, in turn, differentially impacted their ability to effectively monitor and regulate elite political action, and by extension their tolerance for legislative autonomy and means independence. By narrowing the available set of strategic options, the decolonization process put the Kenyan and Zambian legislatures on different paths of internal legislative organizational development and long-run institutionalization.

In Kenya, the decolonization process bequeathed postcolonial presidents a strong administrative structure and a weak independence party in the Kenya African National Union (KANU). A strong administrative structure enabled Kenyan presidents to effectively monitor, regulate, and balance elite political activity. As a result they were able to grant the legislature means independence, without the fear of losing power. At the same time, KANU's weakness foreclosed on the possibility of the party eclipsing the legislature. For most of Kenyatta's tenure (1963–1978), the legislature, and not KANU, served as the focal institutional means of organizing intra-elite politics. This changed under Moi's single-party rule (1978–1992). Then, the strengthening of KANU led to a decline in legislative means independence. This was partially driven by Moi's move to substitute the legislature with KANU as the focal institution of intra-elite politics. These differences in executive-legislative relations meant that the Kenyan legislature was more independent under Kenyatta than under Moi.

Zambia's decolonization process resulted in a weak administrative structure and a strong independence party in the United National Independence Party (UNIP). Zambian independence was marked by a complete reorganization and politicization of the administrative structure in ways that weakened presidential control over administrative officials. The inability to effectively monitor and regulate elite political activity through the administrative system disincentivized presidents from tolerating legislative means independence. In addition, UNIP emerged as both the focal institution governing intra-elite politics and a strong substitute for the legislature. For these reasons, throughout the period under study the Zambian legislature enjoyed lower levels of means independence compared to its Kenyan counterpart.

Table 5.1 *Postcolonial autocratic parliaments in Kenya and Zambia*

Country	Parliament	Acts	Bills Passed (%)	Sittings	Sittings/Act	Budget Share (%)
Kenya	1st	280	71.93	565	2.018	1.009
	2nd	102	67.49	500	4.902	0.5258
	3rd	88	91.53	427	4.852	0.4323
	4th	58	84.06	352	6.069	0.3729
	5th	97	87.39	511	5.268	0.3191
Zambia	1st	291	92.09	268	0.921	0.1746
	2nd	247	97.63	251	1.016	0.2286
	3rd	148	93.08	273	1.845	0.4140
	4th	111	88.10	290	2.613	0.3862
	5th	137	79.65	289	2.109	0.3154

Notes: This table shows temporal aggregations over the first five parliaments in Kenya and Zambia. Parliamentary years calculated inclusive of election years. The fourth column depicts average proportion of bills that became Acts (annually). Sittings are for the entire duration of a given parliament and represent calendar days. The sixth column shows the average number of Sittings per Act in the life of a parliament. The last column shows the average of annual parliamentary budget as a proportion of the national budget. Data are based on author's calculations from *Votes and Proceedings* (various issues) published by the National Assemblies of Kenya and Zambia.

These differences in the political stature and relative independence of the legislature are illustrated in Table 5.1. Measured by the average rate of passage of executive bills (80.5 vs. 90.1) and the number of sittings per bills passed (4.6 vs. 1.7), it is clear that Kenyan legislators enjoyed higher levels of means independence relative to their Zambian counterparts. A higher average number of sittings per year (451 vs. 274.1) afforded Kenyan legislators valuable plenary time to deliberate not only on specific pieces of legislation and policy matters, but also on other matters of state.[1] With the spare time when it was not

---

[1] See Hakes (1970) and Opalo (2014). In terms of sittings per year, Kenya's first parliament bested its peer Commonwealth states in Africa (Hakes, 1970, p. 21). The average of 94.2 sittings per year was well above comparable figures from Ghana (89.6), Malawi (17.6), Nigeria (40.6), Tanzania (29.7), Uganda (80.6), and Zambia (63.2). Further afield, the United States House of Representatives – arguably the strongest and most institutionalized legislature in the world – met for an average of 115.3 legislative sittings per year in its first 25 years of existence, and between 1987 and 2007 averaged about 134 sittings per year. See History, Art, & Archives of the United States House of Representatives, available here: http://history.house.gov/Institution/Session-Dates/100-109/.

debating legislation the Kenyan parliament effectively functioned as the grand inquest of the nation, serving as a check on executive power. In Zambia, legislators barely had plenary time to pass legislation. The limited amount of plenary time spent per bill in Zambia is particular noteworthy because the legislature lacked a functional committee system during this period. Lacking adequate plenary time to deliberate on executive legislative proposals and other affairs of state, the legislature was relegated to serving as a mere constitutional conveyor belt for UNIP's resolutions and policies. It is no wonder that legislators passed nearly all executive bills introduced in Zambia's first five parliaments. In sum, even by the standards of new postcolonial legislatures "like those of Ghana and Kenya, the Zambian Assembly's quantity and quality of debate [were] not impressive" (Tordoff and Molteno, 1974, p. 227). Before proceeding further, in the next section I outline the logics of executive power and intra-elite relations in more detail.

5.2 Executive Power and Elite Balancing

5.2.1 Principal–Agent Relationships and Executive Power

A core argument in this book is that the prevailing intra-elite distribution of power has a significant bearing on executive-legislative relations. Thus, to understand legislative independence and institutionalization is to also understand how chief executives maintain power and balance fellow elites. All chief executives, including autocrats, must rely on regime agents (subordinates) to propagate their power. This is the basis of the principal–agent relationship between chief executives (principals) and regime administrative officials (agents). Chief executives' reliance on regime agents creates a structural source of power sharing throughout the administrative chain of command that comes with the risk of agency loss. Shirking or disloyalty among regime agents can precipitate regime collapse. To mitigate the risk of agency loss, chief executives organize their governance apparatuses in ways that maximize their power relative to regime agents.

However, regime agents always retain some "administrative power" power vis-à-vis chief executives (Greif, 2008, p. 18). This is because regime agents (such as administrative officials) can influence the behavior of chief executives by simply threatening to defy orders. As Egypt's Hosni Mubarak discovered, the unwillingness of security agents to coercively control regime opponents can be costly. In general, regime agents' power is highest if their actions or inactions can influence chief executives' choices. On their part, chief executives seek to tilt the distribution of power away from regime agents. Many achieve this objective through constant reshuffling of cabinet ministers, police, and administrators or the maintenance of parallel agencies staffed by subordinates incentivized to compete against each other. For example, Hassan (2017) finds that the deployment of Kenya's state administrative officials was intended to minimize agency loss. Similarly, Kroeger (2018) finds that extensive and arbitrary cabinet reshuffles are more likely to take place in African states under personalist rule.[2] This approach to power consolidation extends to executive-legislative relations. Chief executives have strong incentives to engineer high turnover rates in legislative elections in order to prevent legislators from developing strong and permanent bases of political support.

All else equal, executive power is determined by chief executives' ability to effectively control the regime agents that comprise their chosen apparatuses of propagating power. For this reason, the structure of principal–agent relationships on which these apparatuses are founded have nontrivial effects on executive power. In effect, they determine the distribution of power between principals (chief executives) and agents (regime administrative officials). In general, chief executives are strongest when they preside over principal–agent structures defined by relationships of command, as opposed to relationships of persuasion. In the former case, agents have limited ability to influence the behavior of principals on account of their limited role in decision-making. Chief executives' subordinates in this case approximate the idea of "perfect agents," and simply executive orders from above. In the latter case, principals and agents jointly determine the content of the orders to be executed. The joint production of orders through negotiation and persuasion means that principals in the latter case necessarily have to rely on agents' support to maintain power.

---

[2] This phenomenon is not limited to Africa. Autocrats the world over infamously orchestrate musical chairs and divisions among their subordinates as a way of consolidating power. For example, Middle Eastern autocrats typically insure themselves against agency loss (coup-proofing) by creating parallel armies and multiple security agencies (Quinlivan, 1999). See also Svolik (2012) for a generalized discussion of intra-elite politics and power consolidation.

Principal–agent relationships of command allow chief executives to discipline or replace regime agents at relatively low cost. This is because such agents ultimately derive nearly all their power from principals. Being "perfect agents" their interests coincide with those of principals. Their limited role as implementers and lack of input in decision-making render them replaceable. This is different from what obtains under principal–agent relationships of persuasion. Under these conditions, the disciplining or replacement of regime agents can be costly. Because of chief executives' reliance on such agents for support in making decisions, the loss of specific agents may diminish their political power and ability to control their own administrative apparatuses.

It follows that chief executives prefer to preside over administrative apparatuses governed by principal–agent relationships of command. However, historical contingencies may force some chief executives to make do with principal–agent relationships of persuasion. Furthermore, even when opportunities to invest in command-based administrative apparatuses arise, chief executives often do so under circumstances not of their own choosing. Intent on maintaining their respective bargaining powers, fellow elites and regime agents at times successfully conspire to curtail such investments. States' established political culture and notions of "how things are done" may also prevent chief executives from completely subordinating regime agents to their will. In general, chief executives seek to boost their executive power by controlling important institutions of state. And, failing to do so, they make important what they can control.

5.2.2 Ruling by Command vs. Ruling by Persuasion

The above simple framework is useful in understanding the differential effects on legislative development of postcolonial strategies of elite control in Kenya and Zambia. In Kenya, Kenyatta relied heavily on the Provincial Administration (PA) to monitor and regulate elite-level politics. This was, in part, because using KANU was not a viable option. Having not been a founder member he only had a tenuous control over KANU (Tamarkin, 1978, p. 298). The PA system was anchored on principal–agent relationships of command. PA officials were directly accountable to Kenyatta and not local political elites (and routinely overruled legislators and cabinet ministers). As such, Kenyatta faced a relatively low risk of agency loss in his efforts to balance, monitor, and regulate elite political action – including in the legislature. This situation enabled Kenyatta to grant the legislature a fair amount of internal organizational autonomy and means independence. This approach extended to legislative elections. Under Kenyatta, elections were "relatively free and democratic affairs" (Throup, 1993, p. 381).

In Zambia, Kaunda relied on UNIP as the primary means of monitoring and regulating elite politics. His preindependence commitment to restructure and subordinate the provincial administrative apparatus to UNIP tied his hands as far as using the administration to monitor and regulate elite politics was concerned. At independence, UNIP absorbed the administrative system and became the primary apparatus through which Kaunda propagated his power. But, Kaunda's use of UNIP came at significant cost. Being a political party, UNIP structure comprised principal–agent relationships of persuasion. Kaunda could not simply fire party members as this would shrink the party's base. This reality exposed the president to agency loss. Continued political support at the local level was always contingent on UNIP's ability to deliver patronage and targeted benefits. Furthermore, Kaunda had to constantly deal with the risk of local capture of party units by local politicians, especially after ethnic factionalism emerged in the party in the late 1960s. To compound matters, any attempts to restructure the agency relationship in favor of the center or discipline local party units risked alienating local party agents and defections from UNIP. Scott (1976) succinctly summarizes Kaunda's structural exposure to agency loss:

For the local UNIP organization, the effect of factionalism was to increase their independence from the centre. Once national leaders became involved in factional politics, party concerns at Freedom House [UNIP headquarters] were neglected. Regional officials found they could rarely contact the top officials at Freedom House; that their own positions and political future depended on factional allegiance rather than performance in office; that the circulars issued by Freedom House were rarely followed up. Increasingly, and particularly after the formation of the UPP [an opposition party], local UNIP officials saw themselves in a favourable bargaining position with the centre (p. 176).

Kaunda's executive power was lowest when he needed UNIP officials the most. Unable to effectively dominate the apparatus through which he propagated his power, Kaunda worked to preemptively put out any and all potential threats to his rule. This meant regular reshuffles of the cabinet and administrators, nationalization of the economy, and the instigation of competition between UNIP and administrative officials. Kaunda's low levels of executive power also predisposed him to deny the legislature means independence. The legislature was subordinated to the party, with UNIP's Central Committee charged with controlling the legislative agenda, vetting candidates for legislative elections, and disciplining legislators that failed to toe the party line (Scott, 1976; Gertzel, 1984; Alderfer, 1997). However, these strategies only worked for so long. When the wave of multiparty politics swept across Africa in the early 1990s, Kaunda found himself unable to tame agency loss as UNIP members defected to the opposition en masse (Riedl, 2014). As a result, he was one of a handful of African presidents who lost the founding multiparty elections of the early 1990s, having garnered a paltry 24 percent of the votes cast in the 1991 presidential election.

Figure 5.1 illustrates a typology of the different strategies of elite control in Kenya and Zambia. As argued above, the decolonization process in Kenya and Zambia differentially endowed the two countries with party types and strengths of administrations. Kenyatta was predisposed to rely on an administration-based means of balancing fellow elites. On his part, Kaunda relied on a party-based means of elite balancing. Moi's tenure presents an attempt to rebalance the means of propagating executive power. In a context in which ethnicity was an important principle of organizing politics, he inherited a PA system dominated by Kenyatta loyalists and Kikuyu coethnics – at the time Kenyatta's brother-in-law, Mbiyu Koinange, was in charge of the PA. To Moi's chagrin, political contingencies meant that a complete reorganization of the PA would take time. As Barkan and Chege (1989) observe, the "pace at which Moi [a Kalenjin] could restructure the regime was necessarily slow as a result of his initial dependence on two senior Kikuyu leaders [Mwai Kibaki and Charles Njonjo] who had been mainstays of the Kenyatta regime" (p. 435). And, so unable to immediately control what was important (the PA), Moi made important what he could control (KANU). To contain the PA, Moi politicized it. At the same time, he invested in strengthening KANU and subordinating the legislature to the party (Widner, 1992; Opalo, 2014). His inability to effectively

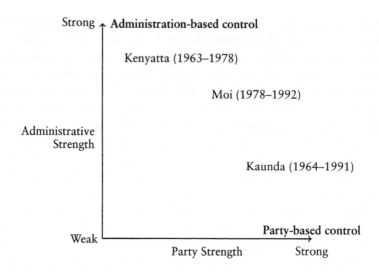

Figure 5.1 Administrative vs. party strength and elite control strategies
Notes: This figure shows the relative strengths of administrative apparatuses and parties in postcolonial Kenya and Zambia. The choice of administrative vs. party-based elite control strategies is conditional on the relative strength and reliability of the administrative structure or ruling political party, which are in turn generated by the contingencies of the decolonization process. *Ceteris paribus*, presidents seek to control elites through a reliably strong system (party or administration). But, failing to control an existing strong system, they make strong what they can control.

propagate his power through the PA and to balance fellow elites predisposed him to limit legislative independence. Like Kaunda, he dominated the legislative agenda, enforced strict party discipline in the legislature, had KANU vet legislative candidates, and ultimately resorted to abolishing the secret ballot and openly rigging elections as happened in the infamous *mlolongo* election of 1988. In short, Moi's overt interference in legislative elections and parliamentary processes was symptomatic of his inability to effectively monitor, regulate, and balance fellow elites through the PA as was the case under Kenyatta.

It is important to emphasize that presidents in both Kenya and Zambia had agency in choosing or investing in specific strategies of controlling their respective elites and legislatures. But, they made these choices and investments under circumstances not of their own choosing. Political developments in the late colonial period limited the menu of options available to Kaunda and Kenyatta. Furthermore, the need to consolidate power in the postcolonial period increased the utility of existing structures of organizing intra-elite politics and propagating executive power since they embodied common-knowledge models of "how politics works." The case of Moi illustrates the manner in which presidents' hands can be tied by precedent and path dependence. The remainder of this chapter provides a deeper analysis of how the dynamics of intra-elite politics and balance of power impacted legislative institutional development in Kenya and Zambia.

5.3 Administration-Based Elite Control in Kenya

5.3.1 Kenyatta's Provincial Administration

British rule in the geographic unit that became Kenya began in 1895. After a decade-long mandate over the territory, the Imperial British East Africa Company (IBEAC) gave way to the Colonial Office. The Provincial Administration (PA) was founded in 1900. As a prefectural field administration structure, its primary function was to maintain law and order and to supervise implementation of colonial policy. The administration was structured around the Governor, Provincial Commissioners (PCs), District Commissioners (DCs), and District Officers (DOs). All were employees of the British Colonial Administrative Service. Below the DOs were Chiefs and Sub-Chiefs, the latter two positions being filled by African recruits that either had authority based on (perceived) local chiefly status or specific training in colonial schools (see Figure 5.2).[3] Unlike most other British colonies, Kenya effectively had direct rule. African chiefs were government bureaucrats with very limited precolonial "traditional" authority (Berman, 1974, p. 231). The structure of the Administration provided a direct link between the African agents of the colonial administration and the Governor. District Commissioners, in partic- ular, were powerful officials whose duties included presiding over African Local Native Councils. By the mid-1940s the PA had evolved into a strong administrative structure that violently perpetuated the

---

[3] The native Authority Ordinance of 1902 paved the way for the appointment of Africans into the colonial administration, Since Kenya lacked centralized precolonial polities besides the Wanga, Whitehall simply invented chiefs in the territory and imbued them with administrative authority.

domination of Africans in the colony in addition to providing public goods and services to European immigrants.

And, then it got stronger. In 1949 African nationalists, frustrated by decades of land alienation, forced labor, forced de-stocking (*kifagio*), exclusion from colonial institutions, and the slow pace toward African self-government, took up arms as part of what became known as the Mau Mau insurgency.[4] At the core of the insurgency were Kikuyu-speaking Kenyans who, at the time, were experiencing the most acute form of land shortage as a result of colonial land alienation. Between 1951 and the Declaration of Emergency in 1952, the PA doubled in size from 184 to 370 officers (excluding African chiefs and sub-chiefs). At the height of the Emergency almost the entire Kikuyu-speaking population of 1.5 million was under surveillance, while virtually the entire rural Kikuyu population was put under a forced villagization program. Tens of thousands of suspected Mau Mau sympathizers were detained. The sheer scale of civilian control in the fight to contain and defeat the Mau Mau insurgency served to strengthen the PA. In particular, it granted District Commissioners immense powers. At the height of the Emergency they could arrest, try, and execute Mau Mau suspects.

The strengthening of the PA was not limited to Kikuyu districts. Fearing the prospects of Mau Mau radicalism "infecting" non-Kikuyu districts, the administration strengthened its monitoring of potential flash points all over the colony (Ogot, 2003, p. 21). The void left following the arrest of the Kapenguria Six and proscription of political parties was filled by the labor movement. As early as 1947 there were several labor strikes and general political unrest among non-Kikuyu Africans. A major strike in Mombasa (March 1947) forced the government to grant workers a sufficient cost of living allowance and a

---

[4] The historiography on the Mau Mau insurgency is vast and varied. Atieno-Odhiambo (1991) reviews the points of contention in the "Mau Mau Debate" among academics and the Kenyan public alike. See Kanogo (1987) on the proximate causes of the rebellion. Beginning among Olenguruone squatters, oath-taking spread to Kikuyu reserves in Central Kenya and provided a basis of achieving a cohesive rebellion against colonialism and land alienation. An estimated 240,000 Africans – many of them Kikuyu speakers – were detained during the Emergency (1952–1960) in a total of 176 detention camps. In the counterinsurgency effort the colonial government had by 1954 recruited about 25,000 Home Guards to supplement the nearly 10,000 British troops deployed (Elkins, 2000; Bennett, 2007; Branch, 2007).

housing allowance. In 1953 Thomas Mboya, then only 23, was elected to lead the Kenya Federation of Labor (KFL). A KFL strike in 1955 paralyzed the port in Mombasa for three days with the participation of over 10,000 workers.

At the same time, African members of the legislative council (MLCs) exploited the government's vulnerability in the face of the insurgency to press for more concessions. Odede Rachelo, MLC for Nyanza, was arrested and expelled from the LegCo for daring to accept the presidency of KAU at a time when the organization was proscribed on account of its alleged links to Mau Mau (Ogot, 2003). Further political pressure during the Emergency forced the colonial government to increase African representation in the LegCo, culminating in the first direct election of Africans to the legislature in 1957. The colonial government was keen to avoid losing the institutionalized political participation of non-Kikuyu MLCs. As Branch (2006) documents, the colonial administration deployed the PA to ensure that only loyalist African elites won seats in the LegCo.

At independence on December 12, 1963 Kenyatta inherited the PA intact. As Gertzel (1966) observes, Kenyatta chose to "use the Provincial Administration rather than the party machine (KANU) as his major link with the people" (p. 202). Although the independence constitution created a regionalist structure of government, the PA remained as the backbone of the Kenyan state and propagated executive power from the Office of the President (OP) through Provincial and District Commissioners and down to the thousands of Sub-Locations all over the country (see Figure 5.2).[5] As direct personal representatives of Kenyatta in the periphery, the PA's officers "were virtually lords in their own realms provided they administered their fiefs efficiently on the regime's behalf" (Barkan and Chege, 1989, p. 438). Their duties included the maintenance of law and order, coordination of the activities of the different government

---

[5] A raft of constitutional amendments in the first few years of independence got rid of the regional structure of government and the Senate (Proctor, 1965; Stultz, 1969); curtailed powers of elected County Councils before subordinating them to the Ministry of Local Government (Stamp, 1986); and gave the PA significant oversight powers over all political activity in the country. These changes gave Kenyatta powers not unlike those of a colonial governor (Okoth-Ogendo, 1972).

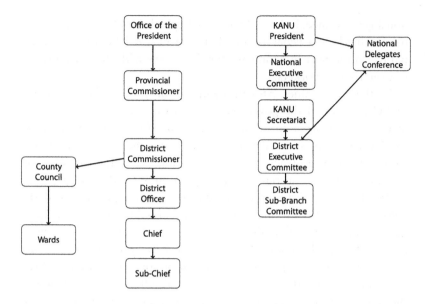

Figure 5.2 The structures of the Provincial Administration and KANU

Notes: For much of the period between 1963 and 1990 Kenya had 8 Provinces, 41 Districts, 150–180 Divisions, and over 3,000 Locations and Sub-Locations. PCs and DCs were directly appointed by the president. The DOs and their subordinates were appointed by the Public Service Commission in conjunction with the Office of the President. Chiefs in Kenya were Civil Servants. County Councils were composed of locally elected Ward Councillors, with limited and taxation and policy powers. KANU's most active units were the branches, which produced national politicians that served as district spokespeople. Cabinet ministers were often district political supremos. The PA and KANU were distinctly separate entities, with the former having precedence over the latter.

departments at the local level, and the monitoring of all political activities.

In many ways, Kenyatta's PA approximated an ideal-type principal–agent relationship of command with perfect agents. Indeed, the postcolonial administration "[wielded] very much less power in the Central Government than it did in the past [under colonialism]" (Gertzel, 1966, p. 210). As a result, local PA officials had little to no administrative power vis-à-vis Kenyatta. To guarantee maximum discretionary powers, the PA had vaguely defined mandates legalized under various colonial-era laws, including the Chiefs' Authority Act (1939), Public Order Act (1966), Preservation of Public Security Act (1960), the Police Act (1960), and the Public Collections Act

(1960). The latter Act was selectively applied by the PA to regulate Harambees (self-help community fundraisers), an important avenue through which MPs built their popularity through the initiation of local development projects. The PA was reinforced by the coercive capacity of the Administration Police and the General Service Unit, both of which were separate from regular police and close to the Office of the President (N'Diaye, 2002).

To monitor, regulate, and balance elite political activity, the PA was empowered to issue licenses for political meetings, *barazas* (local community meetings), and Harambees. The discretionary powers of the PA officers allowed them to selectively apply rules to buttress machines loyal to the president and to harass politicians whose local preferences were at variance with those of the president through the licensing process (Alila, 1986). Legislators and other politicians that were out of favor with the president were routinely denied such licenses. While Kenyan political elites were allowed to compete with one another, they could only do so as long as they did not undermine Kenyatta's authority.

Naturally, legislators opposed their political subordination to the PA.[6] On numerous occasions they petitioned Kenyatta to subordinate the PA to KANU, or at the very least rein in the DCs. In 1965 Martin Shikuku (MP, Butere) moved a motion to subordinate civil servants in the constituency to Members of Parliament. In the same year, Senator D. Oruko Makasembo (Central Nyanza) moved a motion to establish political heads in Kenya's provinces. Both motions failed (Gertzel, 1966, p. 206). In response to such calls Kenyatta invoked the principle of bureaucratic neutrality, insisting that PA officials were impartial professionals, like "doctors," adding that "who would presume to tell a doctor how and where to operate on a sick person?"[7] He particularly "opposed efforts to require civil servants to become members of the party and sought to repel politicization of the civil service ranks" (Widner, 1992, p. 71). The PA thus remained ostensibly "depoliticized" and, more importantly, loyal only to Kenyatta. This

---

[6] Kenya National Assembly, Official Record, June 12, 1973, Cols. 15–16.
[7] John Okumu and Frank Holmquist, "Party and Party-State Relations," in *Politics and Public Policy in Kenya and Tanzania*, ed. Joel Barkan (New York: Praeger, 1984), pp. 53–54, cited in Widner (1992, p. 71).

shielded the PA's field officers from agency loss through political capture by KANU supremos in the districts.

Examples abound of Kenyan legislators whose political wings were clipped by the PA. In November 1970 a Kenyatta critic, Juma Boy (MP, Kwale Central), had his meetings canceled by the Kwale DC who accused Boy of campaigning against government-initiated Harambee projects. Complaining in the National Assembly, Boy claimed that due to the DC's directive he "[could] not hold any public *baraza* or public meetings in [his] constituency, even including meetings covering self-help projects." Joining in the debate, A. O. Araru (MP, Moyale) opined that "[w]e should know from our Government why, if a Member of Parliament wants to speak to his constituents, he has to go and ask permission from somebody else. What sort of law is that, Mr. Speaker?" Also contributing to the same debate, Paul Ngei (Cabinet Minister for Housing) expressed concern over the role of the PA in regulating politics, arguing that "it is high time that Government policy came in so that we know where representatives of the people stand," adding that the police, and not the PA, should regulate political activity based on security considerations.[8]

The PA's powers extended to the lowest geographic units of administration – the locations and sub-locations. The Chief "was the local manifestation of the dominant state – effecting edicts on behalf of the provincial administration, which itself was an extension of the ubiquitous office of the president" (Ndegwa, 1998, p. 199). Retaining many elements of their colonial antecedents, these local government administrators and their assistants had the power to maintain order, prevent crime, arrest suspects, mandate work or services from the public (not too dissimilar form forced labor under colonialism), and to monitor local political activity.[9] In the words of the Attorney General Matthew Muli, Chiefs and Sub-Chiefs were "the eyes of the Government in matters which perhaps the police or the District Commissioner

---

[8] Kenya National Assembly, Official Record, December 18, 1970, Cols. 1965–1972.

[9] The process of appointing Chiefs and their assistants was technically supposed to incorporate local input. But, in reality, and perhaps reflecting the fear of agency loss, the Office of the President (OP) and senior PA officers determined who became Chiefs and Sub-Chiefs (see Kenya National Assembly, Official Record, July 28, 1972, Col. 536).

[could not] be available at the material [*sic*] to tackle."[10] For example, after 1966 when Odinga and Kaggia left KANU to found the Kenya People's Union (KPU), chiefs championed Kenyatta's efforts to contain the party. Chiefs enforced a ban on all meetings held by KPU in Siaya, the home district of Odinga.[11]

Interestingly, despite the harsh extra-parliamentary treatment of party members, KPU MPs remained vocal in the legislature. Before the party was eventually banned in 1969, Kenyatta's strategy of dealing with the opposition was to ethnically isolate its members by turning KPU into a district party (limited to Siaya and other Luo districts), deny party members economic opportunities, and to effectively deploy the provision administration to ensure that political opposition from party members did not transmogrify into outright subversion of the regime (Mueller, 1984).[12]

Members of Parliament (MPs) routinely complained about Chiefs' excessive use of force and arbitrary powers. On one occasion O. G. Migure (MP, Mbita) informed parliament that "[t]hese chiefs, with the colonial mentality they have, say, 'Now look, if so-and-so is of such-and-such clan, I will make sure that his people pay the graduated personal tax in that area.'"[13] Despite their low rank within the PA, Chiefs knew that they could defy incumbent legislators because they derived their power from neither MPs nor voters. Their authority and power was "delegated from the Office of the President and President Kenyatta personally" (Bienen, 1974, p. 38).

The structure and functions of the PA did not change when Kenyatta died in August 1978 and was replaced by Moi. For example, Chiefs

---

[10] Kenya National Assembly, Official Record, November 16, 1983, Col. 300.

[11] See Government of Kenya Annual Report: Siaya District, 1969. The KPU defectors were forced to seek a fresh mandate from their constituents. In the "Little General Election" that ensued KPU won only 9 out of 29 seats contested. Kenyatta used the PA to ensure that the KPU was limited to Odinga's political backyard in Luo Nyanza.

[12] It is important to note that even after the elimination of KPU, political participation in Luo Nyanza remained severely restricted, with Kenyatta's PA playing an important role in deciding election outcomes. However, this is the exception that proves the rule. Odinga's radical-populist brand of politics was not just about the open airing of views and competition for state resources. He sought to challenge the very legitimacy of Kenyatta's authority, the latter having chosen the conservative route of managing Kenya's postcolonial economy.

[13] Kenya National Assembly, Official Record, June 20, 1972, Col. 209.

retained their monitoring functions and were used to ensure that "radical" university students opposed to Moi's regime were effectively surveilled. In addition, university students that were expelled after the coup attempt in 1982 were required to report to their home area Chiefs weekly, and to obtain certificates of good conduct from the Chiefs before they could be readmitted into university.

But, while broadly retaining the structure and functions of the PA, Moi also had to stamp his authority on the administration. To this end he sought to alter its ethnic composition, weaken PCs, and explicitly politicize the position of DCs. As a Kalenjin, Moi understood the risk of agency loss in an administration dominated by Kikuyu coethnics of Kenyatta. The legacy of district-cum-ethnic basis of political organization going back to the colonial era endured. However, his desire to rapidly staff the PA with coethnic loyalists was stymied by factors beyond his control. Initially, his security of tenure was predicated on the support of key Kikuyu elites. He appointed a Kikuyu Vice President (Mwai Kibaki) and retained a powerful Kikuyu Attorney General (Charles Njonjo) as a close confidant (Tamarkin, 1979). The presidential transition was thus marked by a significant degree of institutional continuity. However, the imperative to effectively balance fellow elites using loyalists in the PA could not be ignored. This heightened sense of insecurity was reinforced by Moi's perception that significant portions of Kenya's elite class – including the Kikuyu old guard, parliament, the judiciary, and the intelligentsia – were against his rule (Kariuki, 1996). Within a year of taking office Moi had replaced all of the country's 8 PCs and nearly half of the 41 DCs. And, to tame the wider PA he explicitly politicized its operations, including by using it as the main mechanism of patronage distribution and influencing elections (Widner, 1992; Throup, 1993).

The coup attempt against Moi on August 2, 1982 only served to accelerate this process. As Atieno-Odhiambo (2002) documents, in early 1982 Moi faced the real possibility of the return of an opposition party headed by former Vice President Oginga Odinga. His response was to amend the constitution to make Kenya a de jure single-party state in June 1982. Two months later, junior officers in the Kenya Air Force attempted to depose Moi in a failed coup. The events of 1982 served to heighten Moi's sense of political insecurity. In October 1982 he launched the District Focus for Rural Development (DFRD), an initiative that elevated DCs to be powerful local patrons.

On paper, the primary goal for DFRD was to decongest the state, redistribute resources to poorer districts, and take developing planning closer to the people through District Development Committees.[14] But, it also had an important political function. By making DCs the focal authority in the "management of rural development, the President could reduce the power of P.C.s as well as the power of incumbent M.P.s, especially those with regional followings beyond their constituencies" (Barkan and Chege, 1989, p. 440). The choice to use the PA as a conduit for redistributive patronage resulted in the politicization of the administration. This was in contrast to Kenyatta's strategy of organizing intra-elite sharing of governance rents largely through parliament and appointments to parastatals, an approach to elite control that created few incentives for political capture of district-level PA officials.

The overt politicization of the PA was a self-undermining strategy. Instead of enhancing his executive power, it served to increase the risk of agency loss. Politicization of DCs, in particular, exposed them to capture by district KANU bosses that used them to rig elections. PA officials now had multiple principles (the president and district-level political supremos). By the late 1980s Moi's uncertainty over the ability of the PA to effectively monitor and regulate elite political activity forced him to abolish the secret ballot. In the infamous *mlolongo* elections of March 1988, he decreed (though KANU) that voters should queue behind their preferred candidates in an effort to ensure that legislative and party election outcomes mirrored his preferences. However, even after this drastic move he did not feel confident of being able to screen disloyal elites from winning legislative elections. He knew that powerful KANU bosses were in a position to capture local PA officials and use them to win elections. In the end, Moi resorted to openly rigging out popular candidates in both legislative and party elections.[15]

Moi's experience with the PA illustrates how intra-elite politics structure executive-legislative relations. His lack of trust in Kenyatta's PA forced him to take drastic measures in an effort to balance fellow

---

[14] Previously resources followed a simple chain of command going from the national level, to the eight provinces, and onwards to the districts. See Hassan (2014). See also KANU Manifesto, 1983, p. 12.

[15] Sheila Rule, "In One Party Kenya, Election Is Questioned," *New York Times*, March 24, 1988.

elites. As a consequence, he found himself directly interfering in local intra-elite politics in a manner that curtailed legislative means independence. Unable to compete freely for votes, political elites were reduced to being regime agents competing for power and influence with officials in the PA. In other words, the political bargaining for governance rents and power left the chambers of the National Assembly and moved into party circles and the administrative apparatus. This was in contrast to the state of affairs under Kenyatta. Then, elites openly competed at the local level on condition that they did not challenge his authority as president. And, in many ways the PA system served as an interested umpire – in the service of Kenya – but one that was perceived to be largely neutral in local politics. Under Kenyatta, legislative elections "had all been relatively free and democratic affairs" (Throup, 1993, p. 381), and provided a foundation for legislative means independence by imbuing legislators with localized mandates.

Perhaps Moi had to politicize the PA in order to control it. But, the politicization of the PA came at a steep cost. A side effect of empowering DCs to weaken PCs (and MPs) was a reduction in the efficacy of the entire PA as a tool for balancing fellow elites. No longer was the entire administrative apparatus defined by a relationship of command from the president through the PCs, DCs, DOs, Chiefs, and Sub-Chiefs. DCs and other PA officials became exposed to political capture in their competition for power and influence within and across ranks. By the mid-1980s, the PA, and in particular DCs, had become key and overt players in local politics, enough to warrant a reminder from Moi that "[a]nyone who attacks a district officer or a district commissioner attacks Moi."[16] In addition to its politicization, the PA's efficacy was further eroded by the emergence in the early 1980s of a rival structure for balancing elites within and outside parliament. As he struggled to control the PA, Moi also invested in strengthening KANU. To this we now turn.

5.3.2 KANU's (Failed) Evolution into a Mass Party

The Kenyan National African Union (KANU) was founded in Kiambu on March 27, 1960. At the time Kenyatta was still in detention. The

[16] See *Weekly Review,* November 29, 1985, p. 4.

party grew out of a split in the African Elected Members Organization (AEMO), a grouping of African MLCs. Consistent with the district basis of political development in Kenya, KANU was a confederation of district parties. Its founders – James Gichuru, Thomas Mboya, Oginga Odinga, and Julius G. Kiano – "undertook to convert their district associations into branches of the new party" (Mboya, 1965, p. 84). From the beginning, the party was rocked by both ideological and ethnic rivalries. The left wing, led by Odinga (a Luo) and Kaggia (a Kikuyu), advocated for populist policies, including land redistribution as a means of remedying landlessness caused by colonial land alienation. The right wing, led by Gichuru (a Kikuyu) and Mboya (a Luo), campaigned against the idea of giving people "free things."[17]

KANU under Kenyatta was a weakly institutionalized elite party. The party's basic unit was the branch, which coincided with the district (see Section 5.2). Its loose organization meant that KANU Headquarters had little control over the district branches. Constituencies formed the sub-branches of the party. Throughout Kenyatta's tenure KANU sub-branches almost never existed and the National Governing Council seldom met. In 1964 party treasurer, Joseph Murumbi, noted that the party's organization and finances "don't exist" (Good, 1968, p. 116). This sentiment was echoed by the Nyeri DC, who in his annual report in 1965 noted that "the Union [KANU] closed its offices toward the end of 1964 or beginning of 1965 due to financial

---

[17] Scholars of Kenyan politics often neglect the nuances of ethnic politics in the country. Despite the well-documented district-cum ethnic basis of politics in Kenya, it is also true that larger ethnic groups traversed more than one district, and had serious intra-ethnic cleavages based on these divisions. Thus, Luo Nyanza had conservatives in Gem and elsewhere who opposed Odinga's left-leaning politics. Similarly, conservatives in southern Kikuyuland (Kiambu) fought against leftist populists north of River Chania in Kirinyaga, Nyeri, Nyandarua, and parts of Murang'a. Even after Odinga and Kaggia decamped from KANU, populist Kikuyu politicians like Waruru Kanja, Charles Rubia, and Josiah M. Kariuki continued calls for land redistribution. Layered onto these intra-ethnic divisions have been the imperatives to build inclusive national coalitions – a bedrock of of what Ogot (2003) calls the *National Project*. These efforts began with the founding of the East African Association in 1921 and culminated with the founding of KADU and KANU in 1960. Even during KANU's hegemony, factional politics spawned KANU A and KANU B, both of which were multiethnic coalitions. More recently, elections since 2002 have been marked by strong multiethnic national coalitions. The point here is that the ethnic basis of political mobilization has never been a barrier to the emergence of multiethnic coalitions or parties.

difficulties. It is impossible to know what is the Branch's official status when there is no office to which enquiries can be made."[18] In general "Kenyatta eschewed an important role for KANU" (Tordoff, 2002, p. 131), and as a result the party lacked any strong connections with voters, many of whom remained primarily loyal to their specific district (ethnic) political patrons. The only time that Kenyatta appeared to be directly involved in party affairs was in March 1966 when, with Mboya's help, he maneuvered to force Odinga and his allies out of the party at the infamous Delegates Conference in Limuru (Mueller, 1984).

It is worth noting that Kenyatta had agency, and could have invested in strengthening KANU instead of relying on the PA as described above. However, the prevailing circumstances stacked the odds in favor of the choice to use the PA as the primary means of balancing fellow elites. His benign neglect of KANU can be attributed to several factors. First, he was not a founding member of the party, and therefore was never involved in the initial ideological fights between its dominant factions. Second, despite his credentials as a national independence hero, Kenyatta never completely shed the image of being a Kikuyu nationalist. He was a founding member of the Kikuyu Central Association (KCA) and a staunch Kikuyu traditionalist (Kenyatta, 1965; Tamarkin, 1978). He therefore lacked the ability to directly engage non-Kikuyu party members, instead relying on district-level power brokers who sat atop localized electoral machines. Third, strengthening KANU in the immediate postindependence period would have meant strengthening the party's left-wing faction. Kenyatta's ideological conservatism made him fear "that the grassroots membership of the party harboured radical sympathies, and so made sure it had little to do with the business of government" (Branch, 2011, p. 71).[19] Riding on the decolonization wave, at the time KANU's

---

[18] Government of Kenya, Annual District Report: Nyeri. Government Printer, 1965.

[19] Throughout his political career Kenyatta was allied with Kenya's wealthy and conservative establishment. He did so for both ideological and personal reasons. In addition to his belief in an ideology of individual discipline and economic self-reliance (Berman and Lonsdale, 1998), he had married into two powerful chiefly families in Kiambu. His third wife, Grace Wanjiku, was the daughter of colonial era Senior Chief Koinange wa Mbiyu. His fourth wife, Ngina Muhoho (Mama Ngina), is the daughter of Chief Muhoho wa Gathecha.

radical branch was in ascendance, having successfully created the Lumumba Institute to train KANU cadres with Soviet assistance (Good, 1968).[20] Fourth, having inherited a strong provincial administrative apparatus may have created disincentives to invest in KANU's organizational strengthening. In other words, Kenyatta took the path of least resistance in his quest to effectively balance fellow elites.

KANU's weakness outside of parliament benefited backbencher MPs. The party could not effectively enforce party discipline. For instance, Gertzel (1970) notes that "[t]he organizational weakness of the party and the governmental restrictions on party activity" enabled parliament to become "popularly acknowledged as an established institution having a tradition of lively, critical debate" (p. 9). Backbenchers dominated the KANU Parliamentary Group (PG), which was an arena for logrolling arrangements among legislators and on occasion managed to defeat executive motions and legislative proposals. In many respects the PG "remained the one viable party entity for considering and influencing government policy" (Good, 1968, p. 122). While important bills were discussed within the PG before presentation on the floor of the house, for the most part "matters were discussed in caucuses ... only after confrontations in parliament between Government and backbenchers" (Hakes, 1970, p. 168). The legislature, and not the party, was the first port of call for most intra-elite debates over policy. While the merger of KANU and KADU in 1965 neutralized the populist wing of the former, it did not completely silence its backbenchers. Voting patterns on the few Divisions (roll-call votes) recorded in the National Assembly indicate that intra-KANU cohesion remained relatively low (Opalo, 2014, p. 68). For instance, in 1969 backbenchers forced a delay of debate on the year's budget estimates over disagreements over remuneration of cabinet ministers. In the prolonged gratuities debate that followed backbenchers managed to gain a 5 percentage point increase in the Government contribution to their social security benefits. Overall, in the First Parliament (1963–1969) backbenchers defeated the

---

[20] Odinga, in conjunction with a number of Kikuyu populists (especially outside Kenyatta's home district of Kiambu) advocated for land redistribution to the landless (mostly Kikuyu) who were dispossessed under colonial rule. Kenyatta, Mboya, and Gichuru led the conservative "anti free things" coalition. The first omen of what was to come of this ideological contest was the assassination of one of its leading lights, Pio Gama Pinto, in February 1965.

Government on 44 motions initiated by their Front Bench colleagues (Hakes, 1970).

The party's weakness also made parliament the arena for internecine battles among senior politicians in Kenyatta's cabinet. Consider the "Kenyatta Succession" debates in 1968 after the 77-year-old suffered a stroke in May. Had KANU been stronger, the contest to succeed Kenyatta would have taken place within the party. Instead, the contest took place in parliament. Having trounced KANU's left wing, a new cleavage emerged within the party's right wing – between those for and against Mboya. An alliance between Vice President Moi and Attorney General Charles Njonjo emerged to block Mboya from succeeding Kenyatta. On May 28, Njonjo introduced a constitutional amendment bill designating the Vice President as the automatic successor in case a sitting president died in office for the remainder of the term. Previously, parliament had the power to elect a new president in such a case. The bill also raised the minimum age to be eligible to be president from 35 to 40. These two provisions nakedly targeted Mboya (Okoth-Ogendo, 1972). At the time he was 38 and his faction was ascendant in parliament. Mboya's allies successfully defeated the second amendment and watered down the first. In the bill that eventually passed on June 25, the minimum age limit remained at 35, while the authority of interim presidents was radically curtailed, with elections mandated to take place within 90 days of a president's death.

The conduct of the Kenyatta Succession debate in parliament reflected a broader elite consensus on the supremacy of the legislature as the focal arena for organizing politics. The words of Ronald Ngala, uttered during the debate on abolition of the Kenyan Senate in 1966, summarized these sentiments:

I would, however, like to make it quite clear that in Kenya the parliament is supreme and this is why all these changes from the beginning, since independence, 1963, all the constitutional changes have been brought con-stitutionally to this House, to this parliament for the Members themselves to make the change. All the changes have been made by the Parliament itself. Therefore, indeed we should be very grateful to the President for observing the fact that the Parliament is supreme in Kenya.[21]

---

[21] Government of Kenya, Official Record of the National Assembly, December 21, 1966, Col. 3060.

This was not just cheap talk. Under Kenyatta, parliament functioned as an important arena for sharing governance rents. Because of legislators' relative means independence, Kenyatta was often forced to negotiate with legislators and offer them board appointments in return for their support of his administration (Hornsby, 1985). As a sign that these appointments were about the distribution of rents, MPs were often appointed to boards whose mandates overlapped with constituents' interests. For example, MPs from maize-growing areas served on the Maize and Produce Board. The same was true for the Pyrethrum, Coffee, Wheat, and Cotton marketing boards. The membership of 15 out of the 18 agricultural marketing boards in existence in 1969 included at least one incumbent legislator (Hakes, 1970, pp. 277–285). While MPs did not receive substantial remuneration for their membership on these boards, they got fringe monetary benefits and opportunities to conduct private business with the parastatals on whose boards they sat. Serving on these boards also enhanced their ability to engage in cooperative logrolling arrangements with fellow legislators in an effort to serve their constituents' interests.

Appointment to parastatal boards granted legislators a chance to control their own political destinies. With access to state resources, they could fend off challengers by showcasing their ability to deliver on development projects, make Harambee contributions, and provide job opportunities to lucky constituents. These forms of clientelism and constituency service were the currency of legislative politics. This implicit promotion of a separation of mandate further reinforced legislators' means independence. As Rouyer (1971) notes, Kenyatta's tolerance, coupled with KANU's weakness, meant that any Kenyan legislator was "more likely to guarantee the continuation of his career by attacking unpopular Government policies than acting as its emissary" (p. 73). Parliamentary independence was invigorated with the formation of the Kenya People's Union (KPU), which in 1966 welcomed 29 KANU MPs to its ranks (Hakes, 1970). Following these defections parliament passed a constitutional amendment mandating fresh elections in the 29 constituencies. In the "Little General Election" campaigns of 1966, Kenyatta deployed the PA to ensure that the party received little support outside of Odinga's stronghold of Nyanza Province. Only nine KPU members got reelected (Mueller, 1984). But, even with these diminished numbers the party remained relevant in parliament. As leader of the opposition, Odinga assumed chairmanship of the Public Accounts Committee and KPU's motions were prioritized over those of KANU backbenchers by Speaker Slade. In the end, however, KPU's challenge proved too much even for Kenyatta, and the party was banned and its members detailed in late 1969.[22] Unlike the case of independent KANU legislators, KPU threatened Kenyatta's authority as president.

Having vanquished Odinga and the KPU threat, Kenyatta's tolerance of legislative independence was again on display in 1970. Backbenchers in the new parliament successfully revived Parliamentary Committees in order to strengthen their input on legislation. Jean-Marie Seroney (MP, Tinderet) was adamant that "[i]n this Session, we are going to insist on our right to participate in the process of legislation and if the Ministers are going to instigate the rejection of our Bills then they can expect the same treatment when they bring their own Bills."[23] Seroney's vocal criticism of the executive was rewarded when after the 1974 elections backbenchers elected him as Deputy Speaker against Kenyatta's wishes. It also presented Kenyatta with his biggest test of legislative means independence. As Mazrui (1979, p. 35) observes:

[I] in the first half of 1975, the Kenya Parliament was probably the freest remaining Legislature on the African Continent. It was possible in the Kenyan Legislature to hear very blunt criticisms of government policies, passionate denunciations of particular ministries, and even accusations of corruption, nepotism, and abuse of power levelled against some of the highest-ranking political figures in the nation – with the sole exception of the President himself.

The murder of Josiah M. Kariuki (MP, Nyandarua) on March 2, 1975 marked the beginning of a low period in legislative independence in Kenya. Kariuki was a nationallypopular critic of the administration. The link of his murder to Kenyatta and his allies thus came naturally, and seriously dented Kenyatta's legitimacy. As expected, parliament was eager to investigate the matter, and on March 14 appointed a 15-member select committee headed by Elijah Mwangale (MP, Bungoma East). In a show of legislative independence, the committee's report to

---

[22] Emman Omari, "Tears and Blood as Big 2 Face Off," *Daily Nation*, August 13, 2013.

[23] Government of Kenya, Official Record of the National Assembly, March 29, 1972, Col. 269.

parliament fingered close associates of Kenyatta, including his brother-in-law Mbiyu Koinange. This prompted Vice President Daniel arap Moi and Attorney General Njonjo to move a motion blocking its adoption by the House. But, backbenchers pushed back, and defeated the motion. A minister (Masinde Muliro) and two assistant ministers (John Keen and Peter Kibisu) also voted against Njonjo's motion, and were promptly fired by Kenyatta.[24]

Shaken by the reaction of both the public and political elites to Kariuki's murder, Kenyatta became less tolerant of legislative means independence. His inability to enforce party discipline through KANU led him to use coercion against critical legislators. In violation of the principle of parliamentary immunity, Seroney and Martin Shikuku (MP, Butere) were both jailed in October 1975 for the simple crime of declaring that KANU was dead and promptly lost their seats. In defense of the supremacy of parliament, Shikuku also warned that Kenyatta and his allies were trying to kill parliament "the way KANU has been killed."[25] Six years earlier Kenyatta had sought to silence Shikuku by having him elected KANU Whip in parliament. In many ways Seroney and Shikuku were right. KANU under Kenyatta was an elite party that barely existed below the district level, and whose members were primarily loyal to their respective district politicians and not the party itself or its national leadership. In the 15 years of Kenyatta's tenure (1963–1978), the party held national executive elections only once (in 1966).[26]

---

[24] See Ellen Otzen "Kenyan MP's Murder Unsolved 40 Years on," *BBC*, March 11, 2015. See also Tamarkin (1978) and Amutabi (2010).

[25] See *Weekly Review*, May 31, 1976, p. 5. Other MPs jailed for their independence in parliament included George Anyona, Peter Kibisu, Chelagat Mutai, and Mark Mwithaga (Hornsby, 1985).

[26] Nationwide grassroots elections were held in 1976 and executive elections held in October of 1978 (Kenyatta died in August) and in June of 1985. Sporadic District elections continued to take place, while the president appointed officials running the party secretariat. The District elections were often used to weed out regime critics, while maintaining loyalists. For example in Kiambu James Gichuru served as Party Chairman between independence and when he died in 1982. After Gichuru's death the position remained vacant until the KANU elections of 1985 when Njenga Karume, with the support of President Moi, was elected "unopposed" despite Kiambu being one of the more competitive electoral districts in Kenya (see *Weekly Review*, January 4, 1985, p. 4).

The decline in legislative means independence during this period is evident in Figure 5.1. The rate of passage of executive bills in the Third Parliament (1975–1979) jumped to 91.53 percent, up from 67.49 percent in the Second Parliament. This represented a significant decline in Kenyan legislators' ability to influence legislation. In this regard, Kenyatta's response to legislative assertiveness beginning in 1975 corroborates a core argument of this book: that only chief executives that are confident in their ability to effectively balance fellow elites can tolerate legislative means independence. When it became necessary to put legislators on a shorter leash to preserve his authority, he was able to do so on account of his ability to project power via the PA.

Moi's accession to the presidency in 1978 changed KANU's fortunes. Central to his grip on power was the reorganization of KANU with a view of weakening both senior politicians commanding district electoral machines and the leadership of Kenyatta's PA (Widner, 1992, p. 151). A number of specific moves defined this overall strategy. First, despite Kenya having been a de facto single-party state since the banning of KPU in 1969, in 1982 parliament changed the constitution to make the country a de jure single-party state under KANU. Hence, all legislators had to be KANU members and expulsion from the party meant expulsion from the legislature. Second, the party revised its electoral rules to weaken MPs at the branch level. Branch officials (district-level) now had to have also been elected at sub-branch levels. The effect of these rules was to lock out wealthy district-level politicians that thrived on Harambee-fueled electoral machines. Third, Moi launched the District Focus for Rural Development (DFRD), in late 1982. Under DFRD, newly created District Development Committees (DDCs) dominated the distribution of development resources. Moi's design was to bypass MPs (especially those with a national stature) in the allocation of development resources. This was reinforced by a decree limiting politicians' Harambee activities to their own districts (Barkan and Chege, 1989; Kanyinga, 1998). In 1985 he ordered the PA to arrest "anybody found to be engaging in political campaigns in districts other than their own irrespective of his status."[27] To enforce these changes both among elites and in the grassroots, the KANU Disciplinary Committee was created in 1986 and the KANU Youth

---

[27] See *Weekly Review*, July 5, 1985, p. 21.

Wing empowered. The former kept incumbent legislators in check while the latter, clad in red uniforms, "operated as the de facto police in many parts of the country" (Mwangola, 2007, p. 147).

Under Moi, the Kenyatta-era "neutrality" of the Provincial Administration became a thing of the past. Civil Servants (including PA officials) were required to be KANU members. The PA thus took charge of the collection of party dues, registration of members, and directly intervened in local elections.[28] While Kenyatta almost exclusively governed through the PA and the wider Civil Service, the politicization of these entities under Moi served to strengthen KANU. Thus, the party became "a vehicle for transmitting the views of the president to the grassroots and for controlling the expression of interests within the country and their influence over policy" (Widner, 1992, p. 158).

KANU's ascendance under Moi came at parliament's expense. According to Kariuki (1996), "Parliament steadily became a purely advisory body, most members being fearful of critising the president's actions, for critics were frequently purged and stripped of political standing" (p. 76). The party, and not the legislature, became the focal arena for negotiating intra-elite power sharing and distribution of rents. Moi's direct meddling in local elections took away legislators' ability to cultivate localized bases of political support and made them regime agents. The establishment of the KANU Disciplinary Committee sounded the death knell of legislative means independence. The legislature thus became little more than a constitutional conveyor belt for resolutions dictated by Moi. During this period the share of executive bills passed by parliament remained high (see Figure 5.1). By late 1986 Moi was confident enough to proclaim that KANU was "supreme" over parliament.[29] The old idea of parliamentary supremacy, a central tenet of intra-elite politics in Kenya going back to the colonial era, was dead.

---

[28] For instance the DC for Taita Taveta reported that in 1987 58,791 of residents were registered KANU members against 57,827 registered voters. The report state that "[t]he year 1987 was characterized by intense political activity in the form of KANU recruitment drive and the registration of voters exercise. The district recorded a very high percentage in the registration of voters exercise while the KANU recruitment drive recorded a commendable percentage." See Government of Kenya, District Annual Report: Taita Taveta. Government Printer, 1988. By 1988 KANU claimed to have 4 million registered members, out of 5.6 million registered voters.

[29] See *Weekly Review*, November 21, 1986, p. 9.

Ultimately, and despite Moi's best attempts, the quest to transform KANU into a powerful mass party failed. The resiliency of district-based politics proved insurmountable. While the organizational capacity of the national party was certainly strengthened, the elevation of KANU only served to exacerbate its internal factional politics and empower district bosses that won elections. The party "remained a collection of patrons, and did not develop a membership-based infrastructure" (Cheeseman, 2006, p. 226). The politicization of the PA also backfired, at it exposed PA officials to political capture and limited Moi's ability to effectively monitor fellow elites.[30] In other words, Moi was faced with the specter of agency loss from both KANU and the PA. Unable to reliably use either the PA or KANU to balance fellow elites, in 1986 Moi was forced to abolish the secret ballot in KANU primaries. The *Mlolongo* (queue) Rules required voters to queue behind their preferred candidates, in a bid to cow voters into backing Moi's preferred candidates. However, this was not enough to screen independently wealthy and powerful KANU district bosses.

In this regard the case of Murang'a District is instructive. In the 1988 elections, Moi wanted to oust Mbiiri legislator Kenneth Matiba, a powerful KANU boss in Murang'a District. For most of the 1980s, Matiba had served Moi as a counterweight to powerful Kikuyu elites from Kenyatta's home district of Kiambu (such as Charles Njonjo). But, after Moi hounded Njonjo out of parliament and KANU, he moved to sideline Matiba on account of his wealth and political independence. The first chance to do this was the 1988 *Mololongo* elections. However, knowing what was coming, Matiba deployed a helicopter to capture images of his queues and distributed them to the media (Throup, 1993). He handily won reelection and forced Moi's hand into reappointing him to the cabinet. Next were the KANU branch elections in December 1988.[31] Then, Moi conspired with PA officials to install Joseph Kamotho as branch chairman, despite Matiba's popularity. Matiba resigned from the cabinet in

---

[30] For example, in Kirinyaga District of Central Province, the DC, one Antony Oyier, was accused of being coopted by an MP from the District, James Njiru, and was using Chiefs and their Assistants to skew the KANU registration drive in favor of the MP ahead of the 1985 election – see *Weekly Review*, June 7, 1985, p. 9.

[31] Mutegi Njau "Matiba Group in Another Boycott," *Daily Nation*, December 7, 1988.

protest in a move that began the end of KANU's dominance. Fearful of such a powerful backbencher, Moi expelled Matiba from KANU and parliament. The fallout from the *Mlolongo* elections led to a tumultuous three years in Kenyan politics that culminated in the abolition of single-party rule in 1991.

In the final analysis, Moi's strengthening of KANU and politicization of the PA reflected a desire to have a trusted means of monitoring and balancing fellow elites. Unable to control what was powerful (the PA), he worked to make powerful what he could control (KANU). This resulted in "slowing the process of institutional development not only in the legislature but also in the bureaucracy itself" (Widner, 1992, p. 163). The risk of agency loss within both KANU and the PA led him to drastically limit the domain of legitimate political action by legislators within and outside of parliament – the effect of which was to deny the legislature means independence. Seen this way, Moi's moves to weaken the PA and strengthen KANU were not dissimilar to Kaunda's relationship with UNIP and his provincial administration. As I show below, Kaunda, too, faced an administration with dubious loyalty and chose to weaken it while at the same time strengthening the ruling party.

5.4 Party-Based Elite Control in Zambia

5.4.1 UNIP and the Party-State in Zambia

At UNIP's founding in August 1959 Kenneth Kaunda was in prison. In January 1960 he took over the party and capitalized on popular opposition to federation and the color bar in Northern Rhodesia to create a strong independence movement. To this end he tapped into his extensive connections with local political machines developed during his ANC days. Although not uniformly strong throughout Zambia, UNIP permeated both rural (villages) and urban areas (cells comprising every 25 houses). Because of his firm grip on the party, at independence UNIP became Kaunda's preferred means of monitoring and balancing Zambia's elites. But, as I show below, Kaunda's reliance on UNIP exposed him to agency loss and directly contributed to his loss of power in 1991.

UNIP's overwhelming political dominance came at the expense of the Zambian legislature. For most of Kaunda's tenure (1964–1991), the party was the only game in town, and served as the focal arena for organizing intra-elite politics and the distribution of governance rents. Initial threats to the party's (Kaunda's) hegemony from the ANC (that had considerable support in Central and Southern Provinces), the United Party (with a stronghold in Barotseland, Western Province), and the United Progressive Party (in the Copperbelt and Northern Provinces) were met with legal and extra-legal suppression. In 1972 Zambia became a constitutional single-party state. At the apex was UNIP, towering above all state institutions including the National Assembly.

It is important to note that like Kenyatta and Moi, Kaunda had agency in choosing specific strategies of consolidation power and balancing fellow elites. Yet, his menu of options was limited by factors beyond his control. Fractious racial politics in Northern Rhodesia forced UNIP-allied nationalists to commit to the dismantling of the colonial administrative apparatus after independence. It did not help matters that the postcolonial field administration and local government apparatuses were staffed by Europeans and collaborationist African chiefs (and councils) with dubious loyalty to Kaunda and UNIP. Under the circumstances, Kaunda was forced to restructure Zambia's field administration and subordinate it to UNIP. The resulting politicization of the field administration exposed its officials to political capture, thereby diminishing Kaunda's executive power. Thereafter, the principal–agent relationship between Kaunda and administration officials became not one of command but of persuasion.

The mass-party character of UNIP was also not entirely of Kaunda's making. Rapid urbanization in the Copperbelt beginning in the 1930s (and later along the line of rail) gave political development in Zambia a multiethnic character long before Kaunda (Zelniker, 1971; Mijere, 1985). The political salience of race in Northern Rhodesia was in part a factor of geography, having been influenced by racist administrations in Southern Rhodesia and South Africa. In his quest for political power, Kaunda made the best of the geographical accident of Zambia's location. Federation with Southern Rhodesia and Nyasaland provided a potent populist mobilization tool. Northern Rhodesia's strained race relations significantly lowered the costs of multiethnic mobilization. After independence, Kaunda's inability to effectively control Zambia's field administration and local governments and use them to balance fellow elites left him little choice but to empower what he could control – UNIP. The party's populist origins gave him a direct connection to ordinary Zambians, and allowed him to exploit his personal popularity to keep fellow elites in check.[32]

Kaunda's direct access to voters through UNIP's organizational apparatus made Zambian legislators into agents of his regime and not champions of their constituents' specific interests. Individual legislators dared not develop independent power bases. Many routinely lamented having to "get clearance from the Party's regional office each time they visited places in the constituencies" (Alderfer, 1997, p. 96). To enforce party discipline, a 1966 constitutional amendment mandated legislators to seek a fresh mandate from voters on defecting from the party that sponsored them to the legislature. Mass loyalty to the party, and not particular politicians per se, enabled Kaunda to use the party's apparatus to balance fellow elites. He made this clear at the 1967 party conference, stating that "the constituency belongs to the party ... a UNIP Member of Parliament is part and parcel of the whole, and does not therefore carry out his own policies in the constituency," adding that "we believe that the people have a right to make claims to their government through their party. This they do naturally through the party leadership at all levels and that is why Members of Parliament go where the party sends them" (Momba, 2005, p. 105). Kaunda left very little room for legitimate political action among legislators that was not in direct service to the party.

In many ways UNIP lived up to its billing as "one of the most organizationally developed mass parties in Africa" (Helgerson, 1970, p. 277). Its structure was as follows (see Figure 5.3). The Central Committee was composed of the president, prime minister, three presidential nominees, and 20 officials elected every five years by the General Conference. The General Conference met every five years and brought together 600 delegates from Zambia's nine provinces and all

---

[32] For example, when faced with elite ethnic factionalism that threatened UNIP's hegemony, Kaunda briefly resigned on February 5, 1968. Fearing the public's reaction, the same elites begged Kaunda to remain in office. "Unknowingly, the Kaunda image they [elites] created became equated to that of the nation, and was therefore above them. It was too late when they realised that they had created a 'Frankenstein's Monster'" (Phiri, 2001, p. 231). Besides his nationalist credentials, Kaunda (the son of a Malawian immigrant), was seen by the public to be above the country's fractious ethnic politics.

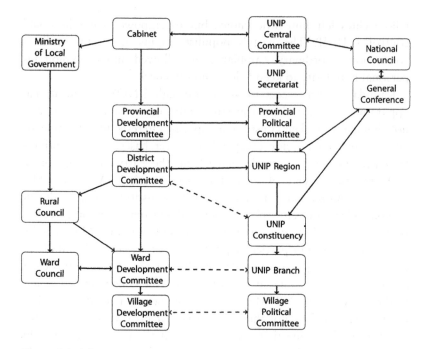

Figure 5.3 Administrative and party structures in Zambia

Notes: This figure shows the structure of UNIP and Provincial Administration in Zambia. The figure shows both UNIP's depth in Zambian society and the overlapping functions between administrative and UNIP units. The main subnational unit of UNIP was the Region (District). Twenty-four officials (representing the party, women, and youth leagues) comprised the UNIP constituency, elected for three-year terms. The 24 officials of the branch were elected annually. Urban sub-branches were called Section Political Committees. This description is based on the 1973 UNIP constitution and various other sources. See Bates (1971), Bond (1976), Scott (1976), Bratton (1980), and Sandbrook (1993).

members of the National Council. The National Council met twice a year, and was composed of all regional officials, members of the Central Committee, district governors, and representatives of women, youth groups, and the trade unions. The Regional Offices mapped onto districts, and were composed of three members appointed by the Central Committee to coordinate subregional activities. At the Constituency level, officials were elected every three years at the Constituency Annual Conference – ten from each branch, four from the main body of the party, and three each from the youth and women's leagues. Officials were elected annually, and comprised eight representatives each for women, youth, and the main body of the party. The lowest unit of the party was the Section Committee (urban) or Village Council (rural) and each had six officials elected annually.

It is worth highlighting that UNIP's organizational strength varied by province, and that its hegemonic status was contested (Larmer, 2006). The party was weakest in the Southern and Western Provinces because of the historical dominance of the ANC and the Lozi royal line, respectively. The founding leader of the ANC, Harry Nkumbula, hailed from Southern Province. The Lozi elite spurned UNIP in 1969 after Kaunda abrogated the Barotseland Agreement of 1964.[33] Despite its variegated presence, UNIP nonetheless shaped the behavior of political elites throughout Zambia. The fact that "service in the lower echelons of the party organization became a virtual prerequisite to more senior posts in the party bureaucracy" boosted the party's organizational strength by creating strong incentives for careerism among officials (Scott, 1976, p. 92). Every region, constituency, and branch had 24 paid officials.

In the rural Kasama District alone, UNIP controlled 2,880 jobs. In addition, possession of a party card "was a minimum condition for employment in Kasama in state, parastatal, or local authority sectors" (Bratton, 1980, p. 253). This, in effect, granted UNIP control over approximately 5,000 state jobs in Kasama. Similarly, in urban Lusaka the party maintained over 40,000 local offices at the section, branch, and ward levels in 1985 (Bates and Collier, 1995, p. 117). These party officials had preferential access to state jobs and loans from the state-owned National Commercial Bank (created in 1969). To project UNIP's power, uniformed youth militants (cadres) policed markets, bus stops, and workplaces and punished anyone accused of disrespecting Kaunda or the party.

---

[33] Throughout the colonial period Barotseland had enjoyed considerable autonomy as a protectorate within the wider Northern Rhodesia colony. The Barotseland Agreement agreement granted the Lozi elite considerable autonomy vis-à-vis Lusaka as a precondition for complete incorporation into independent Zambia (Caplan, 1968). In 1969 Barotseland was renamed Western Province, and its administrative system restructured to conform to the rest of Zambia.

The party's slogan was "It Pays to Belong to UNIP." And with good reason. Kaunda's Mlungushi Declaration (announcing Zambia's adoption of socialism) in 1968 and the subsequent nationalization of the Zambian economy put UNIP at the apex of the country's patronage networks. Two years later the government established the Zambia Industrial and Mining Corporation (ZIMCO), a giant holding company of state-owned enterprises that at its peak controlled over 117 firms and 70 percent of the economy, including in Zambia's mining industry (Ndulo, 1974; Turok, 1981; Mumeka, 1987; Szeftel, 2000).[34] The subordination of the entire economy to the party's Central Committee made UNIP the focal arena for intra-elite bargaining over policy and governance rents. Later Kaunda barred politicians from engaging in private business, thereby reinforcing their dependence on UNIP for patronage (Simutanyi, 1996). Within the first 15 years of independence, the number of public sector workers in Zambia increased from 1,357 in 1963 to 254,610 (126,260 in the regular Civil Service and 128,350 in parastatals). Political considerations ensured that the average wages were 60 percent higher in parastatals than in the private sector. A cabinet minister summarized UNIP's economic strength thus: "without UNIP the various opportunities which we now think we want to protect, to hoard, could not have been there at all. Without the Party the bank manager could not see you to negotiate an overdraft for anything" (Szeftel, 1982, p. 7).

UNIP's Central Committee, and not parliament, was the key policymaking arena. The committee made policy, while the cabinet was charged with implementation. Parliamentary immunity was formally abolished in 1975 when UNIP's disciplinary committee acquired powers to censure legislators for statements in the National Assembly. After 1972 Kaunda merged the cabinet and Central Committee under his control. Between 1973 and 1988 he nominated committee members after which they were elected by acclamation, unopposed

---

[34] In addition to nationalizing the economy, Kaunda subordinated the trade union to UNIP. An Act of Parliament created the Zambia Congress of Trade Unions (ZCTU) in 1965 and mandated all trade unions to affiliate with the congress. In 1971 UNIP, through the Industrial Relations Act, effectively banned all industrial strikes (Larmer, 2005). The adoption of single-party rule in 1972 subordinated ZCTU and affiliated unions to UNIP, effectively neutralizing the threat of unions to Kaunda's political dominance.

(Momba, 2003, p. 39). Kaunda dictated policy to UNIP, after which the party's agenda got a constitutional rubber stamp in the National Assembly (Tordoff, 1977*a*; Bates and Collier, 1995; Alderfer, 1997). In the words of UNIP's Chief Whip in 1968, "we [UNIP MPs] have got various levels at which these problems are sorted out and discussed. And by the time we come here, we have more or less sorted our differences on our side" (Momba, 2005, p. 104). In effect, "the dominant institution in the one-party state was not the party but the presidency, in which resided enormous power" (Gertzel, 1984, p. 102).

Despite UNIP's extensive reach and dominance, Kaunda was never fully confident in his ability to effectively balance fellow elites through the party. This is for the simple reason that his relationship with local UNIP units was one of persuasion and not command. As a result Kaunda found himself constantly bargaining with subordinate units of the party, especially when he needed them the most – as when opposition to his rule gained traction. Furthermore, the concentration of power within UNIP provided enormous upside to capturing key party organs. As happened within KANU under Moi, different factions within UNIP jostled for power at the local and national levels. One early example was the 1967 UNIP Annual Conference that saw the emergence of two competing alliances dominated by Zambia's four main sociolinguistic groups – Bemba, Tonga, Nyanja, and Lozi (Scott, 1976, p. 107). A Bemba–Tonga alliance led by Simon Kapwepwe (a Bemba) squared off against a coalition of senior Nyanja and Lozi politicians led by Vice President Reuben Kamanga (a Nyanja). At the core of the conflict was a contest over the sharing of governance rents within UNIP. The Kapwepwe faction argued that despite having fought for independence, his supporters (mostly Bembas) were being sidelined in favor of more educated non-Bembas. Kapwepwe defeated Kamanga for the position of UNIP Vice President, thereby forcing Kaunda to demote Kamanga and elevate Kapwepwe to the position of Vice President. Kapwepwe's faction also won key positions in party organs, including the Central Committee, where out of 11 members 8 were Bemba and 2 were Tonga (Dresang, 1974).

This particular intra-UNIP conflict exposed the inherent weakness of Kaunda's party-based system of balancing fellow elites. A key source of the weakness was that Kaunda's executive power depended on the very people he at times needed to discipline within UNIP.

This principal–agent relationship of persuasion afforded UNIP agents significant administrative and bargaining powers. As Kaunda fought to contain Kapwepwe's power, different UNIP units – especially in its heartland (Copperbelt and Northern Provinces) – wavered in their loyalty. Eventually Kaunda pushed Kapwepwe out of the party, leading him to form the United Progressive Party (UPP) in 1971. Ominously for Kaunda, a sizable proportion of UNIP officials – the very agents he needed to project power and punish dissent – were captured by Kapwepwe and defected to UPP. Included among the defectors were rank and file members of the Mineworkers' Union of Zambia (MUZ) who associated Kaunda's economic policies (especially nationalization of the mines) with declining living and working standards (Larmer, 2006, p. 297). In a panic, UNIP doubled local officials' salaries. However, this scarcely guaranteed their loyalty to Kaunda. Aware of their bargaining power vis-à-vis UNIP Headquarters, "local officials were quick to point out that, while they whole-heartedly supported the party and government, there were certain improvements urgently needed in their areas" (Scott, 1976, p. 168). The UPP's very credible threat to Kaunda's regime forced his hand into imposing single-party rule in 1972.[35] Thereafter, a chastened Kaunda was only able to maintain power via a delicate balancing of ethnoregional elite interests (Lindeman, 2011). At the same time, he worked to legitimize his rule to Zambians by carefully cultivating an ideology of Zambian Humanism, a project that merged capitalist, socialist, and populist elements, and espoused an elevated role for the state in the management of social and economic affairs (Scarritt, 1979; Parpart and Shaw, 1983).[36]

Kaunda's at once autocratic and precarious hegemony was parliament's loss. Lacking confidence in his ability to effectively balance fellow elites acting collectively in the legislature, he chose to deny

---

[35] Kaunda banned UPP in February 1972 and detained its leaders. He then appointed a commission led by his Vice President, Mainza Chona (1970–1973), to outline an institutional path to a single-party "participatory democracy." The Chona Commission's recommendations were adopted in the 1973 constitution that formally made Zambia a single-party state under UNIP.

[36] In legitimizing his rule Kaunda was also aided by geopolitical factors. UNIP exploited Southern Rhodesia's unilateral declaration of independence (UDI) in 1965 and the wars of liberation in Southern Africa to cast critics as would-be traitorous collaborators with racist White minority governments in Angola, Rhodesia, and South Africa (Macola, 2008, p. 24).

the institution any form of means independence. According to one legislator's succinct summary, "I don't think [the government] gives a two-penny damn what parliament says or thinks" (Helgerson, 1970, p. 276). The risk of agency loss within the party apparatus forced him to stamp out dissent from all quarters in Zambia, starting with parliament. An early warning came in 1965 when UNIP MPs voted to suspend Edward Liso (MP, Namwala) for criticizing Kaunda in the National Assembly (Phiri, 2001, p. 231). Unlike Kenyatta's initial approach to Odinga's KPU in 1966, he denied the ANC the status of Official Opposition and Harry Nkumbula the right to chair the Public Accounts Committee and form a shadow cabinet.

After banning the opposition in December 1972, Kaunda shifted towards engendering loyalty within UNIP ranks.[37] He personally appointed key party and government officials, "from the Secretary-General of the Party, the Prime Minister, Members of the Central Committee and Cabinet Ministers right down to Regional Party functionaries" (Chikulo, 1988, p. 45). UNIP exploited its monopoly to rid parliament of any legislators "with interests inimical to the state" (Alderfer, 1997, p. 95). Legislators had to get permission from its National Secretary before touring their own constituencies (Helgerson, 1970, p. 286). To further restrict the influence of fellow elites, in 1980 Kaunda restricted the franchise in local elections to card-carrying UNIP members who were incentivized to support the regime. He knew that despite UNIP's legal electoral monopoly, voters could distinguish between "UNIP" and "independent" candidates (Bratton, 1980, p. 227). In 1982 he abolished party primaries, and charged the Central Committee with the selection of candidates for legislative elections. In the words of party Secretary-General Mainza Chona (1978–1981), "thorough preparations were made to ensure that loyal and dedicated members were chosen" (Chikulo, 1988, p. 45).

To maintain power while governing with a legislature, Kaunda needed to balance the institution. The contingencies of preindependence political development bequeathed him a powerful mass party in UNIP, on which he anchored his rule. However, the nature of principal–agent relationships between Kaunda and UNIP units provided a structural limitation to Kaunda's executive power. His

---

[37] Existing opposition parties ceased to exist with the dissolution of parliament ahead of the 1973 General Election.

need for their loyalty as UNIP members granted local UNIP units and administration officials considerable bargaining power vis-à-vis Kaunda. Unsure of his capacity to effectively balance an independent legislature, he balked at the idea of legislative means independence. UNIP, and not parliament, became the focal arena for organizing intra-elite politics. But, UNIP was unequal to the task. Economic headwinds in the 1980s forced a wave of privatizations that led to widespread public discontent with the Zambian government, and the weakening of UNIP's powers over the distribution of patronage (de Walle, 2001, p. 82). However, the party's internal principal–agent structures limited the degree to which Kaunda could exert control over local units. This became vivid once the Zambian Congress of Trade Unions (ZCTU) and the Mineworkers' Union of Zambia (MUZ) joined the protest against economic mismanagement, structural adjustment programs, and Kaunda's administrative decentralization program (Mijere, 1985; Larmer, 2006). The party's structural inability to project Kaunda's power was evident when in 1991 it proved unequal to the task of stemming mass defections by elites to the Movement for Multiparty Democracy (MMD). In the subsequent election, Kaunda garnered a paltry 24 percent of votes in the presidential election. Unlike Moi, who still maintained a modicum of separation between the PA and KANU, Kaunda had placed all his eggs in one basket. And, when the party lost favor with the masses and elites alike in the wake of economic crises in the 1980s, the entire apparatus came tumbling down. To shed more light on UNIP's ineffectiveness as a tool of monitoring and balancing fellow elites, we now turn to the structure and functions of the PA in Zambia between 1964 and 1991.

5.4.2 Politicization of the Provincial Administration

The unified administration of Northern Rhodesia (Zambia) became a reality in 1911 with its capital in Livingstone. Before that separate administrations under the British South African Company (BSAC) managed Northwestern Rhodesia (headquartered in Kalomo between 1899 and 1907, then Livingstone afterwards) and Northeastern Rhodesia (headquartered in Fort Jameson/Chipata). BSAC entered the territory that became Northern Rhodesia in 1890 with the signing of the Barotse Concession with King Lewanika (Phiri, 1991, p. 19). In 1924 the Colonial Office took over the colony from BSAC and in

1935 moved the capital to Lusaka. Before the discovery of copper, Northern Rhodesia was largely a labor reserve for Katanga and southern Africa's mines. The railway from Livingston to Broken Hill (Kabwe) was completed in 1906 and extended to Ndola in 1909. Initially, agriculturalist European immigrants settled along the line and marketed their produce in Katanga. Others experimented with tobacco in the east and coffee in the higher altitudes of the northeast.

The Northern Rhodesian Provincial Administration (PA) included a Governor, Provincial Commissioners (PCs), and District Commissioners (DCs), some of whom were holdovers from the BSAC era (Davidson, 1974, p. 37). The colony comprised eight provinces and dozens of districts (44 at independence). Due to the precolonial strength of the Lozi and Bemba, Northern Rhodesia had indirect rule anchored on Native Councils accountable to DCs. Like in Kenya, the PA "was the lynch-pin of central government control [and] possessed extraordinary discretionary power" (Chikulo, 1981, p. 57). "Native Administration" in the urban Copperbelt took the form of Urban Advisory Councils. In addition, the Municipal Corporations and Townships Ordinance of 1927 and the Mine Ordinance of 1933 empowered mining firms to run and provide public goods and services in the Copperbelt's towns.

Zambia's postcolonial administrative legacy was weak. Federation (1953–1963) stunted administrative development under colonialism, as important state functions – including agriculture, education, and health services – were managed from Salisbury (Harare). Under federation Northern Rhodesia had a dual-track Civil Service – the African and European Civil Services. The European Civil Service had features of a formal bureaucracy, and comprised officials under the direction of the federal government and Whitehall (Dresang, 1975). The African Civil Service mainly focused on administration and African agriculture and health. However, agencies in charge of African affairs were woefully underfunded, undertrained, and understaffed (Tordoff, 1980). Key departments were handed to Zambia in January 1964, barely nine months before independence. Racial polarization compounded these problems. At independence, there was a "deeply held suspicion of the bureaucracy among the politicians that was born out of their experience of a white-dominated colonial bureaucracy." The extra-institutional nature of Zambian nationalism under UNIP also alienated African bureaucrats within the African Civil Service.

Many "did not trust politicians, mainly due to political antagonisms they experienced during the terminal years of colonialism" (Chikulo, 1981, pp. 57–58). Thus, the stage was set for a conflict between UNIP and the colonial administrative apparatus.[38]

Unlike in Kenya, where Kenyatta took "steps immediately after independence to assert African control over a strong provincial administration," in Zambia Kaunda and UNIP elites "felt it would best demonstrate [their] independence by weakening and restructuring the system of field administration" (Dresang, 1975, p. 120). Not only did Kaunda change the titles of field administrators (from District and Provincial Commissioners to District Secretaries and Resident Secretaries, respectively), he also stripped them of their responsibilities and authority. Their previous functions as top civil servants in the district and provinces, including the all-important law and order functions, were transferred to other agencies under line ministries. In addition, a Resident Minister (a politician) became the overall head of the provinces, and chaired the Provincial Development and Information Committees. This was unlike in Kenya, where Provincial Administration – from the Sub-Chief to the Provincial Commissioner – was directly managed by a single minister in the Office of the President, and was backed by the coercive apparatus of the Administration Police. In effect, Kaunda reduced once-powerful positions in Northern Rhodesia's Provincial and District Administration apparatus into little more than glorified reporting offices.

In retrospect, Zambian independence made administrative restructuring ineluctable. Kaunda's brand of nationalist politics and the urgent need to subordinate the administration to UNIP left little room for postcolonial administrative continuity like that obtained in Kenya. In July 1964 Kaunda broke up the colonial Provincial Administration. The Local Government Act (1965) centralized rural administration, and took significant powers away from chiefs. After 1968 UNIP membership was a requirement for Civil Servants. The renamed Provincial and District Administration (hereafter PA) lost most of

---

[38] The subordination of the administration to UNIP created tension between professional Civil Servants and party apparatchiks in the face of heated competition over policy and for jobs and patronage. Scott (1980) notes that "by 1971, the conflict, especially in the rural areas where UNIP was strong, had been resolved in favor of the party" (p. 143).

its functions, which were reallocated to other state departments and ministries. Significantly, politicians replaced Civil Servants as heads of provincial and district administrations. Provincial Ministers and Resident Secretaries replaced Provincial Commissioners. District Secretaries/Governors replaced District Commissioners. Several incumbent legislators served as administrators in these capacities (Hakes and Helgerson, 1973).

Following the imposition of single-party rule, in January 1976 the UNIP Central Committee took over the PA. The Local Government Act (1980) further reorganized local administrative units, placing them all under the District Governor. The Act also abolished the Mine Ordinance of 1933 and placed the management of Copperbelt towns under UNIP. These changes effectively fused UNIP and administrative units at the subnational level in Zambia (Mukwena, 1992, p. 237). Accompanying the politicization of the administration was its empowerment to function as a channel for patronage distribution. Provincial Development Committees, District Development Committees, Ward Development Committees, and Village Development Committees were created and charged with the task of steering the development agenda within their jurisdiction (Ollawa, 1977; Tordoff, 1980).

The postcolonial restructuring of Zambia's PA diminished Kaunda's executive power and his ability to effectively monitor and balance fellow elites. While ostensibly done to create a loyal and centralized developmentalist administration, the unintended consequence of the reorganization was to alter the principal–agent relationship between Kaunda and administration officials from one of command to one of persuasion. Because important administration officials were also UNIP members, they were implicated in intra-UNIP politics and exposed to factionalism and local capture. As Dresang (1975) observes, the "role confusion enhanced the importance of departmental authority, the personal characteristics of supervisory officials, and the local environments within which party [UNIP] and government units operated" (p. 124). In other words, local officials – both within UNIP and the Zambian PA – had significant administrative power vis-à-vis Kaunda. Kaunda's frustration with his inability to fully control the administration was evident in his habit of reminding administrators and other Civil Servants of their duty to be loyal to UNIP and his administration. In an address on December 23, 1968 he sounded a warning to state officers:

I cannot see how I can continue to pay a police office or a civil servant who works for [opposition leader] Nkumbula ... How dare they bite the hand that feeds them? They must learn that it pays to belong to UNIP. Those who want to form a civil service of the opposition must cross the floor and get their pay from Harry Nkumbula.[39]

Kaunda understood the risk of agency loss in an administration staffed by officials of dubious loyalty. Yet, his solution – politicization and subordination of the administration to UNIP – worsened the situation and diminished his executive power. Unlike in Kenya, where the PA was directly accountable to the president, Zambia's administration officials had split loyalties between Kaunda and local UNIP politicians. Their critical role as the base of the party further strengthened their bargaining power vis-à-vis Kaunda. It was "difficult to discipline erring District Governors, District Secretaries and other officers due to the [need to] use of political 'fall backs'" (Mukwena, 1992, p. 246). While Kenyatta and Moi (to a large extent) could hire and fire their administration officials at will, Kaunda could not do so without risking widespread loss of political support. Stated differently, disciplining disloyal or ineffective Zambian administrators meant weakening the party. Alderfer (1997) succinctly captures Kaunda's dilemma: "[T]hese detentions [of suspected UPP supporters] and others throughout the Second Republic simply weakened UNIP's organizational and administrative operations at the local level. Kaunda's mass detentions hit UNIP's leadership in the mining towns on the Copperbelt especially hard. The party seemed to turn against itself" (p. 21).

The proverbial last straw was the Local Government Act of 1980. The Act fused UNIP and administrative functions in District Councils (Chikulo, 1985). It also disenfranchised non-UNIP members in council elections. Although the Act applied throughout Zambia, its effect was acutely felt in UNIP's heartland in the Copperbelt that had hitherto been insulated from Kaunda's administrative reforms. For decades, mining firms ran mining towns under the Municipal Corporations and Townships Ordinance of 1927 and the Mine Ordinance of 1933. The 1980 Act put UNIP in charge of mining towns. This move jeopardized mineworkers' benefits (they had to be UNIP members to get benefits) and exacerbated corruption and other inefficiencies

---

[39] See Phiri (2001), p. 232.

that plagued UNIP. The ZCTU and, in particular, the MUZ and the Civil Servants Union of Zambia (CSUZ), bitterly opposed the bill. Nonetheless, the bill passed after the Prime Minister threatened to expel any MP who voted against it (Mijere, 1988). But, a decade later its passage proved to have been a pyrrhic victory for Kaunda. Disregard of unionized workers' concerns unleashed elite and mass defections in the Copperbelt, and catapulted ZCTU's leader (Frederick Chiluba) to the Zambian presidency in 1991 atop the MMD. In effect, Kaunda lost the 1991 presidential election in 1980.

Kaunda's at once hegemonic and precarious tenure created strong incentives against granting legislators means independence. As discussed in the previous section, UNIP's Central Committee took over legislative functions and closely regulated legislators' extra-parliamentary political actions. The fusion of the party and state restricted the domains of legitimate political action. Criticizing the party meant criticizing the state, and vice versa. And, since Kaunda saw himself as the embodiment of both the party and the state, any criticism of the party or state was taken as a direct attack against the president. In this manner Kaunda's lack of sufficient executive power condemned the Zambian legislature to subservience to UNIP and organizational underdevelopment on account of its lack of means independence.

In the end, UNIP and the administration collapsed under their own weight. The more Kaunda tried to centralize power under UNIP, the more he exposed himself to the risk of agency loss. It is worth reiterating that the administrative reforms between 1964 and 1991 were ineluctable. At independence, Africans filled only 4.5 percent of the 848 existing administrative and professional positions in the Civil Service. This stark reality meant that administrative restructuring through Africanization – to enhance loyalty to Kaunda and UNIP – necessarily meant downsizing of the administration. There simply were not enough trained Zambians to replace departing European immigrants in key administrative positions. Thus, between 1964 and 1966 Zambia's Provincial Administration shrank by two-thirds (Chikulo, 1981, p. 61). To compound matters, the politicization of the rump administration to guarantee its loyalty further eroded its ability to effectively carry out its duties and to project Kaunda's executive power. Aware of his structural inability to effectively balance any emergent centers of power, Kaunda's reaction to these developments was to redouble the concentration power in his own hands. The "growing chaos in the government machinery" forced Kaunda to take "personal control of a vast range of government activity. He brought the Foreign Affairs, the Civil Service, Defence and the running of the country's major commercial and industrial enterprises under his wing" (Phiri, 2001, p. 229). The end result was a highly centralized and bloated party-state administration that made Kaunda at once powerful and vulnerable to agency loss.

Perhaps much of this was unavoidable. Besides UNIP, Kaunda had few other options through which to consolidate power and implement his ambitious developmental agenda. Unlike Kenyatta and Moi (and most African presidents) he lacked an ethnic base upon which to build a loyal administrative or security apparatus. The charged racial politics of decolonization foreclosed on the possibility of using the PA as the primary means of projecting power. In the end, he had to use UNIP, a fact that exposed him to the risk of agency loss. Having put all his eggs in one basket, when UNIP lost sway with Zambians he had no recourse. The fusion of the party and state meant he could not distance himself from the failings of either entity. In the eyes of Zambia UNIP was the only game in town. In the end, this left Zambian elites with no option but to defect from UNIP in the face of an economic crisis and the wave of multipartyism that followed the collapse of the Soviet Union. Unlike Kenyatta or Moi, when they did so Kaunda lacked a loyal administration with which to balance fellow political elites. The party-state simply fell apart.

5.5 Conclusion

Legislative organizational development and institutionalization does not take place in a vacuum. The relative power of other key institutions of state play an important role in structuring the contours of legislative operational independence and overall institutional strength. This is particularly true in postcolonial contexts, such as in Kenya and Zambia, where the ability of chief executives to effectively balance fellow elites acting collectively in legislatures conditions the likelihood of legislative means independence. In effect, executive power dictates the upper bound of legislative independence and institutionalization. All else equal, strong chief executives are more likely to govern with relatively independent legislators compared to their weaker counterparts.

In this chapter, I have used material evidence from Kenya and Zambia to demonstrate how intra-elite politics conditions executive-legislative relations and the likelihood of legislative means independence. Focusing on the organizational structures of the two countries' ruling parties and state administrations, I have shown how chief executives' differential ability to balance fellow elites (executive power) made possible legislative means independence in Kenya but not Zambia. I have argued that a greater reliance on the state's administrative apparatus to balance fellow elites in Kenya mitigated against the risk of agency loss and bolstered presidents' executive power. In Zambia, reliance on the ruling party exposed the president to agency loss since local party units could be captured by elites of dubious loyalty to the president. Keeping within this same approach, I have shown how changes in Kenya following Kenyatta's death diminished Moi's executive power, and led to his curtailment of legislative means independence in Kenya.

I attributed these structural differences in executive power to the two countries' colonial endowments. Kenya inherited a weak elite party (KANU) and a strong provincial administration with strong loyalties to the president. Unable to control KANU, Kenyatta opted to use the provincial administration to monitor and balance fellow elites. The resultant boost to executive power made possible Kenyatta's decision to grant the Kenyan legislature means independence for much of his tenure. After a culture of legislative means independence was established, Moi's attempts to subordinate the legislature were only partially successful. On its part, Zambia inherited a weak and disloyal (to Kaunda) administrative structure and a strong mass party (UNIP). This forced Kaunda to use UNIP as the primary means of managing elite politics. To increase loyalty in the administration, he reorganized and subordinated it to UNIP. The unintended consequence of these strategies of power consolidation was a reduction in Kaunda's executive power. Unsure of his ability to balance fellow elites in the legislature, Kaunda responded by denying the institution means independence and condemning it to organizational underdevelopment.

These differences in executive power and executive-legislative relations put the Kenyan and Zambian legislatures on different trajectories of institutional development for the first 25 years of independence. Means independence created incentives for Kenyan legislators to invest in internal organizational mechanisms of handling intra-parliamentary bargains – such as rule-bound parliamentary practice, plenary debates, and structured contribution to policy through a parliamentary group. It also reinforced an intra-elite political culture that recognized parliament as the focal arena for bargaining over policy and the sharing of governance rents. In Zambia, the legislature functioned as a constitutional conveyor belt for policies passed by UNIP's Central Committee. UNIP, and not parliament, was the focal arena for intra-elite politics. Zambian legislators' rational response to their lack of legislative means independence was to not invest in the institution's organizational development. The next chapter provides analyses of specific quantitative measures of legislative means independence in Kenya and Zambia, and how they varied across the two countries and over time.

6 | *Legislative Institutionalization in Time*

6.1 Institutional Change and Legislative Independence

On January 27, 1993, President Moi abruptly prorogued the Kenyan National Assembly after the first sitting of the first multiparty parliament under his rule. In response, Paul Muite (MP, Kabete), accused Moi of developing "cold feet at the eagerness with which the opposition was ready to get down to work in Parliament."[1] In retrospect, Moi had good reason to be concerned about the new parliament. Kenya's Seventh Parliament was both hostile to Moi's legislative agenda and eager to assert its institutional independence. And, so in an effort to limit the erosion of his unilateral executive authority through legislative oversight, Moi chose to limit the number of legislative sittings. At the time, he had constitutional powers to call, prorogue, and dissolve parliament.

But, legislators pushed back, and seven years later stripped him of these powers with the establishment of the independent Parliamentary Service Commission (PARLSCOM) in 2000. PARLSCOM is the bedrock of the Kenyan legislature's institutional autonomy. Before 2000, parliament had the administrative status of a department within the executive branch. Thereafter, PARLSCOM acquired exclusive authority over the drafting of the legislature's budget, the remuneration of staff and legislators, and all legislative capital investments. It also appoints the Clerks of the National Assembly (and since 2013 the Senate). Article 127 of Kenya's 2010 Constitution further cemented the gains enshrined in the Parliamentary Service Commission Act (2000). After 2000 Kenyan presidents lost the power to strategically ration the amount of time available to legislators for debate on legislation and scrutiny of executive actions. The achievement of formal

---

[1] See "Moi Suspends Kenya's Multiparty Parliament, Prospect of Sharing Power with Opposition Gave President 'Cold Feet,' Activist Says," *Reuters News Agency*, January 28, 1993.

administrative autonomy from the executive branch was a significant milestone in the process of legislative institutionalization in Kenya. It was also a vivid illustration of how a rebalancing of executive-legislative relations can result in increased legislative autonomy and assertiveness.

The Zambian experience was different. Despite the end of single-party rule, the Zambian legislators proved unable to exploit their new-found political freedom in a bid to strengthen the legislature. As a result, the institution remained largely subservient to the executive branch. Zambian legislators' inability to rebalance executive-legislative relations under multipartyism was driven, in part, by the fact that the legislature "failed to develop the organizational structure and institutional resources that a more autonomous role in policy making and policy review would require" (Bach, 1999, p. 192). The first three decades without means independence had stunted the organizational development of the Zambian legislature, and deprived legislators the institutional foundation upon which to build their new-found political independence from the executive branch.

This chapter documents differences in postcolonial legislative institutionalization in Kenya and Zambia. I provide quantitative measures of the variation in levels of legislative means independence in the two countries, as well as the divergence in their legislatures' trajectories of institutional development following the end of single-party rule. These measures advance the thesis that autocratic presidents' ability to effectively balance fellow elites conditioned their willingness to tolerate legislative means independence. I also argue that these differences in organizational development under autocracy explain the divergent trajectories of legislative development in Kenya and Zambia following the end of single-party rule in both countries.

The core claim herein is that the nature of political development under colonialism and strategies of elite control deployed by autocratic presidents put legislatures in Kenya and Zambia on different trajectories and rates of institutional development. Both parliaments became institutionalized over time – for example by becoming differentiated from the executive through organizational cohesion and operational independence, gaining internal complexity and differentiation, having established committee systems, and in the increasing importance of

Standing Orders as the source of rules governing legislative processes.[2] But, the rate of change was different. In Kenya, institutional continuity at independence and administration-based strategies of elite control bequeathed the postcolonial legislature with institutional memory and means independence. In Zambia, institutional discontinuity at independence and party-based strategies of control stunted postcolonial legislative development. For these reasons, the rate of postcolonial legislative institutional development was faster in Kenya than in Zambia.

In the next section, I document the data-generating processes underlying the different rates of legislative institutionalization and strengthening in Kenya and Zambia. I measure legislative institutionalization and strengthening using five observable indicators: (i) the number of legislative sittings per year, (ii) the share of executive bills that get passed per year, (iii) the proportion of the annual budget allocated to the legislature, (iv) remuneration of individual legislators, and (v) the exercise of presidential rule-making authority through subsidiary legislation. These measures capture critical legislative characteristics, functions, and outputs. They also capture the nature of executive-legislative relations.

6.2 Measuring Legislative Independence and Strength

Throughout this chapter I use original data from Kenya and Zambia covering the postindependence period between 1964 and 2014. I collected the data over a year of fieldwork at the Archives and National Assembly libraries in Nairobi and Lusaka. Important sources included various issues of Parliamentary Hansards (official verbatim reports of legislative debates), Votes and Proceedings publications by the respective National Assemblies, the Annual Budget Estimates presented to parliaments in the two countries, and official government gazette notices. I measure legislative sittings in days of legislative

---

[2] Burnell (2002) documents legislative institutional reforms in Zambia after 1999 that, among other things, sought to strengthen parliament's committee system. Similarly, Barkan and Matiangi (2009) and Opalo (2014) document the institutional development of the Kenyan legislature during and after the end of single-party rule – including the strengthening of its committee system, the establishment of a Parliamentary Budget Office, and intra-legislative commitment to rule-bound engagements as defined in the Standing Orders.

sessions (meetings) within a given calendar year – from the day parliament is called to the day it adjourns *sine die* at the end of the calendar year. I also document counts of legislative bills and Acts and annual budget estimates by the calendar year of publication. Since throughout the period of analysis all bills required clearance from the Attorney General (in the drafting stage), I consider all bills considered in plenary to have been approved by presidents (through their appointed Attorneys General). Data on legislative remuneration come from the relevant bills (and Acts) in the two countries' legislatures (standardized in dollar terms). The economic data (GDP) in my analyses are from Heston, Summers, and Aten (2002).

I present all the data on a calendar year basis. This necessitated some adjustments in the dataset construction. For instance, the fiscal year spans two calendar years in Kenya (July to June), but coincides with the calendar year in Zambia (January to December). I assign budget estimates to the year in which they are published and presented to the National Assembly in both countries. From the budget estimates I calculated the share of budgetary allocation to the National Assembly – for both recurrent and development expenditures. The data do not include supplementary estimates submitted in the middle of the fiscal year, which almost exclusively contain appropriation votes for executive departments. The data on remuneration of legislators are from bills presented to the respective National Assemblies in various years. The data on statutory instruments and subsidiary legislation are from the gazette notices in both countries.

6.2.1 Frequency of Legislative Sittings

For legislatures to pass laws or sanction chief executives in constitutionally binding ways, they must assemble. For this reason, plenary time is the most important legislative resource. Resolutions from assembled legislators generate common knowledge on the collective preferences of political elites and the general performance of the chief executive. For this reason, chief executives have strong incentives to control the amount of time available for legislators to scrutinize their performance in plenary or to influence the distribution of political power and governance rents. One way of doing this is by rationing legislative plenary time during periods when legislators are critical of the executive branch – as shown in the example of Moi at the beginning of this chapter.[3] As I show in Table 2.4, across much of Africa presidents continue to enjoy constitutional powers to call, prorogue, and dissolve legislatures.

On their part, legislators prefer to have control over the number of legislative sittings. All else equal, they prefer to have as many sittings as possible. This is for four reasons. First, regularized meetings of legislators is the cornerstone of the intra-elite commitment underpinning executive-legislative relations. When assembled, legislators can credibly threaten to collectively punish presidents that renege on intra-elite arrangements to share power and governance rents (Myerson, 2008). Second, legislators have pecuniary incentives to meet. In most countries they earn sitting allowances when in session. Third, public assemblies enable legislators to voice the policy preferences of their constituents, and in so doing signal effort in a bid to win reelection. Regularized meetings also facilitate the professionalization of individual legislators and their specialization on specific issue areas. Finally, legislative sittings create *time* for legislative activities – both with regard to regular lawmaking and the political tasks of balancing chief executives and signaling effort to constituents.

Therefore, the observed frequency of legislative sittings is a by-product of strategic interactions between presidents and legislators. This is true for Kenya and Zambia. In both countries, presidents had the power to call, prorogue, and dissolve parliament for most of the period under study. Yet, they exercised this power differentially – in a manner that reflected the prevailing nature of intra-elite politics and balance of power. As shown in Figure 6.1 (left graph), the Kenyan legislature had relatively more sittings per year than its Zambian counterpart. As argued in previous chapters, this difference was driven by the fact that the Kenyan legislature was the focal arena for intra-elite bargaining over policy, political power, and governance rents. It also had means independence. Both roles created demands for plenary time – a fact that is reflected in the high number of legislative sittings. The Zambian legislature's historical subordinate role as a constitutional conveyor belt for policy proposals from the United

---

[3] This is a strategy that is as old as legislatures. English monarchs limited meetings of the early parliaments to periods when they needed to raise revenue. It took the deliberate efforts of elites in the Long Parliament (1640–1660) to strip the monarch of the power to be the sole determinant of the legislative calendar (Worden, 1971).

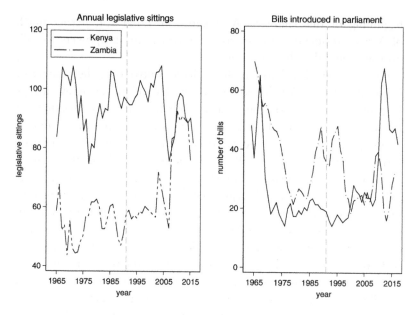

Figure 6.1 Legislative sittings and bills introduced

Notes: Graphs based on author's calculations. The graphs depict three year-moving averages. The Zambian legislature historically held fewer sittings despite handling more bills than its Kenyan counterpart.

National Independent Party (UNIP) is demonstrated in its relatively low number of sittings per year. It was not until after 2005 that the number of legislative sittings in Zambia began to catch up to those in Kenya. These differences in the number of sittings per year are remarkable, especially because the Zambian legislature handled more bills per year that its Kenyan counterpart (Figure 6.1, right graph).

Examples abound from Kenya and Zambia of presidents influencing the number of legislative sittings for political benefit. For example, in 1965 Kenyatta failed to summon the Kenyan parliament for nearly three months (March to June). When he was constitutionally forced to call parliament by the budget appropriation process, legislators and Speaker Humphrey Slade (a holdover from the colonial legislative council) complained against what they considered to be executive overreach. Kenyatta had to reassure that his actions were not in bad faith. And, "[a]fter this experience, the Government was, on the whole, reluctant to create tensions by delaying unduly the summoning of Parliament" (Hakes, 1970, p. 195). Sittings per year would then rise for the remainder of the First Parliament.

Two factors disrupted this delicate executive-legislative balance. First, the National Assembly's loss of two invaluable institutionalists – Mboya and Slade – eroded the institution's standing as a rule-bound arena of intra-elite politics. Mboya was assassinated in July 1969 and Slade retired in 1970. Second, KANU backbenchers got bolder in their criticisms of Kenyatta and his government – especially following the high-profile political assassinations of Mboya (1969) and Kariuki (1975). Perhaps the most vivid expression of backbencher independence was the election of Jean-Marie Seroney, a vocal Kenyatta critic, as Deputy Speaker in 1975. At the first sitting of the Third Parliament on November 6, 1974, backbenchers defied Kenyatta's stated opposition to Seroney and nominated him for the position of Deputy Speaker unopposed. Kenyatta reacted to this by proroguing the National Assembly indefinitely. But, when he recalled parliament four months later in February 1975, Seroney was again nominated unopposed and subsequently elected Deputy Speaker. As the embodiment of parliamentary defiance, Seroney played an important role in the creation of the committee that investigated Kariuki's assassination and the release of a report that fingered Kenyatta's associates for the murder (Kyapoya, 1979). Kenyatta's reaction to the Third Parliament's robust independence was to limit the number of sittings (see Figure 6.1) and to jail vocal legislators who overstepped the boundaries of legitimate political action (Hornsby, 1985).

Moi's accession to the presidency in 1978 resulted in an increase in the number of legislative sittings. This was for three reasons. First, Kenya's political culture of the "Supremacy of Parliament" survived Kenyatta. Legislators therefore expected to hold a relatively high number of sittings as part of "how politics works." Second, Moi enjoyed goodwill among legislators at the beginning of his tenure. This was in no small part because he released many of the political prisoners (including legislators) jailed in the last five years of Kenyatta's rule (Branch, 2011, p. 141). Finally, in 1982 Moi imposed single-party rule – and with it the ability to enforce strict party discipline within parliament. By increasing his ability to meddle in intra-legislative affairs and select pliant legislators, Moi was able to accommodate Kenyan legislators' demands for a relatively high number of sittings (per established political culture) without exposing himself to criticism or any adverse action by legislators acting collectively.

Like Kenyatta and Moi, Zambia's Kaunda also rationed legislative sittings to cater to his political interests, albeit without the constraint of having an inherited political culture of the "Supremacy of Parliament." Despite handling more bills per year, the Zambian legislature met fewer times than its Kenyan counterpart. This reality afforded Zambian legislators very little time to debate or amend legislation. Between 1964 and 1991 the legislature averaged 1.34 sittings per bill introduced, compared to 3.84 in Kenya (1963–1992). In the early postcolonial period, legislators spent time voicing the concerns of constituents. However, over time legislators "largely abdicated their role as communicators of demands from constituency to government [and] instead tended to become agents in communicating government policies to the country" (Hakes and Helgerson, 1973, p. 342). To avoid criticism in the legislature and because the institution's work had been usurped by UNIP, Kaunda simply prorogued parliament for extended periods. For instance, in 1984 he failed to call parliament for over eight months in the face of a rapidly deteriorating economy (Alderfer, 1997, p. 65).

Consistent with the implications of changes in executive-legislative relations, the end of single-party rule led to an increase in the number of legislative sittings in both countries (the exception being Frederick Chiluba's second term in Zambia). Freed from the stranglehold of single-party rule, legislators in both Kenya and Zambia were willing to fight for calendar autonomy. However, this did not stop chief executives from strategically using their power to determine legislative calendars. As shown above, Moi prorogued the National Assembly indefinitely following its first sitting in 1993 to avoid criticism from legislators. Even Mwai Kibaki – Moi's successor under more democratic conditions – prorogued parliament indefinitely after it emerged that opposition legislators were planning to table a confidence motion against his government in late 2005.[4]

A more dramatic contest over parliamentary sessions played out in Zambia in April of 2001. Then, Kaunda's successor, Frederick Chiluba, prorogued parliament indefinitely (and against protests from

---

[4] Njoroge Kinuthia, "Kibaki Shuts Parliament," *Daily Nation*, November 24, 2005.

legislators) in order to evade an impeachment motion. Legislators accused Kaunda of gross violation of the constitution for plotting to change it via a referendum in order to be able to run for a third term.[5] When Chiluba refused to call parliament, legislators invoked the Speaker's powers to call parliament during emergencies (a third of legislators had to sign on to the petition). Out of 158 legislators, 65 signed the petition to call parliament to debate Chiluba's impeachment. In the end, Chiluba relented when it became clear that he would be impeached. He renounced any intention to run for a third term and endorsed his Vice President, Levy Mwanawasa, as his successor.

These examples illustrate the inherent political significance of legislative sittings and the critical importance of calendar autonomy for legislative independence. This fact was not lost on legislators in Kenya and Zambia. For example, Kenyan legislator Mukhisa Kituyi (MP, Kimilili) sought to rally his colleagues to support calendar autonomy thus:

We have to regain our right to set the timetable for Parliamentary Business. We have recently gone through a very crazy exercise, where Parliament is adjourned for two months and when we come back, in total contravention of our Standing Orders, by the last Thursday of October, we have not finished 20 Supply days in the Vote on Account … If we really repossessed the control of the timetable of Parliament, we would not be holidaying and gallivanting with people begging for money in Harambees at the time we are supposed to discuss the Budget in Parliament.[6]

Kituyi was right. The ability to ration legislative sittings was an important mechanism through which presidents limited legislators' input in the policymaking process. And so, led by Oloo Aringo (MP, Alego-Usonga), Kituyi and his institutionalist colleagues worked hard to realize their dream of complete calendar autonomy. They finally succeeded in 2000 with the establishment of PARLSCOM, which established the Kenyan legislature as an administratively separate branch of government with the power to control its own budget and calendar without interference from the executive branch. These achievements were enshrined in Chapter 15 of the 2010 Constitution.

---

[5] "MPs Petition Speaker to Impeach Chiluba," *The Post*, May 4, 2001.
[6] See Republic of Kenya, Kenya National Assembly Official Record, November 4, 1998, Col. 2113.

The Zambian legislature did not fare as well in this regard. It took 25 years following the end of single-party rule for legislators to pass the Parliamentary Service Act (2016). However, two years after the passage of the bill the executive had yet to issue the enabling Statutory Instruments (rules and regulations), thereby prolonging parliament's administrative subordination to the executive branch.[7] The Act would have enabled legislators to manage parliamentary affairs – including the appointment of the Clerk of the National Assembly – through the Parliamentary Service Commission (PSC). Instead, the president is still the effective administrative head of parliament on account of his powers to appoint the Clerk under Article 3(1) of the National Assembly Staff Act (1991).[8] The continued weakness of the Zambian legislature in the multiparty era is illustrated by the fact that despite constitutional amendments in 2016, legislators failed to entrench either legislative calendar or budgetary autonomy from the executive branch. Articles 75 and 81 of the Zambian constitution retained presidential powers to call, prorogue, and dissolve the National Assembly.[9] Furthermore, the Parliamentary Service Act (2016) grants the executive dominance in PARLSCOM through government representatives. Excluding the Speaker, five of the ten members of the commission are government appointees – including the leader of government business, Minister of Finance, and three ruling party legislators (Article 11). Even following the operationalization of the Act, Zambian presidents will retain control over the legislature (including its budget) through the PSC. This is unlike the situation in Kenya, where PARLSCOM's members are elected by and are exclusively accountable to parliament.[10]

In Table 6.1 I empirically demonstrate the differences in the political significance of legislative sittings in Kenya and Zambia. Specifically, I statistically analyze the correlation between the number of bills introduced and legislative sittings. Under conditions of legislative means independence (i.e., with significant legislative input in the lawmaking process), the number of bills introduced ought to be positively correlated with the amount of plenary time available to

---

[7] "Parliamentary Service Commission Act Not in Force – Lubinda," QFM Radio, July 15, 2018.

[8] Republic of Zambia, National Assembly Staff Act (1991).

[9] See the Constitution of Zambia Amendment Act, No. 2 (2016).

[10] The Constitution of the Republic of Kenya, Article 127.

legislatures (the number of legislative sittings). To test this claim, I estimate the Ordinary Least Squares (OLS) model:

$$sittings_t = \alpha + \beta_0 sittings_t + \beta_1 bills_t + \lambda X_t + \epsilon_t$$

where *Sittings* represent the number of days (in year t) that the legislature assembles. The lagged dependent variable ($Sittings_{t-1}$) accounts for the fact that the number of sittings may be influenced by the previous year's sittings. X is a vector of control variables that also influence the number of sittings. These include relative legislative independence after the end of single-party rule (*Post – 1991*), *Election Year*, the share of the budget allocated to the legislature (*Budget Share*), and the rate of economic growth (*GDP Growth*). The end of single-party rule ought to be positively correlated with legislative sittings because multipartyism increases the bargaining power of legislators, means independence, and the possibility of greater input in the lawmaking process. Election years are negatively related with legislative sittings due to the demands of campaigns. The level of funding available for legislative activities is positively correlated with the number of legislative sittings. Finally, by creating demand for new rules and regulations, economic expansion ought to be positively correlated with the number of legislative sittings.

The important takeaway from Table 6.1 is the difference in the correlation between the number of bills introduced and legislative sittings in Kenya and Zambia. In Kenya, there is a positive and statistically significant correlation between the number of bills passed and legislative sittings – suggesting that legislators had means independence and played a meaningful role in the lawmaking process. In Zambia, on the other hand, there is no statistically significant correlation between the two variables. As expected, legislatures are likely to have more sittings under multiparty politics – on account of the increase in legislators' bargaining power and political stature. However, this result is stable for Kenya across multiple specifications but not Zambia. The time demands of campaigning yield the negative correlation between election years and the number of legislative sittings shown in the table. Because sittings require resources (not least for legislators' sitting allowances), the share of the budget allocated to the legislature is positively correlated with the number of sittings. However, the point estimate is statistically significant in the case of

Table 6.1 *Determinants of legislative sittings per year*

	Kenya			Zambia		
	(1)	(2)	(3)	(4)	(5)	(6)
Sittings$_{t-1}$	−0.0985	−0.0411	−0.124	−0.00169	0.0846	0.0602
	(−0.52)	(−0.24)	(−0.67)	(−0.01)	(0.45)	(0.37)
Bills	0.564**	0.534**	0.447*	−0.125	−0.143	−0.139
	(3.05)	(3.15)	(2.21)	(−0.85)	(−1.14)	(−1.12)
Post-1991	12.44∗∗	12.22**	9.953	11.08*	9.155*	−0.495
	(2.96)	(3.11)	(1.55)	(2.40)	(2.32)	(−0.13)
Election Year		−10.27*	−10.33*		−13.01*	−10.04*
		(−2.27)	(−2.36)		(−2.66)	(−2.25)
BudgetShare			3.658			30.81***
			(1.06)			(3.85)
GDP Growth			0.845			−0.274
			(1.56)			(−0.77)
Constant	88.46∗∗∗	86.02***	89.59***	59.57***	58.54***	46.37***
	(4.78)	(5.23)	(4.95)	(4.05)	(4.68)	(4.00)
N	38	38	38	41	41	37

t statistics in parentheses.
* $p < 0.05$, ** $p < 0.01$, *** $p < 0.001$.
Notes: Coefficient estimates are from OLS regressions. The number of legislative sittings is positively correlated with the number of bills introduced in Kenya but not in Zambia. This is suggestive of legislative means independence in the lawmaking process in Kenya but not Zambia.

the Zambian legislature but not its Kenyan counterpart. Finally, there does not appear to be a statistically significant correlation between economic growth and legislative sittings.

6.2.2 *The Politics of Passing Legislation*

When in session, lawmaking is the primary duty of legislators. Yet, the number of bills passed is often a product of strategic interactions between legislators and presidents. In the specific cases of Kenya and Zambia, for much of the period under study presidents enjoyed important agenda-setting powers and acted as important gatekeepers in the legislative process. Due to their Westminster inheritance, presidents in both countries monopolized the introduction of money bills (bills touching on taxation and government spending), as well as the drafting of legislation (through Attorneys Generals' offices). In addition to curtailing legislators' power of the purse, the former constitutional provision severely limited the scope of legislative input in the lawmaking process (and capacity for oversight). The latter practice ensured that all bills (including private members' bills) had to get the direct approval of the executive branch before introduction. In Zambia, the constitution expressly mandated the Attorney General to approve bills before their introduction in the legislature.[11]

In addition to their agenda-setting powers, Kenyan and Zambian presidents were able to persuade or coerce legislators into passing their legislative proposals. They did this by appointing legislators to the cabinet, diplomatic, and executive positions (Hakes and Helgerson, 1973; Bach, 1994). For example, in 1986 72 of 170 Kenyan legislators (42.4 percent) held appointments in the government either as ministers or assistant ministers.[12] In Zambia, by 1990 105 out of 120 legislators (87.5 percent) held at least one position in the executive branch (Bates and Collier, 1995, p. 128). The possibility of being appointed to executive positions incentivized legislators to be loyal to ruling parties and presidents in both countries, and provided a powerful tool through which presidents could determine legislative outcomes.

Figure 6.2 shows the trends in the size of cabinets (ministers) in Kenya and Zambia. Two important observations are worth highlighting. First, it is clear that for much of the autocratic period (before 1991), Kaunda consistently appointed relatively more cabinet ministers (as a share of total legislators) than his Kenyan counterparts. Second, the number of Kenyan ministers rose sharply after Moi succeeded Kenyatta. Both observations suggest a greater need by Kaunda and Moi to exert executive control in their respective legislatures (i.e., curtail legislative means independence). And, as I show in Figure 6.3 below, this was reflected in the relatively high shares of executive bills passed under both Kaunda and Moi. The share of legislators in the cabinet remained steady even after transition to multipartyism in Zambia. In Kenya, there was a decrease in the share of legislators in the cabinet – partly driven by the increase in the number of legislators, but also because the presence of opposition

---

[11] See Constitution of the Republic of Zambia, 1996, Article 213 (5) (c).
[12] Republic of Kenya, Official Record of the National Assembly, March 4–April 30, 1986.

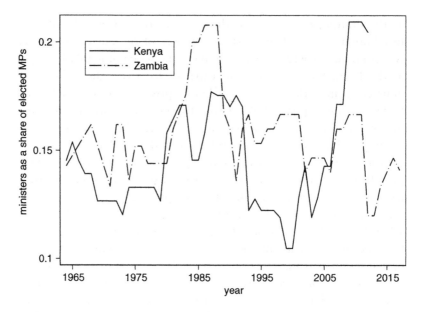

Figure 6.2 Buying support: cabinet sizes in Kenya and Zambia
Notes: Graph indicates the share of legislators appointed to the cabinet (ministers) in Kenya and Zambia. In the autocratic period, Kaunda consistently appointed a larger share of legislators to the cabinet than his Kenyan counterparts. In Kenya, Moi appointed a larger share of legislators to the cabinet than Kenyatta. Graph based on author's calculations.

legislators diminished the pool of available potential ministers. It was not until Kibaki's National Rainbow Alliance Coalition (NARC) government (2003–2007) and the Government of National Unity (2008–2013) – formed following the 2007–2008 post-election violence – that the share of legislators in the cabinet matched their pre-1992 levels in Kenya.

It is fair to say that for most of their histories the Kenyan and Zambian legislatures were reactive institutions that lacked ends independence. The procedural and extra-legislative strategies of gatekeeping highlighted above restricted legislators' ability to pass bills that were at variance with presidents' preferences. That said, the two legislatures were not completely irrelevant. By virtue of their constitutional monopoly over legislation, presidents had incentives to only introduce bills that they deemed to have a high

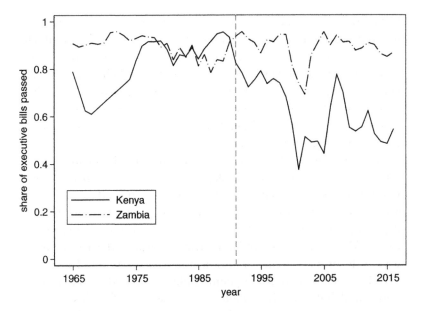

Figure 6.3 Multipartyism and divergence in share of bills passed

Notes: Figure shows the three-year moving average of the share of executive bills passed by parliaments in Kenya and Zambia. The vertical line depicts the point of transition to multiparty politics. There is a clear structural break in Kenya following transition. The transition in Zambia lags by a decade and is not as pronounced as in Kenya. It also ceases following the end of the Mwanawasa presidency in Zambia. Graph based on author's calculations.

probability of getting passed.[13] In addition, under conditions of legislative means independence (as obtained in Kenya), intra-legislative

---

[13] The process of passing legislation in Kenya and Zambia is as follows. The First Reading introduces a bill into the legislature before it is assigned to a departmental committee. At the Second Reading (the most important stage), legislators vote on the general contours of the bill and refer them to the committee for further amendments. At the Third Reading, legislators review amendments coming out of the committee and give final approval before presidential assent. For most of the period under study, committees in Kenya and Zambia were weak, with most of the legislative work done in plenary. This situation limited legislators' ability to specialize in the affairs of specific departments or line ministries, and therefore be able to provide substantive input before passage of presidential legislative proposals. Notice that throughout the different stages of passing bills, legislators can either vote against bills at the Second Reading, or allow the bills to die a slow death in committee.

deliberations at times revealed new information on bills (e.g., distributional implications), leading to their withdrawal. All else equal, subjecting legislative proposals to further negotiation in the legislature (means independence) increased the likelihood that bills would be rejected, amended, or let to die slow deaths in committee stage.[14] An observable implication of this claim is that even when legislatures lacked ends independence, means independence depressed the share of executive bills passed.

This is evident in Figure 6.3. Consistent with the claim that the Kenyan legislature had means independence and its Zambian counterpart did not, the trend data show that legislators passed executive bills at lower rates in Kenya compared to Zambia. In addition, the rates of passage of executive bills was lower under Kenyatta than under Moi. KANU's weakness under Kenyatta elevated the legislature to serve as the primary arena for intra-legislative bargains (and associated logrolling). On occasion bargaining failures resulted in the death of presidential bills. KANU's dominance under Moi foreclosed on the intra-legislative bargains as the legislature lost its means independence. Indeed, consistent with the pattern shown in Figure 5.1, the rate of passage of executive bills under Moi in the single party era is indistinguishable from the rate in Zambia under Kaunda.

The organizational dominance of ruling parties explains the similarity between Kaunda's Zambia and Moi's Kenya under single-party rule. In Zambia, UNIP served as a substitute to the National Assembly. Due to the dominance of UNIP's Central Committee, Zambian legislators scarcely had any say on laws passed by the National Assembly. Kaunda openly advocated for extra-legislative bargaining over legislation, and expected legislators "to use the offices of the district governors, other party officials, and other government officials at the district level rather than raise ... issues in the national assembly" (Momba, 2005, p. 105). Stated differently, Kaunda preferred legislative input in the policymaking process outside of channels protected by the constitution or the cloak of parliamentary

---

[14] Examples of government bills that had to be withdrawn in the face of insuperable opposition in the legislature include the Constitution of Kenya (Amendment) Bill No. 2 (2001) and the Constitution of Kenya (Amendment) Bill No. 32 (2007). In Zambia these include the Lands Bill (1994), Constitutional Officers (Emoluments) Bill (1995), and the State Security (Amendment) Bill (1999) (Momba, 2005, p. 113).

immunity. This approach to lawmaking generated the consistently high rates of passage of executive bills shown in Figure 6.3. It also denied legislators means independence and the incentives to invest in legislative organizational development.

The advent of multipartyism fundamentally altered executive-legislative relations in Kenya and Zambia. Multiparty politics created the possibility of both means and ends independence. This is for the simple reason that ability of legislators to gain membership through parties other than KANU or UNIP eroded presidents' ability to enforce party discipline. The loosening of party discipline, in turn, boosted legislative means independence by enabling legislators to freely express themselves in plenary. As shown in Figure 6.3, an observable implication of this development was the reduction in the share of executive bills passed.

However, legislators' ability to exploit their new-found political and institutional freedom was conditioned by their respective legislatures' historical organizational development. As shown in previous chapters, on the eve of multipartyism, the Kenyan legislature was more organizationally developed than its Zambian counterpart. As a result, Kenyan legislators had a stronger organizational foundation upon which to build their quest for both means and ends independence. This organizational difference is observable in the precipitous decline in the share of executive bills passed after 1991 in Kenya but not in Zambia. The decline in bills passed in Kenya is especially remarkable since Moi's KANU retained legislative majorities throughout his last decade in power (1993–2002). His successor, Kibaki (2003–2013), faced an even harder time. Having to govern with a coalition government, he had the least legislative success of Kenya's three presidents at the time – with only 56.5 percent of bills proposed getting passed. It is also during Kibaki's presidency that legislators acquired ends independence, and started proposing and passing bills against the publicly stated preferences of the president.

The Zambian legislature, too, experienced a decline in the share of executive bills passed, albeit not as precipitously as obtained in Kenya. The first Movement for Multiparty Democracy (MMD) term (1992–1996) saw a steady decline in the share of bills passed. This was halted, in part, by UNIP's boycott of the 1996 General Election – effectively handing the MMD unchallenged control of the legislature. Thereafter, the MMD behaved like the new UNIP. For example, Burnell (2003) observes that "[w]ell into the 1990s the view could still be heard (and not just from ministers) that the MPs' function is to interpret the official policies and implement government programmes in the constituencies. In short, MPs are agents of the executive" (p. 58).[15] This changed when it became clear that Chiluba intended to abolish presidential term limits via a constitutional referendum. The resultant backlash stalled nearly all legislative activity, a fact reflected in a decline in share of bills passed during this period. The departure of Chiluba came with a return to levels of passage of executive bills last seen under Kaunda. Despite multipartyism, executive-legislative relations in Zambia are still clouded by the country's political culture of ruling party dominance in parliament.

Recent constitutional amendments present more evidence of the differential effects of multipartyism in Kenya and Zambia. Kenya's 2010 Constitution was the culmination of decades of intra-elite struggles to tame presidential powers. The new constitution established formal separation of powers between the executive and the legislature. Legislators cannot serve as cabinet ministers (Article 152 (3)). Under Article 109 of the Kenyan Constitution, "any bill may originate in the National Assembly." The president can only introduce legislation via proxies in the legislature. The only restriction applies to money bills – that can only be introduced in "accordance with the recommendation of the relevant Committee of the Assembly after taking into account the views of the Cabinet Secretary responsible for finance" (Article 114 (2)).[16] In Zambia, constitutional amendments did little to alter the nature of intra-elite politics and balance of power. The 2016 constitution continues the historical melding of the Westminster and presidential systems. Zambian legislators serve in the cabinet (Article 116), a fact that enables executive domination of the legislature through the Front Bench. Under Article 64 (1) "[a] Member of Parliament or Minister may introduce a Bill in the

---

[15] This view of the role of the legislature had deep roots in the UNIP era. For instance, in 1975 Kaunda reminded legislators that "[p]olicies and decisions made by the [UNIP] National Council are expressions of the people's will ... they are the wishes of the majority and should therefore be respected" adding that "if it is legislative action that is needed to implement a policy decision on the National Council, the National Assembly as an Arm of the Party, must act accordingly, without question" (Momba, 2005, p. 108).

[16] Constitution of the Republic of Kenya (2010).

National Assembly." However, only ministers can introduce money bills (Article 65 (1)).[17] These procedural differences in the introduction of bills are evidence of structural changes in the nature of executive-legislative relations after the advent of multipartyism in Kenya but not in Zambia.

6.2.3 Budget Autonomy and Remuneration of Legislators

Successful conduct of legislative work requires material resources. Poorly funded legislatures ineluctably become politically and organizationally weak institutions. Such legislatures lack resources for research, staff, remuneration of legislators, and other activities. Most African legislatures fit this description. For example, out of eight legislatures surveyed in 2012, seven had an average of only 6 researchers (South Africa was the outlier with 69 researchers).[18] Low research capacity renders African legislatures powerless in the face of chief executives with structural informational advantages and significantly more staff.

The lack of fiscal autonomy is a key cause of legislative weakness in Africa. It is also inherently political.[19] Control over budgets enables African presidents to intentionally limit legislative effectiveness by rationing the amount of resources at their disposal. It is for this reason

---

[17] Constitution of the Republic of Zambia (2016).

[18] Benin had a grand total of zero researchers for its chamber of deputies. The other seven countries were Ghana (3), Kenya (4), Namibia (3), Nigeria (6), Tanzania (5), Uganda (15) and Zimbabwe (14). See "Do Parliaments Matter? African Legislatures and the Advance of Democracy," Heinrich Boll Foundation, 2012, available here: http://ke.boell.org/sites/default/files/perspectives_22012.pdf.

[19] Take the example of the Ghanaian parliament. Between 2001 and 2004 the executive routinely failed to disburse the full amount of funding allocated to the legislature in the national budget – an average of 81 percent of the total was disbursed over the entire period. This deliberate underdisbursement of fiscal resources to the Ghanaian legislature happened despite the fact that the constitution (Article 179 (2)) and the Parliamentary Service Act (No. 460 of 1993) expressly barred the Minister of Finance from altering the parliamentary budget after submission by the Speaker. Interestingly, in late 2002 the Speaker, Pete Ala Djetey, after public confrontation with the president, managed to get a concession from the executive that the legislature's budget would not be doctored by the Finance Ministry. For his troubles, the president declined to renominate Djetey for the Speakership two years later (Lindberg and Zhou, 2009).

that the demand for fiscal autonomy has been central to the quest for legislative independence in Kenya and Zambia. However, for a long time such demands were resisted by chief executives keen on retaining a key lever of legislative control. As noted above, constitutions and Standing Orders in both countries barred legislators from originating money bills. This reality granted presidents in both countries the power to ration or threaten to ration resources in a bid to elicit legislative subservience. However, these barriers worked better at deterring legislators in Zambia than in Kenya.

As early as 1970, Kenyan legislators, led by Jean-Marie Seroney (MP, Tinderet), demanded for budgetary independence from the executive branch. Five years earlier Kenyatta had transferred control over the legislative budget to the executive as part of his postindependence bid to consolidate power. In a motion tabled in parliament on March 20, 1970, Seroney argued that "the National Assembly must, as befitting its said dignity and privileges, be a self-accounting unit independent of any Government Ministry or Department."[20] As evidence of the lasting influence of Kenya's intra-elite political culture of legislative independence, Seroney cleverly invoked the Kenyan legislature's rich institutional inheritance going back to the colonial era:

Now, at that time, the Legislative Council, although a small place, was a self-accounting unit; and that meant that all financial matters affecting the officers of this House and Members of this House, were handled in the Legislative Council. This process, Sir, continued until we got our *Uhuru* [independence] ... The National Assembly was a self-accounting unit. But something happened, Sir, in 1965, and our financial affairs were removed and placed under the President's Office ... I think it was manipulated, administratively, so that now we are treated as though we were just a minor Government department under the President's Office.[21]

While the clamor for fiscal autonomy faded in tandem with the decline in legislative means independence in Kenya in the 1970s, Seroney's cause found new champions after 1992. In 1997 Peter Anyang' Nyong'o (nominated MP) emphasized that a politically and

---

[20] Republic of Kenya, Official Record of the National Assembly, March 20, 1970, Col. 1647.
[21] Republic of Kenya, Official Report, National Assembly, Vol. XIX, First Session, March 20, 1970, Cols. 1649–1650.

fiscally autonomous PARLSCOM would "ensure that this Parliament functions autonomously of the Executive."[22] Just under two years later, Moi finally gave in to a constitutional and statutory codification of PARLSCOM. On May 12, 1999, Peter Oloo Aringo formally moved a motion to establish PARLSCOM. Aringo's bill passed that November, and in early 2000 Seroney's dream of legislative fiscal autonomy – through PARLSCOM – became reality. Presently, the Kenyan parliament prepares and passes its budget independent of the executive. It is worth noting that legislative budget autonomy in Kenya has since 2010 been anchored on parliament's overall *power of the purse*: the executive merely submits estimates of revenue and expenditures to the legislature, which then determines the actual voting heads and has power of *virement*.[23]

The Zambian legislature has been less successful in this regard. The nature of executive-legislative relations in postcolonial Zambia fostered an intra-elite political culture that conditioned legislators to seldom "affect any changes to proposed government revenues or expenditures" (p. 129). It is telling that as late as 2016, when Zambia had a constitutional review process, the legislature only managed to get the power of *virement* but not full budget autonomy from the executive branch (unlike the case in Kenya since 2000). The Zambian president, through the Finance Minister, maintained the power to ration the amount of resources available to legislators.[24] Therefore, it is not surprising that Zambian legislators' salaries and benefits did not increase at the same rate as happened in Kenya following the end of single-party rule.

Figure 6.4 shows trends in the availability of legislative financial resources – both for legislatures' operational budgets and the remuneration of legislators. Similar to the case of legislative sittings and share of bills passed, the graphs show similarities between Kenya under KANU's single-party dominance and Zambia under UNIP. In addition, the advent of multipartyism in both countries was followed

---

[22] Republic of Kenya, Official Report, National Assembly, November 4, 1997, Col. 3233.
[23] To facilitate legislative handling of the budget process, in 2007 PARLSCOM established the Parliamentary Budget Office (PBO). The legislature's budget powers are anchored in Article 221 of the Kenyan Constitution (2010) as well as the Public Finance Management Act (2012).
[24] See Constitution of Zambia Act No. 2 (2016), Article 202.

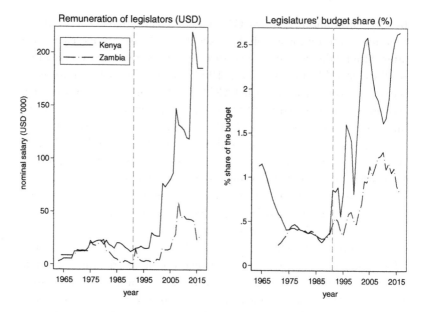

Figure 6.4 Financial resources for legislators and legislatures
Notes: The graphs depict the nominal remuneration (in US dollars) of legislators (including salaries, benefits, and allowances) and the three-year moving averages for legislative budget share (%). The main observations are: (i) the structural breaks that occur in both the budget share and remuneration of legislatures around the transition point in 1991, and (ii) the differential in the rates at which the breaks occur in Kenya and Zambia. On both measures Zambia lags Kenya by about a decade. Graphs based on author's calculations.

by an increase in the bargaining power of legislators – observable as an increase in the share of budgets allocated to legislatures and the remuneration of legislators. Finally, the rate of increase in these two measures was faster in Kenya than in Zambia. This, too, reinforces the argument that the relatively higher level of organizational development of the Kenyan legislature on the eve of multipartyism put Kenyan legislators in a better position (relative to their Zambian counterparts) to exploit their new-found political freedom.

6.2.4 Exercise of Executive Rule-Making Authority

Executive rule-making in presidential systems – whether through decrees, executive orders, or subsidiary legislation – is universally accepted as a key feature of presidential power (Punder, 2009). Kenya and Zambia are no different. In line with their Westminster inheritance, the two countries' presidents have historically maintained the power to engage in executive rule-making via "subsidiary legislation." However, the two countries differ in the degree to which the legislature can regulate the incidence of executive rule-making. In Kenya, the legislature – via enabling legislation – can delegate rule-making authority to the executive branch. In theory, Kenya's Legal Notices (subsidiary legislation) remain subordinate to the enabling legislation, and can be revoked by parliament. Zambia's presidential rule-making authority is more expansive. Despite the fact that they derive their power from parent legislation, Zambia's Statutory Instruments cannot be revoked by parliament. These powers rest in the Constitutional Court, whose members are indirectly appointed by the president.[25] These nominal constitutional checks notwithstanding, observable executive rule-making in both countries often deviates from the spirit of the parent legislation. For example, presidents have historically exempted cronies from important clauses of legislative statutes, thereby violating the universalist intent of legislation.[26]

Despite the inherent risk of agency loss, there are a number of reasons why legislators may delegate rule-making authority to presidents. These include the fact that legislators lack sufficient time to anticipate every possible scenario while drafting legislation; the executive has superior expertise and information on the process of implementing statutes; and in some cases legislators may delegate to the executive in order to avoid legislative gridlock. In addition, legislators may leave it up to the executive to determine the onset of specific clauses of legislation (as in the example of Zambia's Parliamentary Service Act above), or to be able to waive the operationalization of specific clauses of legislation as a matter of policy. However, in all such cases, executive rule-making remains subject to legislative oversight. Ultimately, legislatures

---

[25] According to the Constitution of Zambia (2016), the Judicial Service Commission recommends judges for presidential appointment. Article 5 of the Service Commissions Act (2016) empowers the president to appoint all members of the Judicial Service Commission.

[26] In both Kenya and Zambia, subsidiary legislation (Legal Notices or Statutory Instruments) are issued by the president and the cabinet. Because members of the cabinet serve at the pleasure of presidents in both countries, throughout my analyses I assume that the executive branch is a unitary actor.

retain constitutional monopoly over lawmaking. This implies that the realized levels of executive rule-making reflect executive-legislative balance of power. It follows that unilateral executive rule-making ought to be inversely proportional to the level of legislative involvement in the policymaking process (means independence).

The example of Kenya is illustrative. Before 2010 Legal Notices (subsidiary legislation) acquired legal force upon gazettement. Thereafter, such rules could only be annulled by the courts. This meant that parliament's ability to regulate executive rule-making was dependent on judicial independence – that at the time did not obtain in Kenya (Mutua, 2001). Unchecked by parliament, presidents misused their rule-making powers to exempt cronies from taxes, strategically delay the onset of legislation, and to dish out public resources to supporters (Opalo, 2019). The end of single-party rule created opportunities for Kenyan legislators to reassert parliament's position as the supreme lawmaking authority and the focal arena for bargaining over the distribution of governance rents. Kenyan legislators began to openly criticize specific instances of executive rule-making. The most prominent of these attempts to curtail executive rule-making was the 2004 motion by Amina Abdalla (nominated MP) to establish a dedicated parliamentary Delegated Legislation Committee. In contributing to the motion, Abdalla made clear the motion's goal:

[T]he Executive has been able to abuse these [rule-making] powers. This means that in the long run, we end up spending time at Committee Stage amending Bills so that they are perfect in serving our people. Afterwards, bureaucrats in a particular Ministry bring up a detailed document that provides hurdles for the implementation of the same ... I am proposing the set up of a mechanism to ensure that we are able to scrutinize things so that we do not pass beautiful Acts that are not implementable.[27]

Supporting the motion, Bonaya Godana (MP, North Horr) argued that unchecked executive rule-making "erodes the very principle of Parliament as the ultimate authority for legislating for this land."[28] Abdalla's motion passed, and became part of the National Assembly's Standing Orders. Parliament eventually passed the Statutory

---

[27] Republic of Kenya, Official Report of the National Assembly, October 6, 2004, Col. 3389.
[28] Republic of Kenya, Official Report of the National Assembly, October 6, 2004, Col. 3399.

Instruments Act No. 23 (2013) that empowers the Committee on Delegated Legislation to scrutinize and nullify executive rules that run afoul of parliament's legislative intent. Section 21 of the Act imposes automatic revocation of all subsidiary legislation after ten years of issuance (unless extended). Simply stated, after 2013 the Kenyan legislature had both the legal and political powers to regulate the incidence of executive rule-making.[29]

Zambian presidents, too, have historically exploited their rule-making authority to bypass parliament, routinely issuing Statutory Instruments before parliament votes on the "parent" legislation – especially on matters relating to the budget (Burnell, 2002, p. 296). But, unlike in Kenya, Zambian legislators have yet to develop robust checks on executive rule-making in the multiparty era. The power to review Statutory Instruments rests with the Constitutional Court whose members are indirectly appointed by the president.[30] Parliament's Standing Orders (No. 123 and 154) empower legislators to merely report unconstitutional subsidiary legislation to the Chief Justice.[31]

Figures 6.5 and 6.6 show trends in the instances of executive rule-making (along with Acts) in Kenya and Zambia, respectively. The trends in Acts illustrate the structural "demand" for executive rules in the normal process of implementing statutes. Figure 6.5 reveals an interesting relationship between Legal Notices and Acts in Kenya. Under periods of high levels of legislative means independence – under Kenyatta and in the multiparty era – the number of Legal Notices issued appear to track the number of Acts gazetted. This is suggesting evidence that there was relatively minimal issuance of excess Legal Notices (i.e., more than is required for smooth implementation of statutes) during these periods. However, during periods of legislative subservience (under Moi), the number of Legal Notices appears to have had no correlation with the number of Acts gazetted. After engineering KANU's dominance over parliament, Moi was able to issue excess Legal Notices without fear of legislative sanctions.[32] Another interesting observation is that even in the multiparty era,

---

[29] See Republic of Kenya, Statutory Instruments Act No. 23 (2013).

[30] Constitution of the Republic of Zambia (2016), Article 67 (4).

[31] Republic of Zambia, National Assembly Standing Orders (2016).

[32] An egregious example of Moi's abuse of power was the Finance Minister's Legal Notice No. 240 of 1985 that stated that "income of the President derived from the use of agricultural land owned by him shall be exempt from tax."

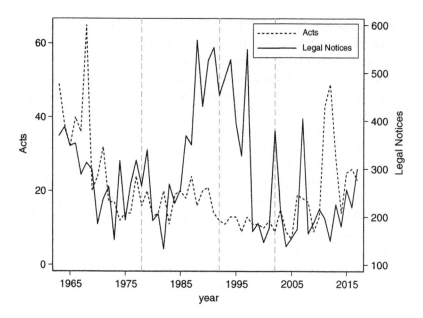

Figure 6.5 Trends in executive rule-making in Kenya

Notes: Vertical lines indicate Moi's succession to the presidency (1978), the end of single-party rule (1992), and Moi's retirement (2002). The issuance of Legal Notices substantially increased under Moi, an era characterized by legislative weakness in Kenya. Election years are also characterized by an increase in presidential rule-making.

election years (1992, 1997, 2002, 2007, and 2013) are characterized by increases in the number of Legal Notices issued. This is evidence that Kenyan presidents have continued to use Legal Notices as means of providing targeted benefits to electorally important constituencies.

Executive rule-making in Zambia depicts a different trend. Despite having unchecked rule-making powers, Figure 6.6 shows that Zambian presidents have, since the late 1960s, published steadily fewer Statutory Instruments. Furthermore, this decline closely matches that of the number of Acts. The joint decline in the number of Acts and Statutory Instruments suggests that executive rule-making in Zambia is largely driven by the demand for rules in the process of implementing legislative statutes. That said, there is a discernible difference in the levels of executive rule-making across regimes. The number of both Statutory Instruments and Acts were high in the immediate postindependence period, followed by a decline and general

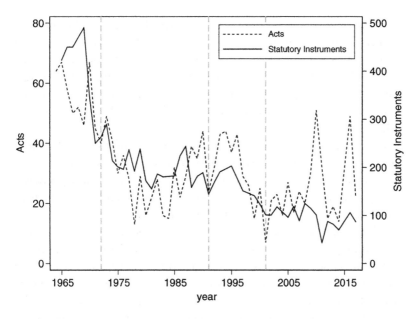

Figure 6.6 Trends in executive rule-making in Zambia

Notes: Vertical lines indicate the imposition of single-party rule (1972), the end of single-party rule (1991), and Chiluba's retirement (2001). There is a steady secular decline in the issuance of Statutory Instruments in Zambia in a manner that is not discernibly correlated with regime changes.

stability during UNIP's single-party dominance. Consistent with the general argument in this book, the advent of multipartyism in 1991 led to a further decline in the issuance of Statutory Instruments under Chiluba before reaching an apparent steady state after 2001. During this period, increases in the number of Acts (such as in 2010 and 2016) were not accompanied by any observable increases in the number of Statutory Instruments issued by the government. Stated differently, despite the close relationship between executive rule-making and legislative statutes, on average, the number of Statutory Instruments issued per legislative statute in Zambia decreased following the end of single-party rule.

6.3 Conclusion

This chapter has documented the longitudinal variation in measures of legislative institutionalization and strength in Kenya and Zambia. The data show impacts of changes in executive-legislative relations and balance of power on observable indicators of legislative institutional characteristics and outputs. These characteristics and outputs include the number of legislative sittings each year, the share of the budget allocated to the legislature and the remuneration of legislators, the share of bills passed in the legislature, and the incidence of executive rule-making.

The data generally support the core theses of this book. First, during the autocratic and single-party eras (1964–1991), the Kenyan legislature enjoyed higher levels of legislative means independence and political stature relative to its Zambian counterpart. It held more sittings per year (despite handling fewer bills) and passed smaller proportions of executive bills introduced in the legislature. The holding of more legislative sittings per year illustrates the political significance of the Kenyan legislature as the focal arena for intra-elite bargaining over policy and the sharing of governance rents during the autocratic era. The Zambian legislature, on the other hand, held fewer sittings while passing more bills per year, in part because it served merely to give a constitutional rubber stamp to UNIP's policies. The Kenyan legislature's passage of a smaller share of executive bills introduced signals means independence. Intra-legislative debates and bargaining in Kenya increased the likelihood of executive bills dying before passage. In Zambia, UNIP's overwhelming dominance ensured that nearly all executive bills got passed.

Second, longitudinal changes in executive-legislative relations in Kenya and Zambia are reflected in the data. In Kenya, Moi's presidency brought a departure from Kenyatta's tolerance of legislative means independence. His general insecurity of tenure and inability to effectively monitor and balance fellow elites led him to curtail legislative means independence. As a result we observe an increase in the share of executive bills passed under Moi and the issuance of executive Legal Notices. Similarly, following the end of single-party rule, we see changes in the balance of power between presidents and legislators reflected in a number of measures. In both Kenya and Zambia, legislatures began to hold more sittings per year, acquire bigger shares of the budget, pass smaller shares of executive bills, and curtail executive rule-making (Legal Notices in Kenya and Statutory Instruments in Zambia). At the same time, the remuneration of legislators increased – a reflection of their ability to get a bigger share of governance rents.

Finally, I have shown that institutional development takes time and that the level of legislative organizational development on the eve of multipartyism structured continued legislative institutional organizational development thereafter. Decades of means independence put the Kenyan legislature at a higher level of organizational development relative to its Zambian counterpart. As a result, Kenyan legislators were better able to take advantage of their new-found institutional and political freedom following the end of single-party rule. This is observable in the differential rates of change in the budgets allocated to the legislature, the remuneration of legislators, the share of executive bills passed, and the incidence of unilateral executive rule-making. For all these measures, the rates of change following the end of single-party rule are more rapid in Kenya than in Zambia.

Overall, the evidence in this chapter depicts two increasingly institutionalizing legislatures – albeit at different rates. The institutional trajectories of the Kenyan and Zambian legislatures fit the indicators of legislative institutionalization identified by Polsby (1968): (i) well boundedness and differentiation from the external environment, (ii) internal differentiation and complexity, and (iii) rule-bound and universalistic criteria of conducting internal business (p. 145). This chapter illustrates a trend in which the Kenyan and Zambian legislatures have increasingly become differentiated from chief executives (by having independent Parliamentary Services and passing smaller shares of executive bills), internally differentiated (by obtaining more funds for staff, research, and committee systems), and by adhering to rules governing internal operations (through greater emphasis on Standing Orders and rules emanating from the Parliamentary Services). The next chapter examines a further indicator of boundedness – barriers to entry – through an examination of the electoral origins and consequences of legislative institutionalization.

7 | *Electoral Politics and Legislative Independence*

7.1 Introduction

In previous chapters I discussed the political and organizational origins of legislative strength, with a focus on horizontal intra-elite relations. In this chapter I explore the electoral consequences of legislative independence and strength. In particular, I show how changes in the nature of executive-legislative relations impact the ability of incumbent legislators to cultivate independent bases of electoral support. To this end, I compare the electoral performance of incumbent legislators vis-à-vis comparable challengers before and after the end of single-party rule in Kenya and Zambia.

Recall that a separation of mandate – defined as individual legislators' ability to cultivate bases of political support that are independent of chief executives – is a key pillar of legislative independence and strength. Politically independent legislators are likely to assert and reinforce the institutional independence and strength of legislatures – by serving as representatives of their constituents (as opposed to agents of chief executives), providing checks on executive authority without fear of losing elections, and boosting careerism, professionalization, and institutional memory in legislatures by investing in and winning reelection. Through these mechanisms, the political independence of legislators serves to reinforce legislative independence and long-run institutionalization.

All else equal, electorally independent legislators have the ability to pass statutes that are at variance with the preferences of chief executives without fear of retribution. This reality creates strong incentives for chief executives to curtail the electoral independence of legislators. They can do this through control over ruling parties (that nominate legislators), banning of opposition parties (that provide outside options for legislators), denying legislators access to the resources needed to invest in reelection, or simply rigging elections.

208

By engineering high turnover in legislative elections (or purging independent legislators), chief executives who are able to do so can strategically stunt legislative institutional development. Legislatures dominated in this manner are likely to lack institutional memory and be populated by legislators facing disincentives to invest in legislative organizational development and professionalization.

It is important to note that even autocrats face incentives to hold relatively competitive elections (as long as their own power is not threatened). This is because elections under autocracy serve important political and informational functions. First, elections help autocrats to fairly allocate access to governance rents (in the public sector) to elites that are both popular and loyal (Blaydes, 2011). Second, elections enable autocrats to manage intra-elite politics by revealing the implicit cost of coopting or sanctioning particular elites. Electorally popular elites can be coopted to bolster regime legitimacy. Similarly, elites that command power bases independent of the ruling party (and chief executive) and who pose a threat to the regime can be purged. Third, elections provide information on the policy preferences of the wider public. As Gandhi (2008) documents, the survival of autocrats partially hinges on their ability to credibly commit to providing essential public goods and services. Therefore, elections can serve as a fire alarm that alerts the ruler about nonperforming regime agents who might expose the regime to widespread criticism, open elite rebellion, or mass revolutions.

The informational function of elections is conditional on their perceived fairness (Malesky and Schuler, 2011). Perfectly choreographed elections have little informational value. But, completely open autocratic legislative elections come with significant risks. Voters may choose representatives whose policy preferences are at variance with those of the chief executive. Furthermore, openly rigging or annulling such elections ex post may come at a steep cost to the chief executive.[1] In short, autocrats face incentives to hold reasonably competitive legislative elections as long as such elections do not threaten regime stability.

---

[1] In this regard Algeria is instructive. The voiding of the 1991 legislative elections in which the Islamic Salvation Front (FIS) defeated the ruling National Liberation Front plunged the country into a costly civil war (Martinez, 2000).

For example, Blaydes (2011) finds that in Mubarak's Egypt a "majority of the 444 [legislative] electoral contests are generally competitive" (p. 53). Similarly, Throup (1993) notes that, "the 1963, 1969 and 1974 elections under Kenyatta ... had all been relatively free and democratic affairs" (p. 381). Barkan (1987) echoes this sentiment, stating that "[c]ontrary to the conventional wisdom about elections in authoritarian systems, elections in Kenya count" (p. 232). Localized competition for legislative seats was the norm in Zambia, too, albeit under the watchful eye of the United National Independence Party (UNIP) Central Committee (Chikulo, 1988; Posner, 2005). Under single-party rule, "politics were shaped by conflict and competition within UNIP rather than between parties. And the nature of UNIP ensured that there was plenty of this kind of competition" (Szeftel and Baylies, 1992, p. 78).

My point of departure in this chapter is that legislative elections in Kenya and Zambia, under both autocracy and democracy, were not epiphenomenal.[2] The two countries are among a small group of African countries that have continuously held regular and fairly competitive legislative elections since independence.[3] Like autocrats elsewhere, in the single-party era presidents in Kenya and Zambia held fairly competitive legislative elections with a view of recruiting new elites to the legislature, incorporating representatives of different ethnic groups in the center, purging critical incumbents, and generating information on regime performance and the policy preferences of elites and the masses alike.

The end of single-party rule loosened presidential influence on legislative elections. The presence of opposition parties provided outside options through which elites could win seats in the legislature. This enabled incumbent legislators to invest electoral careers and cultivate independent bases of political support without fear of retribution from chief executives. In this chapter, I use electoral data from Kenya and

---

[2] This is an accepted truism in the wider literature on the politics of legislative elections. Even autocrats are often incentivized to conduct free and fair elections as a means of recruiting and regulating elites, credibly promising to share power, or learning about the popularity of regimes – see for example Geddes (1999), Gandhi and Lust-Okar (2009), Blaydes (2011), and Malesky and Schuler (2011).

[3] Throup (1993) discusses the importance of elections as a legitimation device in Kenya during single-party rule. Similarly, Posner (2005) outlines the dynamics of intra-UNIP electoral competition under single-party rule in Zambia.

Zambia to demonstrate that the end of single-party rule occasioned an increase in legislators' ability to exploit their incumbency status in efforts to cultivate a personal vote. I show this by comparing the vote share of incumbent legislators relative to comparable challengers before and after the end of single-party rule.

7.2 The Politics of Legislative Elections

7.2.1 *What Do Voters Want?*

Under both autocracy and democracy, legislative elections create opportunities for voters to evaluate the performance of incumbents. Where incumbents are *Mayhewian* (i.e., seek reelection), elections create incentives for incumbent legislators to engage in *observable* and *attributable* constituency service. And, at each election, the overriding question motivating voters is, *what have you done for me lately?* In order to be able to answer this question satisfactorily, incumbents need to engage in targeted constituency service. As a result, targeted clientelism and other benefits to voters are often the currency of legislative electoral politics.[4] Stated differently, incumbents' investments in passing laws or in broad programmatic policies may not yield as many votes as availing funds for the construction of local hospitals, roads, schools, or wells.

This reality of the electoral relationship between voters and politicians has implications for the political importance of specific legislative functions and the distribution of legislators' effort allocation. All else equal, legislators face very few electoral incentives to perform

---

[4] This electoral relationship holds in both emerging and established electoral democracies. For example, Mayhew (1974) observes in the case of the United States Congress that "If a congressman goes before an audience and says, 'I am responsible for passing a bill to curb inflation,' or 'I am responsible for the highway program,' hardly anyone will believe him" (p. 59). In general, the relationship between voters and their representatives can be modeled as a principal–agent relationship, with the agent (legislators) performing multiple tasks with varying degrees of observability (Holmstrom and Milgrom, 1991). Under such conditions, the legislators have strong incentives to allocate most of their time to the most easily observable and attributable tasks (Mani and Mukand, 2007). For example, Lindberg (2010) notes that Ghanaian "MPs unanimously report personal assistance and community development as what citizens in their constituencies hold them most accountable for" (p. 123). In the study, legislation ranks fourth, below community development and representation of community interests.

their constitutional functions that, from voters' perspectives, are not easily observable and attributable. Therefore, they are likely to underinvest effort in tasks that are unlikely to yield significant electoral returns – such as committee work, universalist lawmaking, or the scrutiny of specific executive functions. It is for this reason that elections are a core pillar of legislative institutional development. The nature of legislative electoral politics determines the types of politicians that win elections to become legislators, their specific incentives and effort allocation while in office, and whether or not they are able to develop stable legislative careers and contribute to overall legislative institutionalization.

The success of clientelism as an electoral strategy is well documented in African politics – from Benin (Wantchekon, 2003), to Ghana (Lindberg, 2010), to Kenya (Barkan, 1979), to Sao Tome and Principe (Vincente, 2014). Much of this reflects the widespread popular belief that political independence (from colonial rule) would bring rapid economic growth and development. Thus, politics became a means through which local communities would bargain for "development" in the form of targeted personal benefits (e.g., payment of school, hospital, and funeral fees) and public goods (e.g., construction of local hospitals, roads, and schools). Most African voters seemed to have internalized Nkrumah's promise to "seek ye first the political kingdom, and all else shall be added unto you" (Nkrumah, 1957, pp. 162–163). This political exchange relationship defined the interactions between voters and politicians in much of postcolonial Africa.[5]

The entrenched clientelistic nature of electoral politics in Africa means that candidates unable to meet voters' demand for targeted benefits seldom win elections. For perspective, Barkan and Mattes (2014) show the extent of voters' demands for clientelistic constituency service. On average, African legislators spend US$38,820 a year on handouts and projects in their constituencies. Yet, the median African legislator earns less than US$50,000 per year, barely enough to finance

---

[5] In addition to legislatures, there is also ample evidence that electoral competition induces chief executives to strategically target specific constituencies with public goods and services in an effort to win votes (Kramon, 2018). See Stasavage (2005) on education expenditures, Briggs (2012) on investments in electrification, Burgess et al. (2009) and Harding (2015) on road construction, and Dionne and Horowitz (2016) on agricultural subsidies.

Table 7.1 *The low reelection rates in African legislative elections*

Country	Election Year	Share Reelected	Country	Election Year	Share Reelected
Botswana	2014	0.35	Namibia	2014	0.42
Comoros	2015	0.13	Nigeria	2015	0.23
Cote d'Ivoire	2016	0.40	Seychelles	2016	0.04
Gambia	2012	0.54	Sierra Leone	2012	0.25
Ghana	2016	0.47	South Africa	2014	0.42
Kenya	2017	0.38	Tanzania	2015	0.32
Liberia	2011	0.28	Uganda	2016	0.39
Malawi	2014	0.30	Zambia	2016	0.33
Mauritius	2014	0.26	Zimbabwe	2013	0.26

Notes: Data from author's calculations (last election before January 2018). Reelection rates are consistently low across Africa, regardless of regime type.

the expensive lifestyles expected of legislators, let alone the clientelistic demands of constituents (Lindberg, 2010).

The yawning gap between voters' demands for targeted material benefits and politicians' ability to deliver on the same partly explains the high levels of turnover in African legislative elections (see Table 7.1) and the institutional weakness of the region's legislatures (Opalo, 2017).[6] It also explains legislative weakness in the region. Voters' strong expectations of targeted clientelistic benefits and "development" projects, created opportunities for presidents to ration fellow elites' access to the financial resources needed to win elections. Loyal candidates invariably had access to state largesse, and could signal their effort by bringing "development" to their communities. Disloyal candidates found themselves outspent by state-sponsored candidates.

Voter demands for visible and attributable "development" projects are a key feature of legislative electoral politics in Kenya and Zambia. In Zambia, "*Tabumoneka*" (we have not seen you here) was a typical

---

[6] Clientelistic demands from constituents overwhelm even relatively well-paid African legislators. For example, despite a gross pay of $13,000 per month, in 2012 more than 100 Kenyan legislators routinely took home net salaries of less than $300 every month due to loans and financial commitments to constituents. See "Debts May Cost MPs Re-election," *Daily Nation*, November 5, 2012, available here: www.nation.co.ke/news/politics/Debts-may-cost-MPs-re-election-/1064-1611480-hc8xnwz/index.html.

refrain during political campaigns throughout the 1970s (Baylies and Szeftel, 1984, p. 46). Despite UNIP's relative success in inserting itself between voters and candidates, Zambian voters still expected their representatives to provide targeted benefits and constituency service (Posner, 2005). In Kenya, the famous *Harambee* (let's pull together) system provided a platform for politicians to showcase their competence at constituency service by bringing pork to constituents. Different types of self-help projects – ranging from schools, to hospitals, to road upgrades – became "the essence of grassroots politics in Kenya" (Barkan and Holmquist, 1989, p. 360). Similarly, Mwiria (1990) notes that "by the late 1960s the Harambee Schools movement had assumed a distinctively political character as local politicians keen to ingratiate themselves with their constituents, began to play a principal role in the establishment of new schools and support of existing ones" (p. 350).[7]

Surveys of Kenyan or Zambian voters under single-party rule are scarce, but available data suggest that voters preferred candidates that delivered targeted material benefits to constituents. For example, Barkan (1979) finds that 71 percent of Kenyan legislators regarded obtaining government projects for their constituents as the most important role; and 79 percent of their constituents chose the same option. Similarly, Wanjohi (1985) finds that voter satisfaction with the performance of incumbent legislators was conditional on their perceived contribution to local development. Survey respondents who were dissatisfied with their representative's development record were 42 percentage points more likely to prefer a different candidate than the incumbent.

Voters' preference for targeted benefits survived the end of single-party rule. When asked in 2005 about how their legislators should spend their time, 45.4 percent of respondents across 18 different African countries wanted their legislators to visit their constituencies at least once a month; while 17.9 percent preferred to see their

---

[7] It is hard to overstate the political and economic significance of Kenya's Harambee self-help system. From 1964 to 1984 about 37,300 Harambee projects were completed, which amounted to around 12 percent of the gross capital formation in the country. Until 1976 nearly 40 percent of the capital development in the rural areas was directly linked to Harambees (Berman, Cottrell and Ghai, 2009). At its peak in the early 1970s the Harambee self-help system contributed upwards of 30 percent of the development investment in Kenya (Mbithi and Rasmusson, 1977).

legislators at least every week.[8] The commensurate breakdown for Zambian voters was 48 percent and 19 percent, respectively; and that for Kenya 50 percent and 30 percent. These data illustrate the importance of constituency service as the primary currency of legislative electoral politics in Kenya and Zambia.

These voter preferences are borne out in the data. In both Kenya and Zambia, legislators with differential access to material resources – cabinet ministers – got reelected at much higher rates than backbenchers.[9] On average, between 1963 and 2007 64 percent of Kenyan ministers got reelected compared to only 41 percent of backbenchers. In Zambia (between 1968 and 2011) the commensurate figures were 44 percent of ministers and only 28 percent of backbenchers. The differential rates of reelection between ministers and backbenchers in both countries were partially driven by legislators' access to material resources for clientelistic benefits and constituency service. As heads of ministries and subordinate state agencies, ministers could directly fund development projects within their domain or provide job opportunities for constituents. For example, Throup (1993) observes that Kenyan ministers were "better placed than their Assistant Ministers or ordinary Members of Parliament to direct development schemes and government projects to their constituencies" (p. 377). Similarly, Kanyinga (1994) documents how after his appointment to the cabinet, "[f]unding was made available for [Arthur] Magugu to organize/initiate a series of major *harambees* in his constituency" (p. 76). The situation was no different in Zambia, albeit under more centralized control of patronage within the UNIP hierarchy. Cabinet ministers often used their positions for both personal and political benefit. For instance, the Land Act of 1975 expressly gave the Minister of Lands "broad discretionary powers to approve both individual transfers and the price at which such transfers occurred" (Szeftel, 1982, p. 11).

---

[8] The question asked, "How much time should your Member of Parliament spend in this constituency to visit the community and its citizens?." See here: www.afrobarometer.org/online-data-analysis/analyse-online.

[9] Kenya's 2010 constitution established a separation of powers by banning the appointment of legislators as ministers. Zambia's 2016 constitution allows for serving legislators to be appointed to the cabinet.

7.2.2 *Intra-Elite Competition under Presidential Shadows*

As noted above, presidential preponderance was an important feature of executive-legislative relations. In Kenya, Zambia, and elsewhere in Africa, postcolonial intra-elite clientelistic electoral competition took place under the watchful eyes of presidents keen on protecting their political power. Thus, the electoral fortunes of incumbent legislators mirrored the prevailing nature of executive-legislative relations. With regards to the election of legislators, presidents faced the problems of adverse selection and moral hazard. They had to ensure that only candidates that were sufficiently loyal were permitted to compete in legislative elections. And, after elections, they had to ensure that the same incumbent legislators did not exploit their institutional platform to undermine presidential authority or the regime. Throughout Africa, presidents converged on single-party rule as a preferred strategy of dealing with both problems. Constitutional single-party rule provided a powerful mechanism through which to screen for loyalty before elections, and to ensure that incumbent legislators remained loyal. The threat of expulsion from the party (and as a result the legislature) kept incumbents in check.

Under these conditions, elites interested in serving as legislators faced a complicated strategic dilemma. On the one hand, they needed to invest in their individual popularity by cultivating support among voters. But, on the other hand, they had to ensure that their efforts were not seen as attempts to build power bases independent of either the ruling party or the chief executive. On account of their access to an institutional platform, incumbent legislators faced special scrutiny. In order to ensure that legislative institutionalization did not outstrip presidential ability to balance legislators, presidents in both Kenya and Zambia worked to deter the emergence of a critical mass of institutionalist legislators. Ambitious and independent legislators that crossed the line and became "too popular" were sanctioned. Some were banned from participating in legislative elections. Others were assassinated.

In Kenya, Thomas Mboya (MP, Nairobi Central) and Josiah M. Kariuki (MP, Nyandarua) were assassinated in 1969 and 1975, respectively. Both were independent legislators with presidential ambitions. Mboya, in particular, was an adept institutionalist who sought to use his influence over fellow legislators to ascend to the presidency. Besides these extreme cases, the Kenya African National Union (KANU) proved useful in screening for loyalty to Kenyatta and Moi. After the banning of Kenya People's Union (KPU) ahead of the 1969 elections, Kenya became a de jure single-party state – a fact that strengthened KANU's powers vis-à-vis legislators. At its zenith during Moi's tenure, KANU's unchallenged supremacy enabled it to make and unmake elites' political careers during nominations for legislative elections. It is telling that as part of his strategy of consolidating power, and dealing with the dual problems of adverse selection and moral hazard, Moi decided to make Kenya a de facto single-party state in 1982. Under both Kenyatta and Moi, independent politicians with national profiles – like Oginga Odinga, Chelagat Mutai, Wasike Ndombi, George Anyona, Martin Shikuku, Jean-Marie Seroney, James Orengo, Koigi Wamwere, and Charles Njonjo – were either expelled from KANU and parliament, or denied the right to run for office (Amutabi, 2010).[10],[11]

Similar tactics were on display in Zambia. UNIP vetted all candidates for legislative elections, only allowing through those deemed to be sufficiently loyal to Kaunda. For example, ahead of the 1978 elections, Simon Kapwepwe, who had grassroots support in the Copperbelt and Northern provinces and posed a serious threat to Kaunda's authority, was disqualified from vying on a technicality. In the same year, 28 winners of primary elections were rejected by the Central Committee, including Arthur Wina, a vocal former minister and

---

[10] Charles Njonjo's swift fall from grace reflected the dangers of cultivating an independent power base under single-party rule. During his heyday in the cabinet he was at the forefront of enforcing discipline within KANU. His favored targets included a number of independent legislators that he later christened the "Seven Bearded Sisters" – James Orengo (MP, Ugenya), Abuya Abuya (MP, Kitutu East), Mwachegu wa Mwachofi (MP, Wundanyi), Onyango Midika (MP, Nyando), Chibule wa Tsuma (MP, Kaloleni), Lawrence Sifuna (MP, Bumula), and Koigi wa Wamwere (Nakuru North). But, by 1983 Njonjo had become too powerful for Moi's liking. He was accused of subversion and expelled from KANU and parliament (Kyapoya, 1988).

[11] Presidential quest to limit the emergence of alternative centers of power in the legislature was partly driven by ethnic considerations. Mboya, a Luo, threatened Kikuyu interests. But, intra-ethnic rivalries also motivated presidents. Kariuki, a Kikuyu, posed perhaps an even greater threat to Kenyatta (a fellow Kikuyu) than Mboya did. Similarly, while Moi sought to check Kikuyu and Luo politicians, he was also keen to ensure that no alternative leaders emerged among his coethnic Kalenjins.

another potential challenger to Kaunda.[12] In 1980 Kaunda banned party primaries altogether and granted UNIP the power to nominate candidates to the legislature. This effectively ended any semblance of a separation of mandate in Zambia. Like Ghana's Nkrumah and Cote d'Ivoire's Houphouet-Boigny before him, Kaunda effectively acquired the powers to simply appoint legislators. Thus, Zambian legislators ceased being representatives of their constituents, and became near-perfect agents of Kaunda's regime.

These examples illustrate the contested (and often contradictory) character of legislative electoral politics under single-party rule. Kenyan and Zambian presidents tolerated competitive elections in order to enjoy their informational benefits and to co-opt fellow elites into supporting their respective regimes. But, they also had reasons to forestall the entrenchment of independent legislators in a bid to avoid the emergence of alternative centers of power. Under the circumstances, presidents' confidence in their ability to effectively monitor and balance fellow elites' political activities – such as the creation and maintenance of local party machines, local distribution of patronage and targeted clientelistic benefits, relationship with the local party and administrative officials, and credit claiming – conditioned their willingness to tolerate relatively free and fair legislative elections. It is for this reason that legislative elections were relatively freer under Kenyatta than Moi in Kenya; and that autocratic legislative elections saw relatively less stringent executive interference in Kenya than in Zambia. Table 7.2 shows an apparent higher tolerance for political entrenchment in Kenya than in Zambia. During the autocratic era, a bigger proportion of Kenyan incumbent legislators were permitted to run for reelection (80 percent) and to get reelected (43 percent) relative to their Zambian counterparts (64 percent and 39 percent, respectively).

The end of single-party rule changed this dynamic. The advent of multiparty politics created outside options for independent legislators in Kenya and Zambia. Having lost their monopoly powers to sponsor candidates to the legislature, both KANU and UNIP lost the ability to make and unmake legislators' political careers. Politically independent legislators in both countries were then able to invest in independent

[12] See David Ottaway, "Kaunda Faces Difficult Election," *Washington Post*, December 10, 1978.

Table 7.2 *Trends in candidacy and incumbent reelection*

Election	Seats	Candidates	Rerunning	Incumbents(%)	Reelected(%)
Kenya					
1969	158	601	136	65	29
1974	158	734	292	89	44
1979	158	746	338	91	47
1983	158	730	386	89	54
1988	188	356	201	68	44
1992	188	751	188	57	28
1997	210	883	239	59	36
2002	210	1035	307	74	41
2007	210	2552	454	85	34
Zambia					
1968	105	181	N/A	N/A(%)	N/A(%)
1973	125	315	58	47	32
1978	125	345	107	58	34
1983	125	760	195	78	47
1988	125	596	257	72	44
1991	125	330	109	54	17
1996	150	595	81	47	35
2001	150	1193	133	41	8
2006	150	701	166	19	6
2011	150	757	158	59	37

Notes: The number of seats indicate the total elected members. Presidents nominated 12 and up to 10 legislators in Kenya and Zambia, respectively. The proportion of incumbents rerunning and reelected is calculated based on the total number of elected legislators.

power bases without fear of retribution from presidents or expulsion from the legislature. Simply stated, political elites in both countries gained greater control over their individual electoral destinies. Incumbent legislators, in particular, were better able to invest in reelection without fear of being perceived to challenge presidential authority. This change was manifested in their ability to outperform comparable challengers (in vote share) in the period following the end of single-party rule (despite an increase in electoral competitiveness).

In the next section I empirically demonstrate this using data on legislative elections in Kenya and Zambia during and after single-party rule. I estimate personal incumbency effects in legislative elections in both countries by comparing incumbents' vote shares with those of comparable challengers. This strategy allows me to observe the changes in *levels* of incumbency advantage during and after the end of single-party rule in Kenya and Zambia. My identification strategy relies on the quasi-exogenous nature of the transition from single-party rule to multipartyism in both countries in 1991. As argued above, the adoption of multiparty politics in Kenya and Zambia was imposed by both domestic (protests) and external (donor pressure) factors at variance with the preferences of either Moi or Kaunda.[13] I exploit the quasi-exogenous changes in regime types (and executive-legislative relations) in both countries to evaluate the causal effect of ruling parties' ability to control incumbent legislators' political careers on their (incumbents') electoral performance. I find that the end of single-party rule was followed by an improvement in incumbents' electoral performance (measured by vote share), despite an increase in the level of competitiveness.

7.3 The Data and Analysis

7.3.1 The Data

To analyze the electoral effects of legislators' political independence following changes in executive-legislative relations, I collected data on the first ten postindependence legislative elections in Kenya (1963–2007) and Zambia (1968–2011). These data come from publications of the respective electoral management bodies in the two countries and published secondary sources.[14] The legislative elections dataset includes candidate-level observations, covering candidates who ran in legislative elections in Kenya (8,357) and Zambia (5,773). Variables in the dataset include candidates' names, party affiliation, vote share, and the turnout rates at the constituency level. Election

---

[13] The combination of domestic protests and donor pressure forced Moi and Kaunda to end single-party rule (Bratton and van de Walle, 1992; Posner, 2005). Zambian legislators passed constitutional amendments to allow for multipartyism on August 24, 1991. Kenyan legislators followed suit in December of the same year.

[14] I thank Daniel Posner for sharing data on legislative elections in Zambia before 1991. I digitized the data from the Kenya National Data Book Publications of the Institute for Education and Democracy. Any errors herein are my own.

turnout data for Zambia are not available before 1991. Kenya and Zambia conduct elections under a Single Member Simple Plurality (SMSP) system every five years.

On average, about 42 percent and 29 percent of all candidates ran in subsequent elections in Kenya and Zambia, respectively. In Zambia, 52 percent of incumbents sought reelection and 29 of all incumbents got reelected. The comparative figures for Kenya are 75 percent and 40 percent respectively.[15] It is also important to note that elections became more competitive after the transition to multipartyism. The average number of candidates in Kenya was four and six before and after transition, respectively. The comparable figures for Zambia are four and five. The increase in competitiveness of elections under mutlipartyism makes the finding of an increase in incumbency advantage after the transition even more remarkable. Greater bargaining power and political independence enabled incumbents to outdo challengers despite the increase in electoral competition.

7.3.2 Estimating Legislative Incumbency Effects

In order to identify how legislative independence conditions incumbency effects in Kenya and Zambia, I estimate incumbency effects during and after single-party rule using a regression discontinuity (RD) design.[16] This design allows me to compare the electoral performance of candidates that barely win elections (incumbents) against that of those that barely lose elections (challengers) across elections. The underlying assumption is that in close elections the leading candidates typically have similar characteristics – in this case broad support at the constituency level and a credible ability to channel targeted clientelistic benefits and development projects to constituents. In my analysis I do not disentangle personal and partisan incumbency effects. Instead, my goal is to compare the *levels* of the joint measure of the two concepts, before and after the end of single-party rule in Kenya and Zambia. The findings herein should thus be viewed as aggregate indicators of

[15] For comparison, in India between 1976 and 2001 55 percent of incumbents sought reelection; and about 50 percent of incumbents got reelected (Uppal, 2009). The commensurate figures for the United States House of Representatives are 88 percent and 90 percent respectively (Lee, 2008).

[16] See Lee (2008).

incumbents' ability to effectively invest in their reelection before and after changes in executive-legislative relations occasioned by regime change. They show how the typical incumbent performed relative to a typical comparable challenger before and after the end of single-party rule in Kenya and Zambia.

Two concerns inform this research design. First, before 1991, KANU and UNIP were the sole legal parties in Kenya and Zambia, respectively. This rendered intra-constituency elections to be contests between *individuals* under the umbrellas of the two parties (Posner, 2005). Second, since the end of single-party rule, Kenyan and Zambian parties have remained volatile and ephemeral (see Table 7.3). The single-party era bequeathed both countries legacies of candidate-centric, as opposed to party-centered, politics. These conditions limit the usefulness of party identification as a meaningful concept in the analysis of incumbency effects in both countries.[17] Even after the end of single-party rule, candidate-centric politics persisted in Kenya and Zambia. Political defections were common, with legislators incurring minimal electoral penalties.

Take the example of Raila Odinga, who served as legislator for Langata Constituency in Kenya between 1992 and 2013. In 1992 Odinga was elected on a Forum for the Restoration of Democracy - Kenya (FORD-Kenya) ticket. But, before the 1997 election he decamped to the National Development Party (NDP) and was reelected. Ahead of the 2002 elections, Odinga's NDP merged with KANU, earning him a spot in Moi's cabinet. But, in the run-up to the 2002 election, Odinga fell out with Moi over the nomination of KANU's presidential candidate, and formed the Liberal Democratic Party (LDP). The LDP then joined the National Rainbow Coalition (NARC), atop which Kibaki won the 2002 presidential election (with Odinga retaining his seat). Two years later Odinga fell out with Kibaki and founded the Orange Democratic Movement (ODM), the party on whose ticket he retained his Langata seat in 2007.

---

[17] Recent works on incumbency effects have sought to disentangle personal and party incumbency effects. The emerging consensus is that incumbency effects are largely personal, rather than party-based. The empirical evidence from established democracies with stable party systems suggests that nearly all of the observable incumbency effects are driven by the personal incumbency advantage, with party incumbency being negligible or negative (Fowler and Hall, 2014; Erikson and Titiunik, 2015; da Fonseca, 2017).

Table 7.3 The rise and fall of parliamentary political parties in Kenya and Zambia

Kenya

Political Party	1992	1997	2002	2007	2013	2017
KANU	100	107	64	15	6	8
FORD-Kenya	31	17		1	10	10
FORD-Asili	31	1	2	1		
DP	23	39		2		
KSC	1	1				
KNC	1				2	
PICK	1			2		
NDP		21				
SDP		15				
Safina		5	2	5		
FORD-People		3	14	3	3	
Shirikisho		1	1			
NARC			125	3	3	
Sisi Kwa Sisi			2	2		
ODM				100	78	62
PNU				44		
ODM-K/Wiper				16	19	19
NARC-K				4	1	
CCU				2	2	
New FORD-K				2	4	
TNA					72	
URP					62	
UDFP					11	
APK					5	
Independents					4	13
FPK					3	
Jubilee						140
ANC						12
Others				8	5	26
Total	188	210	210	210	290	290

Zambia

Political Party	1991	1996	2001	2006	2011	2016
UNIP	25		13			
MMD	125	131	69	74	55	3
National Party		5				
Agenda		2				
ZDC		2				
Independents		10	1	3	3	14
UPND			49		29	58
FDD			12		1	1
Heritage Party			4			
ZRP			1			
PF			1	43	61	80
UDA				26		
ULP				3		
NDF				1		
ADD					1	
Total	150	150	150	150	150	156

Notes: Figures indicate the size of parliamentary parties since 1990. Notice the high levels of party volatility across elections in both countries. Data from the Kenyan and Zambian National Assemblies. Data for Kenya in 2013 and 2017 do not include special seats for women representatives of Kenya's 47 counties.

In summary, between 1992 and 2013 Odinga was affiliated with five different parties and coalitions, an experience that was not atypical for the modal Kenyan legislator. Similarly, in every election since 2002 Kenya's presidents have run for reelection on the ticket of different parties from the ones that nominated them for their first term in office. Kibaki was elected in 2002 on the NARC ticket, and reelected under the Party of National Unity (PNU) ticket in 2007. Uhuru Kenyatta was elected in 2013 on The National Alliance (TNA) ticket, and was reelected on the Jubilee Party ticket in 2017. Personal loyalty to specific candidates, and not parties, is the dominant feature of the relationship between politicians and voters in Kenya.

On this score Zambia is no different (Butler and van de Walle, 1999). While Zambia's party system has been relatively more stable than Kenya's since 1991 (see Table 7.3), the two countries share high rates of defection of politicians (and voters) across parties. The last two decades have been marked by significant volatility among Zambia's parliamentary parties and alliances. For example, between 1991 and 1996, 25 legislators switched parties in Zambia (Burnell, 2001).[18] The net effect of the volatility of parliamentary parties in Kenya and Zambia is that a defining feature of both countries' legislative electoral politics is the enduring ubiquity of candidate-centric politics.

The above discussions highlight the disutility of using party-based means of identifying the electoral effects of incumbency status. In the minds of both voters and politicians, party identification carries very little information beyond signaling the credibility of promises of patronage and clientelistic benefits (Wantchekon, 2003; Kramon, 2018). And, since most legislative elections in both Kenya and Zambia are intra-ethnic contests, ethnicity plays a minor role in determining vote choice. Ultimately, what voters care about is different candidates' individual abilities to credibly signal that they are both able and willing to provide targeted clientelistic benefits and channel resources to their constituencies for local development. For this reason, the empir-

---

[18] Party volatility and party switching were not unique to Kenya and Zambia in this period. Goeke and Hartmann (2011) document similar patterns across much of Africa. They also find that as a result of the widespread prevalence of party switching in the region 54 percent of African states have passed laws banning party switching in an effort to instill party discipline within parliamentary parties (p. 269).

ics in this chapter focus on individual candidates in Kenyan and Zambian legislative elections; and compare the observable electoral effects of incumbency status during and after the end of single-party rule.

7.3.3 Identification under Regression Discontinuity Design

Regression discontinuity (RD) designs require fairly weak identifying assumptions. The key identifying assumption is that:

$\Sigma[Y_{0i}|X_i]$ and $\Sigma[Y_{1i}|X_i]$ are continuous in X_i at X_0

In other words, that all other unobserved determinants of potential outcomes Y are continuously related to the forcing variable X and "treatment" status is a deterministic function of X. The idea here is that because of the continuity of other variables at the cutoff point X_0, we can reliably assume that average outcomes of units just below the cutoff point are a valid counterfactual for units just above the cutoff – since only treatment status changes discontinuously at the cutoff point. We cannot directly test this assumption, but can empirically determine if it is reasonably satisfied.

RD estimates provide the local average treatment effect (LATE) in the neighborhood of the cutoff point X_0 (Lee and Lemieux, 2010, p. 292). In addition, the validity of inferences from RD designs depends on whether agents are able to perfectly manipulate the forcing variable. This is particularly important when studying elections in contexts where candidates might be able to systematically influence their positions around the cutoff. As stated above, the advantage of RD designs is that their identifying assumptions are fairly weak. What is required for estimates to be valid is not the absence of manipulation, but rather imprecise manipulation (see McCrary, 2008).

The formal treatment of the notion of "imprecise" manipulation of the forcing variable reveals that the assumption of randomness around this cutoff is met as long as candidates do not have complete control over the outcome of elections. Under conditions of imprecise sorting at the threshold, "the treatment in a neighborhood of the threshold is as good as randomized" (Lee and Lemieux, 2010, p. 293). As shown above, conventional accounts of the history of legislative elections in both Kenya and Zambia support the view that elections under both autocracy and democracy in both countries meet these identification assumptions. While political parties – especially UNIP under Kaunda and KANU under Moi – enjoyed significant control over candidate selection and discipline, it is also the case that they permitted fairly competitive electoral contests among loyal political elites. Stated differently, legislative electoral candidates in both Kenya and Zambia were allowed to compete for seats as long as they did not threaten presidents' hold on power.

7.3.4 The Key Variables

My unit of observation is candidate i in period $t + 1$ in constituency j. I run different regressions for Kenya and Zambia. The "treatment" condition is incumbency status, denoting incumbents seeking reelection. I assign challengers to the "control" condition. I only focus on legislative elections that took place during general elections, and ignore any by-elections or other special elections.

The forcing variable is the margin of victory ($MARGIN$) in period t. Because these are multiparty elections, for incumbents ($MARGIN$) is the difference between their vote share and that of the runner-up in period t in constituency j. For challengers ($MARGIN$) is the difference in vote share between candidate i and the winner in period t. Therefore, incumbents in period $t+1$ have positive margins of victory, and their challengers a negative margin of victory. As such, the forcing variable is centered at 0, which serves as the threshold that determines whether a candidate belongs in the treatment ($MARGIN > 0$) or control ($MARGIN < 0$) groups. The outcome variable of interest is the *vote share* of candidate i in constituency j in period $t + 1$. For this variable, the estimated regression discontinuity gap between the treatment and control groups is the electoral advantage that incumbents have over comparable challengers around the cutoff.

These variables are coded as follows. Out of the 13,932 total observations, I matched legislative elections candidates running in period $t + 1$ with their electoral performance at period t. Candidates are considered to have re run only if they run in period $t + 1$ in the same constituency in both periods. Candidates running in a different constituency in the subsequent election are considered as challengers. The dataset has a total of 2,448 and 1,264 complete observations of candidates who ran in both periods for Kenya and Zambia, respectively. I analyze the data separately for Kenya and Zambia, segmented before and after the first multiparty election. I ignore the transition elections – 1992 in Kenya and 1991 in Zambia. My identification of the effects of legislative independence and bargaining power on incumbency effects relies on the quasi-exogenous change in executive-legislative relations in both countries occasioned by the end of single-party rule. This exogenous shock resulted in the return to multiparty politics, which increased the bargaining power and political independence of legislators and their ability to cultivate a personal vote. These changes, I argue, enabled incumbents to make better and bigger investments in reelection. As a result, they were able to outperform comparable challengers.

7.4 Results

I begin by testing whether the requirement of as-if-random assignment at the threshold of the forcing variable is met. Results in Figure 7.1

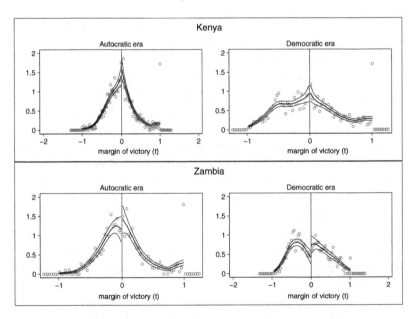

Figure 7.1 McCrary density tests of manipulation of forcing variable

Notes: Density test of manipulation of the forcing variable before and after the end of single-party rule. There is no evidence that politicians could perfectly manipulate election outcomes in Kenya. In Zambia, there is evidence of some manipulation of the forcing variable in the democratic period but not the autocratic period.

Table 7.4 *Manipulation test using local polynomial density estimation*

Method	T	P > |T|
Kenya		
Conventional	1.4540	0.1460
Undersmoothed	1.3023	0.1928
Robust Bias-Corrected	1.5608	0.1186
Zambia		
Conventional	1.7212	0.0852
Undersmoothed	1.0099	0.3125
Robust Bias-Corrected	0.9674	0.3125

Notes: Forcing variable manipulation test for the pooled data using local polynomial density estimation with quadratic local estimation, triangular kernel, and jacknife standard errors.

show (through McCrary [2008] density tests) no statistically significant evidence of perfect manipulation of the forcing variable in Kenya (either under autocracy or electoral democracy). In Zambia, there is no statistically significant evidence of manipulation in the autocratic period, and some evidence of manipulation in the democratic period. However, the distribution of means around the threshold still fall within the margins of error of the density function. These findings lend credence to the assumption that legislative elections in Kenya and Zambia were reasonably competitive and devoid of perfect manipulation. In other words, while presidents could certainly put a thumb on the scale – through endorsements and the financing of preferred candidates (among the selection of party-approved contestants) – there is no evidence that they were able to perfectly influence closely contested legislative elections. A forcing variable manipulation test using local polynomial density estimation (see Table 7.4) confirms these findings.

Next, I visually illustrate the effects of incumbency status on electoral performance during and after the end of single-party rule in Kenya and Zambia. These results are in Figure 7.2. The graphs show vote share in $t + 1$ plotted against the running variable (*MARGIN*). The discontinuities at X_0 capture the local average treatment effects of incumbency status at the threshold. The top panel depicts elections

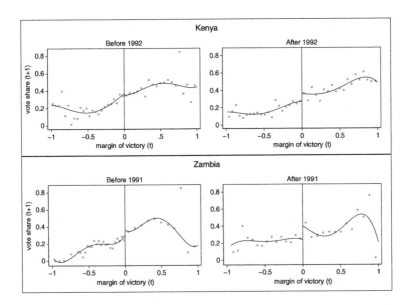

Figure 7.2 RD effect of winning at *t* on vote share at *t + 1* fourth order polynomial

Notes: Graphs show the effects of incumbency status on electoral performance. Points indicate averages within each bin. The lines show the fourth order polynomial fit.

in Kenya before and after 1992, while the bottom panel captures Zambian elections before and after 1991.

In Kenya, there is no clear discontinuity around the cutoff in elections before 1992. In other words, incumbents appear to garner similar vote shares to comparable challengers under autocracy. This changes after 1992. The graph on the right shows a clear discontinuity in vote shares around the cutoff – with incumbents (on the right of the cutoff) garnering a bigger vote share than challengers (on the left). The interpretation of this finding is that after 1992 Kenyans incumbents were able to outperform comparable challengers in legislative elections. This is consistent with the claim that the end of single-party rule empowered legislators to invest in their own reelection without fearing that Moi would sanction their attempts to cultivate independent bases of political support.

In Zambia (lower panel) there appears to be a discontinuity around the cutoff both before and after 1991. However, the discontinuity in the period after 1991 is slightly bigger than before 1991. The

Table 7.5 *RD effect of winning at* t *on vote share at* t + 1

	Kenya		Zambia	
	Before 1992	After 1992	Before 1991	After 1991
Conventional	−0.0393	0.0742[+]	0.0837	0.113
	(−1.33)	(1.88)	(1.60)	(1.43)
Bias-corrected	−0.0491[+]	0.0831*	0.0974[+]	0.141[+]
	(−1.67)	(2.11)	(1.86)	(1.78)
Robust	−0.0491	0.0831[+]	0.0974	0.141
	(−1.44)	(1.82)	(1.59)	(1.53)
N	1,283	988	612	646

t statistics in parentheses.
[+] $p < 0.10$, * $p < 0.05$, ** $p < 0.01$, *** $p < 0.001$.
Notes: Local linear regression point estimates show a penalty to incumbency status before 1992, and a significant electoral boost due to incumbency status after 1992 in Kenya. In Zambia there is a positive incumbency effect both before and after 1991, albeit higher in the latter period.

interpretation of this finding is that Zambian incumbents were able to outperform comparable challengers before 1991 and that this continued after 1991, albeit in a slightly more pronounced manner. One explanation for the apparent strength of Zambian incumbent legislators (relative to challengers) might be the fact that relatively fewer incumbents ran for reelection (52 percent) compared to Kenya (75 percent). This differential selection may have resulted in a situation in which only strong Zambian incumbents ran for reelection and proceeded to outperform comparable challengers. The slightly larger discontinuity around the cutoff in the period after 1991 is consistent with the claim that the end of single-party rule empowered legislators to independently invest in their reelection without fear of being sanctioned by either Kaunda or UNIP.

These findings are confirmed in Table 7.5. Both the conventional and robust local linear regression point estimates of incumbency effects before and after the advent of multipartyism show clear differences in the electoral performance of Kenyan and Zambian legislative incumbents. Before 1992, Kenyan incumbent legislators appear to have been disadvantaged relative to comparable challengers (by about 4 percentage points). These estimates are only statistically significant in the bias-corrected model. However, after 1992, and despite the increase in level of electoral competition, Kenyan legislative incumbents appear to have become advantaged (by about 8 percentage points) relative to comparable challengers.

In Zambia, too, there was a distinct shift in electoral outcomes before and after 1991. Perhaps due to the selection effect outlined above, Zambian incumbent legislators appear to have been advantaged relative to comparable challengers before 1991 – by about 9 percentage points (however, the statistical significance of the point estimates are sensitive to model selection). This changed following the end of UNIP's rule. After 1991 the incumbency advantage increased by about 5 percentage points. This is consistent with the claim that multiparty electoral competition granted legislators political independence and the ability to invest in their reelection without fear of sanctions from the president or the ruling party. Like their counterparts in Kenya, Zambian legislators acquired a greater degree of electoral advantage relative to comparable challengers.

Consistent with the trends in other measures of legislative institutionalization and strength, the structural changes in executive-legislative relations in Kenya and Zambia with the end of single-party rule resulted in an increase in the bargaining power of incumbent legislators. Incumbent legislators were free to invest in their reelection without fear of retribution from the ruling party or the president. And, as a result, incumbent legislators garnered a greater vote share (relative to comparable challengers) under multiparty rule than under single-party rule. Stated differently, the political and organizational independence of the Kenyan and Zambian legislatures after the advent of multipartyism resulted in greater electoral success for incumbent legislators.

7.5 Explaining African Legislators' Quest for Pork

The idea that legislative independence can boost the electoral prospects of incumbents is not new. Mayhew (1974), for example, observes that "if a group of planners sat down and tried to design a pair of American national assemblies with the goal of serving members' electoral needs year in and year out, they would be hard pressed to improve on what exists" (p. 81). The idea here is that empowered legislators have the ability to design intra-legislative organizational structures and provide material resources in a manner that improves their prospects. Recall that what voters care the most about is the answer to the question: *what have you done for me lately?* Regardless of political context, incumbent legislators spend their time in office preparing for this question by channeling specific targeted projects to their constituents. Whether termed as clientelism, pork barrel politics, patronage, or constituency service, such investments achieve the same outcome – signaling to voters that incumbents are exerting effort on their behalf.

An interesting case study of this phenomenon is the spread of constituency development funds (CDFs) across Africa following the end of single-party rule in the early 1990s. Legislative empowerment under multipartyism, coupled with citizen demands for readily identifiable and attributable material benefits, resulted in the creation of dedicated slush funds for constituency-targeted expenditures in a number of African countries. As noted by Barkan and Mattes (2014), just under a quarter of African states have adopted CDFs in part "as a response to constant and intense constituent pressure 'to deliver' both private ... and public goods ... and thus increase their prospects for reelection" (p. 27). It is telling that across Africa only states whose legislators are elected from Single-Member Districts (SMDs) have adopted CDFs.[19]

Kenya and Zambia were no exception. Kenya's towns and cities are dotted with billboards advertising projects funded by the CDF. Kenyan legislators established the CDF in 2003 with a view of obtaining state resources for "development" projects in their constituencies. Previously, MPs mainly funded such projects from personal sources at Harambees. The Constituency Development Fund Act (2003) guaranteed the disbursement of at least 2.5 percent of government revenue to constituency development committees (CDCs) headed by MPs. Through the fund legislators acquired resources to invest in all manner of targeted benefits for their constituents – including road renovations, construction of schools and hospitals, disbursement of bursaries, among other vote-getting investments.

CDF allocations in Kenya are substantial. In the 2012–2013 fiscal year the average constituency was allocated US$1,196,689.91. In 2016 the CDF was renamed the National Government Con-

---

[19] These include Botswana, Ghana, Malawi, Nigeria, Sierra Leone, South Sudan, Swaziland, Tanzania, Zambia, Zimbabwe, and Uganda.

stituency Development Fund. Allocations in the 2017–2018 fiscal year amounted to an average of $868,103.44 per constituency. The Act was intentionally designed to give MPs broad discretion over the membership of CDC members and the choice of projects. Supporting the CDF bill in parliament, one legislator argued that control over CDCs was important "so that the Hon. Member can have significant influence on that committee," adding that "[t]here is no person in that constituency who has a greater stake in its development than the Hon. Member."[20]

The Kenyan CDF demonstrates legislators in independent legislatures can exploit their institutional powers to boost their electoral prospects. The politics of CDF adoption across Africa is illustratative. Recall that chief executives have incentives to limit the political (and electoral) independence of legislators. This is for the simple reason that legislative empowerment and independence necessarily limits executive power. As such, African presidents had incentives to limit the degree of legislative autonomy in the management of CDFs. Presidential control over CDFs created opportunities to limit legislators' ability to establish localized bases of political support upon which they would build independent legislative careers. This is precisely what Tsubura (2013) documents in a study of the politics of CDF adoption across Africa. Legislative institutional bargaining power at the point of creation of CDFs conditioned the specific types of CDF funding and project selection mechanisms. In countries where legislators lacked significant bargaining power at the point of adoption (like Ghana and Zambia), presidents retained control over CDFs – and had discretion over both the disbursement of funds and the types and location of CDF projects. However, in countries whose legislatures had more bargaining power (like in Kenya and Tanzania), legislators ensured that CDF laws mandated fixed budget allocations and granted legislators relative autonomy over project choice.

A closer look into the differences between the Kenyan and Zambian CDFs sheds more light on the variation of CDF adoption across Africa. Between 1995 and 2016, Zambian legislators had very limited control over the committees in charge of CDFs – the CDCs.

[20] Government of Kenya, National Assembly Official Report, November 27, 2003, Col. 4082.

In addition, they shared CDF disbursements with local politicians (chiefs and councillors) and district administrators appointed by the president. Finally, the amounts of CDF cash disbursed varied each year, as the total amount was set at the discretion of the president. A presidential appointee – Minister of Local Government (and Housing Services) – was responsible for allocating funds to specific constituencies through their respective district councils.

This arrangement was not particularly beneficial to Zambian legislators. Zambian presidents retained maximum discretion over the disbursement of CDF funds to constituencies. This essentially made the CDF a means through which presidents could influence legislators through a selective disbursement of funds. For example, in 2015 the Ministry of Local Government and Housing Services simply stopped disbursing funds to some constituencies, citing the lack of proper guidelines on how the funds were to be used.[21] The sharing of funds with other politicians and administrators limited legislators' ability to credibly claim credit for specific projects. Recall that a key part of the electoral utility of targeted benefits is that it makes it easy for voters to observe their legislators' effort. The multiplicity of actors involved in the Zambian CDF introduced noise in the attribution process, thereby making it harder for legislators to claim specific projects. Zambian legislators decried this arrangement. For example, Hon. Davison Mung'andu (MP, Chama South) questioned "the rationale for disbursing the fund through the councils as opposed to disbursing it through the Office of the Clerk of the National Assembly. After all, it is meant for hon. Members of Parliament who have assistants in their constituency offices."[22]

The Kenyan CDF was different. Introduced in 2003, the CDF Act guaranteed predetermined constituency allocations, a monopoly over the funds, and discretion over project choice. Legislators appointed members of CDF committees, and had the final say on projects. The amount disbursed was also fixed in a formula – at least 2.5 percent of government revenue – and charged directly on the Consolidated Fund.

---

[21] Sipiliswe Ncube, "Only 4 Constituencies in N/Western Have Received CDF Since 2015 - Kambita," *News Diggers*, September 19, 2017.

[22] Government of Zambia, National Assembly Official Report, November 2, 2016.

The money was to be shared across constituencies based on population and poverty levels in proportions fixed by a formula. These features allowed Kenyan legislators to be able to claim full responsibility for development projects funded by CDFs.

The differences between the Kenyan and Zambian CDFs were, in part, a function of the timing of their implementation. In 1995 the Zambian legislature was dominated by the Movement for Multiparty Democracy (MMD), having won a landslide four years earlier in 1991. Zambian legislators were therefore not in a position to strike a hard bargain against Chiluba, as a means of asserting their political independence and the separation of mandate. Kenya's CDF was established in 2003, a time when legislative strength in Kenya was in its apogee. PARLSCOM had been created, granting the legislature complete institutional independence from the executive branch. Furthermore, Kibaki had just been elected atop a fractious coalition government and lacked the institutional means of enforcing party discipline. This limited his bargaining power vis-à-vis legislators, both individually and collectively. These conditions made it possible for Kenyan legislators to strike a hard bargain, and acquire for themselves a slush fund independent of executive control. In debates preceding the bill's passage, MPs demanded for control over CDCs "so that the Hon. Member can have significant influence on that committee," adding that "There is no person in that constituency who has a greater stake in its development than the Hon. Member."[23] As illustration of the electoral motives behind the adoption of CDFs, Kenyan legislators banned harambees around elections. Harambees provided a platform through which deep-pocketed challengers could outbid incumbents with readily demonstrable promises of targeted benefits. Simply put, incumbent legislators legislated away an important arena of electoral competition.[24]

Despite their loss in 1995, Zambian legislators did not give up the fight for full control over the CDF. In December 2016 they passed

[23] Government of Kenya, National Assembly Official Report, November 27, 2003, Col. 4082.
[24] Article 16 (1) of the Elections Act (2011) states that "A person who directly or indirectly participates in any manner in any public fundraising or Harambee within eight months preceding a general election or during an election period, in any other case, shall be disqualified from contesting in the election held during the election year or election period."

a resolution to give them the sole authority over the management of the funds. Contributing to the motion, Davies Chisopa (MP, Mkushi South) argued that "the MP should be the central person to regulate, manage, disburse and utilize the CDF."[25] Zambian legislators' determination to control the management of disbursed funds is an important first step in the quest to acquire resources for constituency service and a separation of mandate from the executive branch. However, the executive fought back and retained control over the timing and amounts of funds disbursed.[26]

These accounts of the politics of CDF adoption in Kenya and Zambia illustrate the electoral origins of legislative weakness in Africa. Given voters' expectations of clientelism, targeted benefits, and other forms of constituency service, only politicians who can credibly meet these expectations stand a chance of building long-term legislative careers. Thus far, the dearth of resources for legislators has resulted in high turnover rates in legislative elections across the region. High turnover, in turn, has curtailed the development of institutional memory, careerism and specialization among legislators, and the overall institutionalization of African legislatures.

7.6 Conclusion

This chapter examined the electoral origins of legislative strength. As the primary means of gaining membership in legislatures, elections are an important pillar of legislative strength. Politically secure legislators are more likely to use their legislative institutional authority to check executive power. Because of this, presidents are likely to curtail legislators' political security by influencing their reelection prospects. However, changes in executive-legislative relations that increase legislative autonomy can create opportunities for legislators to invest

[25] See "MPs Vote to Take Control of CDF," available here: https://zambiareports .com/2016/12/14/mps-vote-take-control-cdf/.
[26] Constitutional amendments in 2016 ejected MPs from local councils, thereby completely cutting them off from the activities of CDF committees. Having failed to amend the constitution to regain their membership in local councils, Zambian legislators chose to give themselves discretion in the management of CDF resources. See The Republic of Zambia, National Assembly Official Report, December 14, 2016.

in their political security without fear of influence or sanctions from presidents.

Using data on legislative elections in Kenya and Zambia, I showed that regime changes in both countries in the early 1990s impacted incumbent legislators' ability to cultivate a personal vote, and to outcompete favorable challengers. To this end I employed a regression discontinuity design to estimate the electoral payoff accrued by incumbents (bare winners) on account of being in office (incumbency advantage) relative to comparable challengers (bare losers).

I find that Kenyan and Zambian legislators fared better relative to comparable challengers under multipartyism than under single rule (despite an increase in levels of electoral competitiveness). I attribute this to the political independence afforded to legislators under multiparty politics. While elections under autocracy in both Kenya and Zambia were relatively competitive, they also took place in the shadow of powerful presidents with the power to end the political careers of ambitious and independent legislators. The difficulty of walking a fine line between investing in reelection and not cultivating independent power bases exposed incumbents in both countries to being outflanked by challengers (often backed by chief executives). Incumbents were thus disadvantaged, primarily because of chief executives' desire to limit the political independence of individual legislators.

This changed under multipartyism. The existence of outside options in the form of multiple political parties enabled incumbents to openly invest in reelection without fear of retribution from ruling parties or chief executives. As a result, incumbents in both Kenya and Zambia were able to cultivate a personal vote, and perform better than comparable challengers relative to the single-party era. An examination of the politics of CDF adoption in Kenya and Zambia highlighted the mechanisms through which legislative independence can boost individual legislators' electoral prospects. At the point of adopting CDFs, a relatively more assertive legislature in Kenya was able to only secure resources for clientelistic politics and constituency service but also grant legislators discretion in the choice of projects. In contrast, relative legislative weakness in Zambia resulted in executive control over both the disbursement of CDF funds and the choice of projects.

Overall, this chapter demonstrates that legislative autonomy is predicated on interbranch separation of mandate – whereby individual legislators and chief executives are elected by different sets of voters. The political need to cater to these different sets of voters creates incentives for legislators to check and balance executive power. It is for this reason that there is a strong correlation between legislative strength and independence on the one hand, and individual legislators' political independence and the ability to cultivate power bases independent of chief executives on the other hand. Simply put, politically independent legislators make for strong legislatures, and vice versa.

8 | Conclusion

8.1 Explaining Postcolonial Legislative Development

Over the past two centuries legislatures have become entrenched as one of the three branches of government. As the institutional expression of horizontal accountability, they are the most important pillar of representative democratic government. Legislatures serve as arenas for the representation of mass interests, intra-elite bargaining over policy, as well as the sharing of governance rents. For these reasons, legislative activities have a direct bearing on welfare outcomes for ordinary citizens throughout the world. Laws passed determine social policy, allocate distributional benefits, and structure economic activity. At the same time, institutionalized intra-elite competition within legislatures cements elite consensus and political stability. For these reasons, it is important to understand the dynamics of executive-legislative relations and legislative development.

Nowhere is the study of legislatures more important than in former colonies. In these states, political development over the last five decades has been characterized by the preponderance of chief executives. The ubiquity of "overdeveloped" legislatures led scholars to neglect other institutional centers of power in these states – such as legislatures. Yet, as I show in this book, and contrary to conventional wisdom, postcolonial legislatures have served important roles in structuring political development in these contexts.

Building on existing works on autocratic institutions and democratic transitions, this book explored the politics of legislative development in postcolonial states. To this end, I asked two simple questions: (i) what explains the observed variation in legislative strength in autocratic states? and (ii) under what conditions can democratic legislatures emerge from their autocratic foundations?

Using material evidence from Africa, I answered the first question by showing that contingencies of political development under both colonial rule and autocracy explain contemporary variation in legislative strength and institutionalization in Africa. The colonial experience with legislatures bequeathed postcolonial African states with specific institutional forms and practices, and the associated intra-elite political culture of *how politics works*. Strategies of elite control under autocracy conditioned the organizational development of African legislatures under autocracy. African presidents who were confident in their ability to effectively balance fellow elites acting collectively in legislatures tolerated a modicum of legislative organizational independence. Those that could not stifled legislative organizational development and independence. Following transition from autocracy to electoral democracy in the early 1990s, these differences became apparent, and continue to structure legislative development in contemporary Africa.

My answer to the second question is related to the first. Strong autocratic legislatures provide the foundation for strong democratic legislatures. Legislative institutionalization takes time. And, more often than not, institutional forms and practices survive regime transitions. Therefore, the degree and forms of legislative development under autocracy condition postautocratic trajectories of legislative institutional development. In the African context, organizationally weak autocratic legislatures remained weak following transition to democracy. On the other hand, organizationally strong autocratic legislatures provided the foundation for the emergence of institutionally capable and independent democratic legislatures.

This model of legislative development is a new contribution to the study of autocratic institutions. Much of the current literature operates under the assumption that autocrats are all-powerful, and therefore can optimally institutionalize with a view to sustaining their regimes. My contribution is to endogenize the autocrat's strength, and argue that an autocrat's willingness to institutionalize rule is conditioned by their ability to effectively balance institutions so created.

For instance, it is obvious that weak rulers presiding over weak states do not necessarily provide the best environment for institutional development. What is not obvious is why institutions that limit the power of the ruler do not readily emerge in such contexts. After all, institutions emerge to *constrain* the ruler. Therefore, it would appear that this process would be made easier by the existence of a weak autocratic ruler. Yet, the empirical evidence suggests that weak rulers preside over weak institutions, opting for personalist rule; while strong rulers institutionalize their rule – either through parties or legislatures. This explains the observed empirical regularity of a positive correlation between institutionalized rule and regime stability. Strong autocrats that are likely to stay longer in power are also more likely to govern with institutions.

To test this theoretical supposition, this book delves into the actual mechanics of institutionalized autocratic rule. I begin by providing detailed qualitative evidence from Kenya and Zambia on how the coercive structure of the state and the organizational strength of ruling parties interact to determine the specific strategies employed by autocrats to keep fellow elites in check. I argue, with supporting evidence, that administration-based strategies of elite control (that I characterize as indirect and extra-legislative) are more conducive to the emergence of organizationally independent legislatures. This is because leaders that rely on apolitical administrations to balance fellow elites face lower risks of agency loss. As a result, autocrats that rely on these strategies are more likely to tolerate relatively independent legislatures. Party-based control strategies, on the other hand, stunt legislative development. Party-based control inserts autocrats into the daily operations of legislatures, and creates incentives for the substitution of legislatures with parties. In addition, party-based control exposes presidents to the risk of agency loss. Under these conditions, parties and not legislatures, become focal arenas of intra-elite bargaining and policymaking.

I augment the analytical narratives on legislative development in Kenya and Zambia with analyses of legislative characteristic and outputs – including the frequency of legislative sittings, share of bills passed, legislative budgets, remuneration of legislators, and the exercise of executive rule-making powers. The trends in these data mirror changes in executive-legislative relations in Kenya and Zambia, with structural breaks occurring following the transition from single-party rule to multiparty electoral politics in the early 1990s. I then explore the electoral connection in legislative development. I argue that legislative organizational strength and capacity is a function of the political power of individual legislators. Legislators' power, in turn, depends on their ability to get reelected. From this starting point, I show how autocratic presidents in Kenya and Zambia stifled legislators' attempts to cultivate independent power bases, and how the end of single-party rule freed incumbent legislators to invest in their reelection without fear of executive retribution. I find that while incumbent legislators were disadvantaged relative to comparable challengers under single-party rule, following the transition to multiparty politics they began to outperform comparable challengers. This shift is particularly remarkable given that legislative electoral competition increased under multiparty politics.

Taken together, the body of evidence presented in this book increases our knowledge of institutions and institutional change under autocracy, and the processes through which democratic institutions of limited government can emerge from their autocratic foundations.

8.2 Implications for the Study of Institutions

The findings in this book have important implications for different strands of literature in the fields of political economy and comparative politics. In particular, this book contributes to our understanding of both institutional politics under autocracy and institutional change following autocratic transitions. First, it is important to note that politics does not end with the establishment of autocratic parties or legislatures. By virtue of concentrating elite political action, these institutions pose nontrivial threats to autocratic rule. The analysis of Kenya and Zambia demonstrates the consequences of specific autocratic strategies of balancing elite institutions. Second, the fact that institutional change takes time, and that new institutions often retain vestiges of old institutional forms and functions, calls for a study of how autocratic institutional development impacts postautocratic trajectories of further institutional change. The longitudinal study of legislative development in Kenya and Zambia in the late colonial period, under single-party rule, and in the multiparty era contribute to our understanding of institutional change across regime types.

8.2.1 Autocratic Institutions

Why do some autocrats govern with institutions while others do not? And, what explains the variation in the strength of autocratic institutions? The existing stylized account of institutionalized autocracy posits that autocrats optimally institutionalize with a view to enhancing regime stability (Magaloni, 2006; Gandhi, 2008; Blaydes,

2011; Svolik, 2012). The findings in this book suggest that the causal mechanism may be reversed. Weak autocrats, lacking the ability to effectively balance institutions such as legislatures, and unlikely to have long tenures, are also less likely to institutionalize their rule. The implication is that there are two institutional equilibria under autocracy – strong autocrats institutionalize, while weak ones do not. For example, given the informational and political benefits of governing with legislatures, rulers with robust abilities to monitor and regulate elite political activity and balance legislatures are likely to tolerate not only the existence of legislatures but also their organizational independence. Those unable to effectively monitor and balance fellow elites may find it too risky to tolerate such institutions. The former autocrats are likely to stay longer in office, with or without institutions. The latter are likely to have shorter tenures.

Thus far, scholars have attributed the failure by some autocrats to sufficiently institutionalize to incomplete information. For example, Gandhi and Przeworski (2007) argue that "[f]or whatever reason, some autocrats do err, and as a consequence have institutions weaker or stronger than the threat from the opposition would require" (p. 1289). This book contends that, unable to effectively balance elite institutions (e.g., legislatures), weak autocrats rationally under-institutionalize. Examples abound of weak rulers who deliberately underinstitutionalized in attempts to remain in office. In the African context, these include Samuel Doe of Liberia, Mobutu Sese Seko of Zaire (the Democratic Republic of Congo), and Salva Kiir of South Sudan. The different trajectories of legislative development in Kenya and Zambia demonstrate how presidents' ability to effectively balance elite institutions explains the variation in the strength of autocratic institutions.

8.2.2 *Institutions and Institutional Change*

Under what conditions do democratic institutions emerge from their autocratic foundations? This book addresses this question from different perspectives. First, by historicizing the process of legislative institutional development, it injects the time dimension to the analysis of legislative development in postcolonial states. In doing so, it shows how legislative development under both colonialism and autocracy impacts trajectories of further evolution following transition to democracy.

This is a departure from current theories of political change that emphasize institutional discontinuities as the basis for the emergence of democratic institutions (North and Weingast, 1989; Acemoglu and Robinson, 2006). Noting that new institutional forms and functions are often layered on the old (Thelen, 2004), it argues that autocratic institutions provide the foundation upon which reformers build more representative and responsive democratic institutions. In the case of legislatures, the level of organizational development at the point of autocratic transition often determines the trajectories of legislative development under democracy. The histories of Kenyan and Zambian legislatures demonstrate this fact.

Second, this book explores how variation in styles of autocratic rule structure institutional development under autocracy and following transition to democracy. In doing so it highlights the singular importance of intra-elite politics to institutional development. Conventional wisdom prizes vertical accountability (for example, through elections) as the cornerstone of strong institutions. In line with Ansell and Samuels (2014), this book's findings are a call to appreciate the importance of intra-elite competition and balance of power as a basis for strong institutions. Strong legislatures necessarily constrain chief executives. In addition, the preponderance of executive power in postcolonial states does not mean that legislative tyranny is not possible. The example of Benin in Chapter 3 shows that autocratic presidents lacking the ability to effectively balance fellow elites can be overthrown. Finally, in analyzing the electoral foundations of legislative strength, this book illustrates the ways in which elections can serve to weaken legislatures – through executive manipulation to limit a separation of mandate and high turnovers that limit the extent of legislative institutional memory and careerism among legislators. Ultimately, a normatively desirable executive branch is one that is at once powerful and limited in the use of its powers. The same goes for legislatures. This is the stuff of intra-elite politics.

Lastly, this book contributes to the literature on democratic consolidation by focusing attention on legislatures. Thus far, the vast majority of scholarly works of the *Third Wave* of democratization have focused on presidential elections and their implications for political stability and distributional outcomes (Kim and Bahry, 2008). This literature has paid little attention to legislatures, despite the centrality of these institutions to the effective operationalization of representative democratic government. This book explores how multiparty politics can serve to limit the power of the executive by providing legislators with outside options and autonomy to establish their own independent bases of political support. It argues that politically independent legislators make for strong legislatures with the ability to check and balance chief executives.

8.3 Policy Implications

Due to the significant welfare implications of legislatures, this book project was partly motivated by normative concerns. The idea that strong institutions promote political stability and drive economic development is both intuitive and normatively desirable. To this end, legislatures are the *sine qua non* institutions of representative democratic government. Indeed, the history of the evolution of limited democratic government is one of the rise of legislatures as a mechanism of enforcing both horizontal and vertical accountability; and as the main channel through which governments derive their mandate to govern and enact public policy. Horizontal (intra-elite) accountability through legislatures generates consensus on legitimate forms of political contestation and procedures of public administration. Vertical accountability (between elites and masses) ensures that state institutions are responsive to the policy preferences of the governed. As the embodiment of popular sovereignty, legislatures are therefore indispensable for the proper functioning of modern democratic states. We therefore ought to know more about how these institutions function and evolve in low-income emerging democracies – many of which are postcolonial states.

How can legislatures in emerging democracies be strengthened in order to entrench the principals of interbranch separation of powers and horizontal accountability? What can be done to improve the representative character of legislatures in much of the developing world? And, lastly, what can be done to improve the quality of policy input from legislatures in emerging democracies?

These are important questions that have in the last two decades partially informed democracy promotion programs around the globe. For instance, the United Nations Development Program (UNDP) supports one in three parliaments globally, including 28 African legislatures since 2010. These efforts take the form of technical assistance designed to improve capacity of legislators and staff, promote general institutional reform, improve interbranch relations, and enhance gender balance in legislatures (Power and Shoot, 2014). The World Bank has a Parliamentary Strengthening Program that seeks to promote normatively beneficial reforms; increase ties between parliaments in developing countries; and provide training for legislators and staff in order to improve the oversight capacities of these institutions (Pelizzo and Stapenhurst, 2004). Several donors have similar programs that assist legislatures in emerging democracies on a bilateral basis.

The findings in this book present lessons that could potentially inform the design of legislative strengthening programs such as those run by UNDP and the World Bank. The focus on organizational technical competence holds promise for long-term benefits. Organizational development and internal differentiation are key for the emergence of legislative means independence. Investments in record keeping, research, and understanding of parliamentary rules and procedures can go a long way in laying the foundation for future institutionalization of legislatures. The history of the Kenyan legislature demonstrates that this is true *even* under autocracy. Organizational development serves to regularize internal organizational activities and limit the discretionary powers of party leaders, while at the same time limiting the impact of extra-legislative influences. Simply stated, experience with means independence *over time* contributes to long-term legislative institutionalization, regardless of regime type.

However, the focus on organizational development and normatively desirable reforms may not succeed if not coupled with investment in legislators' political empowerment. One of the key lessons in this book is that politically powerful legislators make for strong legislatures. Therefore, legislative strengthening programs that do not directly address the question of political independence of legislators may not achieve the desired results. This is not an easy goal to achieve. Strengthening legislatures through empowerment of individual legislators necessarily involves an acknowledgment of the intent to reduce the discretionary powers of presidents through credible horizontal oversight. The overtly political nature of this kind of intervention may make it less attractive to both multilateral and bilateral donors who support legislative strengthening programs.

In the same vein, while it may be normatively desirable to increase gender balance in the legislatures of emerging democracies, how this objective is achieved is very important. Should gender quotas be met through election or appointment? To whom should these special representatives be answerable? The evidence presented in this book suggests that if gender quotas are implemented poorly, they may lead to legislative weakening by giving too much power to the appointing authority (typically [male] party leaders). Elections under gender quotas, which anchor representatives in society and provide them an opportunity to cultivate a personal vote, may be the best way to achieve this goal without sacrificing legislative independence.

In the final analysis, legislative institutionalization is fundamentally political and cannot be achieved exclusively through technical assistance and organizational reforms. This means that there is only so much that external assistance can do to strengthen legislatures and reinforce the principles of horizontal accountability and limited government in emerging democracies. Ultimately, legislative strengthening in these contexts will continue to hinge on the accumulated historical experience, the nature of intra-elite politics, and the resultant effects on executive-legislative balance of power.

References

Acemoglu, Daron and James A. Robinson. 2006. *Economic Origins of Dictatorship and Democracy.* New York: Cambridge University Press.

Acemoglu, Daron, Simon Johnson, and James Robinson. 2001. "The Colonial Origins of Comparative Development." *American Economic Review* 91(5):1369–1401.

Ademolekun, Ladipo. 1971. "Bureaucrats and the Senegalese Political Class." *Journal of Modern African Studies* 9(4):543–559.

Ajulu, Rok. 2002. "Politicised Ethnicity, Competitive Politics and Conflict in Kenya: A Historical Perspective." *African Studies* 61(2):251–268.

Ake, Claude. 1966. "Charismatic Legitimation and Political Integration." *Comparative Studies in Society and History* 9(1):1–13.

Alavi, Hamza. 1972. "The State in Post-Colonial Societies: Pakistan and Bangladesh." *New Left Review* 74:59–81.

Alderfer, Philip Wendell. 1997. "Institutional Development in a New Democracy: The Zambian National Assembly, 1964 to 1996." PhD thesis. Michigan State University, Ann Arbor, MI.

Alila, Patrick. 1986. "Luo Ethnic Factor in the 1979 and 1983 Elections in Bondo and Gem." Nairobi: Institute of Development Studies.

Allman, Jean Marie. 1993. *The Quills of the Porcupine: Asante Nationalism in an Emergent Ghana.* Madison, WI: University of Wisconsin Press.

Amutabi, Mauric N. 2010. "Interrogating the Tumultuous Relationship between Parliament and the Executive in Kenya over the Past 45 Years: Retrospection." *Kenya Studies Review* 3(3):17–40.

Anderson, David M. 1993. "Black Mischief: Crime, Protest and Resistance in Colonial Kenya." *Historical Journal* 36(4):851–877.

2005. "Yours in Struggle for Majimbo: Nationalism and the Party Politics of Decolonization in Kenya, 1955–64." *Journal of Contemporary History* 40(3):547–564.

Ansell, Ben W. and David Samuels. 2014. *Inequality and Democracy: An Elite-Competition Approach.* New York: Cambridge University Press.

Arhin, Kwame. 1967. "The Structure of Greater Ashanti (1700–1824)." *Journal of African History* 8(1):65–85.

248

Arriola, Leonardo. 2009. "Patronage and Political Stability in Africa." *Comparative Political Studies* 42(10):1339–1362.

Arrow, Kenneth J. 1951. *Social Choice and Individual Values*. New York: Wiley.

Atieno-Odhiambo, Elisha Stephen. 1974. "The Political Economy of the Asian Problem in Kenya, 1888–1939." *Transafrican Journal of History* 4(1):135–149.

1991. "The Production of History in Kenya: The Mau Mau Debate." *Canadian Journal of African Studies* 25(2):300–307.

2002. "Hegemonic Enterprises and Instrumentalities of Survival: Ethnicity and Democracy in Kenya." *African Studies* 61(2):223–249.

Bach, Stanley. 1994. "Parliamentary Reform in Zambia: Constitutional Design and Institutional Capacity." Prepared for presentation at the XVIth World Congress of the International Political Science Association.

1999. "Political Policy: President and Parliament in Zambia." *Journal of Management History* 5(4):183–196.

Bagehot, Walter. 1867. *The English Constitution*. Cambridge: Cambridge University Press.

Baldwin, Kate. 2010. "Big Men and Ballots: The Effects of Traditional Leaders on Elections and Distributive Politics in Zambia." PhD thesis. New York University, New York.

2015. *The Paradox of Traditional Chiefs in Democratic Africa*. Cambridge: Cambridge University Press.

Barkan, Joel D. 1976. "A Reassessment of Conventional Wisdom about the Informed Public: Comment: Further Reassessment of the 'Conventional Wisdom:' Political Knowledge and Voting Behavior in Rural Kenya." *American Political Science Review* 70(2):452–455.

1979. "Bringing Home the Pork: Legislator Behavior, Rural Development and Political Change in East Africa." In *Legislatures in Development*, ed. Joel. Smith and Lloyd. Musolf. Durham, NC: Duke University Press, pp. 265–288.

1987. "The Electoral Process and Peasant-State Relations in Kenya." In *Elections in Independent Africa*, ed. Fred M. Hayward. Boulder, CO: Westview Press, chapter 8, pp. 213–238.

2009*a*. "African Legislatures and the 'Third Wave' of Democratization." In *Legislative Power in Emerging African Democracies*, ed. Joel D. Barkan. Boulder, CO: Lynne Rienner, chapter 1, pp. 1–32.

2009*b*. *Legislative Power in Emerging African Democracies*. Boulder, CO: Lynne Rienner.

Barkan, Joel D. and Michael Chege. 1989. "Decentralizing the State: District Focus and the Politics of Reallocation in Kenya." *Journal of Modern African Studies* 27(3):431–453.

Barkan, Joel D. and Frank Holmquist. 1989. "Peasant-State Relations and the Social Base of Self-Help in Kenya." *World Politics* 41(3):359–380.

Barkan, Joel D. and Fred Matiangi. 2009. "Kenya's Tortuous Path to Successful Legislative Development." In *Legislative Power in Emerging African Democracies*, ed. Joel D. Barkan. Boulder, CO: Lynne Rienner, chapter 2, pp. 33–72.

Barkan, Joel D. and Robert Mattes. 2014. "Why CDFs in Africa? Representation vs. Constituency Service." In *Distributive Politics in Developing Countries: Almost Pork*, ed. Mark Baskin and Michael L. Mezey. Lanham, MD: Lexington Books, chapter 2, pp. 27–48.

Barkan, Joel D. and John Okumu. 1980. "Linkage without Parties: Legislatures and Constituents in Kenya." In *Political Parties without Linkage: A Comparative Perspective*, ed. Kay Lawson. New Haven, CT: Yale University Press, pp. 123–146.

Barkan, Joel D., Chong Lim Kim, Ilter Turan, and Malcolm E. Jewell. 1984. *The Legislative Connection: The Politics of Representation in Kenya, Korea and Turkey*. Durham, NC: Duke University Press.

Barro, Robert J. 1973. "The Control of Politicians: An Economic Model." *Public Choice* 14:19–42.

1971. *Unions, Parties, and Political Development: A Study of Mineworkers in Zambia*. New Haven, CT: Yale University Press.

Bates, Robert H. and Paul Collier. 1995. "The Politics and Economics of Policy Reform in Zambia." *Journal of African Economies* 4(1):115–143.

Baudais, Virginie and Gregory Chauzal. 2011. "The 2010 Coup d'État in Niger: A Praetorian Regulation of Politics?" *African Affairs* 110(439):295–304.

Baylies, Carolyn and Morris Szeftel. 1984. "Elections in the One-Party State." In *The Dynamics of the One-Party State in Zambia* ed. Cherry Gertzel, Carolyn Baylies, and Morris Szeftel. Manchester: Manchester University Press, chapter 2, pp. 29–57.

Bennett, George. 1957. "The Development of Political Organizations in Kenya." *Political Studies* 5:113–130.

Bennett, Huw. 2007. "The Other Side of COIN: Minimum and Exemplary Force in British Army Counterinsurgency in Kenya." *Small Wars and Insurgencies* 18(4):638–664.

Berman, Bruce. 1974. "Administration and Politics in Colonial Kenya." PhD thesis. University of Michigan, Ann Arbor, MI.

1990. *Control and Crisis in Colonial Kenya: The Dialectic of Domination*. Nairobi: Heinemann Kenya.

Berman, Bruce and John Lonsdale. 1998. "The Labors of 'Mwigithania': Jomo Kenyatta as Author, 1928–45." *Research in African Literatures* 29(1):16–42.

Berman, Bruce J., Jill Cottrell, and Yash Pal Ghai. 2009. "Patrons, Clients, and Constitutions: Ethnic Politics and Political Reform in Kenya." *Canadian Journal of African Studies* 43(3):462–506.

Berry, Sara. 1992. "Hegemony on a Shoestring: Indirect Rule and Access to Agricultural Land." *Africa: Journal of the International African Institute* 62(3):327–355.

Besley, Timothy. 2006. *Principled Agents? The Political Economy of Good Government*. Oxford: Oxford University Press.

Bienen, Henry. 1974. *Kenya: The Politics of Participation and Control*. Princeton, NJ: Princeton University Press.

Blaydes, Lisa. 2011. *Elections and Distributive Politics in Mubarak's Egypt*. New York: Cambridge University Press.

Boix, Carles. 2003. *Democracy and Redistribution*. Cambridge: Cambridge University Press.

Boix, Carles and Milan W. Svolik. 2013. "The Foundations of Limited Authoritarian Government: Institutions, Commitment, and Power-Sharing in Dictatorships." *The Journal of Politics* 75(2):300–316.

Bond, George C. 1976. *The Politics of Change in a Zambian Community*. Chicago, IL: University of Chicago Press.

Bond, George Clement. 1975. "New Coalitions and Traditional Chieftainship in Northern Zambia: The Politics of Local Government in Uyombe." *Africa: Journal of the International African Institute* 45(4):348–362.

Boone, Catherine. 2003. *Political Topographies of the African State: Territorial Authority and Institutional Choice*. Cambridge: Cambridge University Press.

Bormann, Nils-Christian and Matt Golder. 2013. "Democratic Electoral Systems around the World, 1946–2011." *Electoral Studies* 32(2):360–369.

Bowman, Larry Wells. 1971. "Authoritarian Politics in Rhodesia." PhD thesis. Brandeis University, Waltham, MA.

Branch, Daniel. 2006. "Loyalists, Mau Mau, and Elections in Kenya: The Triumph of the System, 1957–1958." *Africa Today* 53(2):27–50.

2007. "The Enemy within: Loyalists and the War against Mau Mau in Kenya." *Journal of African History* 48(2):291–315.

2011. *Kenya: Between Hope and Despair, 1963–2011*. New Haven, CT: Yale University Press.

Bratton, Michael. 1980. *The Local Politics of Rural Development: Peasant and Party-State in Zambia*. Hanover, NH: University Press of New England.

Bratton, Michael and Nicolas van de Walle. 1992. "Popular Protest and Political Reform in Africa." *Comparative Politics* 24(4):419–442.

Bretton, Henry L. 1966. *The Rise and Fall of Kwame Nkrumah: A Study of Personal Rule in Africa*. New York: Praeger.

Briggs, Ryan C. 2012. "Electrifying the Base? Aid and Incumbent Advantage in Ghana." *Journal of Modern African Studies* 50(4):603–624.

Brownlee, Jason. 2007. *Authoritarianism in an Age of Democratization*. New York: Cambridge University Press.

Burgess, Robin, Edward Miguel, Remi Jedwab, and Ameet Morjaria. 2009. "Our Turn to Eat: The Political Economy of Roads in Kenya." Unpublished Manuscript.

Burnell, Peter. 2001. "The Party System and Party Politics in Zambia: Continuities Past, Present and Future." *African Affairs* 100:239–263.

   2002. "Parliamentary Committees in Zambia's Third Republic: Partial Reforms, Unfinished Agenda." *Journal of Southern African Studies* 28(2):291–313.

   2003. "Legislative-Executive Relations in Zambia: Parliamentary Reform on the Agenda." *Journal of Contemporary African Studies* 21(1):47–68.

Burns, Alan. 1966. "The History of Commonwealth Parliaments." In *Parliament as an Export*, ed Alan Burns. London: George Allen and Unwin, chapter 1, pp.13–37.

Butler, K. S. and Nicolas van de Walle. 1999. "Political Parties and Party Systems in Africa's Illiberal Democracies." *Cambridge Review of International Studies* 13(1):14–28.

Callaghy, Thomas. 1984. *The State-Society Struggle: Zaire in Contemporary Perspective*. New York: Columbia University Press.

Caplan, Gerald L. 1968. "Barotseland: The Secessionist Challenge to Zambia." *Journal of Modern African Studies* 6(3):343–360.

Carey, George W. 1978. "Separation of Powers and the Madisonian Model: A Reply to the Critics." *American Political Science Review* 72(1):151–164.

Cartwright, John R. 1978. *Political Leadership in Sierra Leone*. Toronto: University of Toronto Press.

Chabal, Patrick and Jean-Pascal Daloz. 1999. *Africa Works: Disorder as Political Instrument*. Oxford: James Currey.

Chafer, Tony. 2002. *End of Empire in French West Africa: France's Successful Decolonization?* Oxford: Berg Publishers.

Chanaiwa, David Shingirai. 1980. "The Zulu Revolution: State Formation in a Pastoralist Society." *African Studies Review* 23(3):1–20.

Chazan, Naomi. 1979. "African Voters at the Polls: A Re-examination of the Role of Elections in African Politics." *Journal of Commonwealth and Comparative Studies* 17(2):136–158.

Cheeseman, Nicholas. 2006. *The Rise and Fall of Civilian-Authoritarianism in Africa: Patronage, Participation, and Political Parties in Kenya and Zambia Government.* Unpublished DPhil manuscript. Oxford University, Oxford.

Chege, Michael. 1998. "Introducing Race as a Variable into the Political Economy of Kenya Debate: An Incendiary Idea." *African Affairs* 97(387):209–230.

Cheibub, Jose Antonio, Jennifer Gandhi, and James Raymond Vreeland. 2010. "Democracy and Dictatorship Revisited." *Public Choice* 143(2):67–101.

Chikulo, Bornwell C. 1981. "The Zambian Administrative Reforms: An Alternative View." *Public Administration and Development* 1(1): 55–65.

1985. "Reorganization for Local Administration in Zambia: An Analysis of the Local Administration Act, 1980." *Public Administration and Development* 5(1):73–81.

1988. "The Impact of Elections in Zambia's One Party Second Republic." *Africa Today* 35(2):37–49.

Chuunga, S. M. 1968. "Local Government in Zambia before and after Independence." Master's thesis. University of East Africa, University College, Dar es Salaam Dar es Salaam, Tanzania.

Clough, Marshall S. 1990. *Fighting Two Sides: Kenyan Chiefs and Politicians, 1918–1940.* Niwot, CO: University of Colorado Press.

Cox, Gary W. 1987. *The Efficient Secret: The Cabinet and the Development of Political Parties in Victorian England.* Cambridge: Cambridge University Press.

2012. "Was the Glorious Revolution a Constitutional Watershed?" *Journal of Economic History* 72(3):567–600.

2016. *Marketing Sovereign Promises: Monopoly Brokerage and the Growth of the English State.* New York: Cambridge University Press.

Crook, Richard C. 1989. "Patrimonialism, Administrative Effectiveness and Economic Development in Cote d'Ivoire." *African Affairs* 88(351):205–228.

da Fonseca, Mariana Lopes. 2017. "Identifying the Source of Incumbency Advantage through a Constitutional Reform." *American Journal of Political Science* 61(3):657–670.

Davidson, James Wightman. 1974. *The Northern Rhodesia Legislative Council*. London: Greenwood Press.

Davies, Norman. 2005. *God's Playground: A History of Poland, the Origins to 1795*. Vol. I. New York: Columbia University Press.

de Walle, Nicolas van. 2001. *African Economies and the Politics of Permanent Crisis, 1979–1999*. Cambridge: Cambridge University Press.

Dealing, James Ralph. 1974. "Politics in Wanga, Kenya, c. 1650–1914" (Volumes I–III). PhD thesis. Northwestern University, Evanston, IL.

DiMaggio, Paul J. and Walter W. Powell. 1983. "The Iron Cage Revisited: Institutional Isomorphism and Collective Rationality in Organizational Fields." *American Sociological Review* 48(2):147–160.

Dionne, Kim Yi and Jeremy Horowitz. 2016. "The Political Effects of Agricultural Subsidies in Africa: Evidence from Malawi." *World Development* 87:215–226.

Downs, Anthony. 1957. "An Economic Theory of Political Action in a Democracy." *Journal of Political Economy* 65(2):135–150.

Dresang, Dennis L. 1974. "Ethnic Politics, Representative Bureaucracy and Development Administration: The Zambian Case." *American Political Science Review* 68(4):1605–1617.

1975. *The Zambia Civil Service: Entrepreneurship and Development Administration*. Nairobi: East African Publishing House.

Dulani, Boniface Madalitso. 2011. "Personal Rule and Presidential Term Limits in Africa." PhD thesis. Michigan State University, East Lansing, MI.

Dumbuya, Ahmed R. and Fred M. Hayward. 1985. "Changing Electoral Patterns in Sierra Leone: The 1982 Single-Party Elections." *African Studies Review* 28(4):62–86.

Easterly, William and Ross Levine. 1999. "Africa's Growth Tragedy: Politics and Ethnic Divisions." *Quarterly Journal of Economics* 112(4): 1203–1250.

2016. "The European Origins of Economic Development." *Journal of Economic Growth* 21(3):225–257.

Edling, Max M. 2003. *A Revolution in Favor of Government: Origins of the U.S. Constitution and the Making of the American State*. Oxford: Oxford University Press.

Ekeh, Peter P. 1975. "Colonialism and the Two Publics in Africa: A Theoretical Statement." *Comparative Studies in Society and History* 17(1):91–112.

Elischer, Sebastian. 2013. *Political Parties in Africa: Ethnicity and Party Formation*. Cambridge: Cambridge University Press.

Elkins, Caroline. 2000. "The Struggle for Mau Mau Rehabilitation in Late Colonial Kenya." *International Journal of African Historical Studies* 33(1):25–57.

Engerman, S. L. and K. L. Sokoloff. 2000. "Institutions and Factor Endowments and Paths of Development in the New World." *Journal of Economic Perspectives* 14(3):217–232.

Erikson, Robert S. and Rocio Titiunik. 2015. "Using Regression Discontinuity to Uncover the Personal Incumbency Advantage." *Quarterly Journal of Political Science* 10(1):101–119.

Evans-Pritchard, Edward. 1971. *The Azande: History and Political Institutions*. Oxford: Clarendon Press.

Ferejohn, John. 1986. "Incumbent Performance and Electoral Control." *Public Choice* 50:5–25.

Filipovich, Jean. 1980. "Leopold Senghor's Approach to Opposition: A Policy of Reconciliation." PhD thesis. McGill University, Montreal.

Fink, Elisabeth. 2015. "Elections and Political Mobilization in the Time of Decolonization: Voting in Postwar French West Africa." PhD thesis. New York University, New York.

Fish, M. Steven and Matthew Kroenig. 2009. *The Handbook of National Legislatures: A Global Survey*. Cambridge: Cambridge University Press.

Fletcher-Cooke, John. 1966. "Parliament, the Executive, and the Civil Service. In *Parliament as an Export*, ed. Alan Burns. London: George Allen and Unwin, chapter 6, pp. 142–165.

Fowler, Anthony and Andrew B. Hall. 2014. "Disentangling the Personal and Partisan Incumbency Advantages: Evidence from Close Elections and Term Limits." *Quarterly Journal of Political Science* 9(4):501–531.

Fraser, Andrew, R. H. Mason, and Philip Mitchell. 1995. *Japan's Early Parliaments, 1890–1905: Structures, Issues, and Trends*. Routledge Japanese Studies. London: Routledge.

Fuentes, Claudio. 2015. "Shifting the Status Quo: Constitutional Reforms in Chile." *Latin American Politics and Society* 57(1):99–122.

Furedi, Frank. 1973. "The African Crowd in Nairobi: Popular Movements and Elite Politics." *Journal of African History* 14(2):275–290.

Gandhi, Jennifer. 2008. *Political Institutions under Dictatorship*. Cambridge: Cambridge University Press.

Gandhi, Jennifer and Ellen Lust-Okar. 2009. "Elections under Authoritarianism." *Annual Review of Political Science* 12:403–422.

Gandhi, Jennifer and Adam Przeworski. 2007. "Authoritarian Institutions and the Survival of Autocrats." *Comparative Political Studies* 40(11):1279–1301.

Garcia-Ponce, Omar and Leonard Wantchekon. 2015. "Critical Junctures: Independence Movements and Democracy in Africa." Working Paper.

Gardinier, David E. 1982. "France in Gabon Since 1960." *Proceedings of the Meeting of the French Colonial Historical Society* 6:65–75.

Geddes, Barbara. 1999. "Authoritarian Breakdown: Empirical Test of a Game Theoretic Argument." Working Paper. University of California, Los Angeles.

Gehlbach, Scott and Philip Keefer. 2012. "Private Investment and the Institutionalization of Collective Action in Autocracies: Ruling Parties and Legislatures." *Journal of Politics* 74(2):621–635.

Gertzel, Cherry. 1966. "The Provincial Administration in Kenya." *Journal of Commonwealth and Comparative Studies* 4(3):201–215.

1970. *The Politics of Independent Kenya*. Nairobi: East African Publishing House.

1984. "Dissent and Authority in the Zambian One-Party State." In *The Dynamics of the One-Party State in Zambia*, ed. Cherry Gertzel. Manchester: Manchester University Press, Chapter 4, pp. 79–117.

Gewald, Jan-Bart, Marja Hinfelaar, and Giacomo Chiozza, eds. 2011. *Living the End of Empire: Politics and Society in Late Colonial Zambia*. Leiden: Brill Academic Publishers, chapter 1, pp. 7–16.

Goeke, Martin and Christof Hartmann. 2011. "The Regulation of Party Switching in Africa." *Journal of Contemporary African Studies* 29(3):263–280.

Good, Kenneth. 1968. "Kenyatta and the Organization of KANU." *Canadian Journal of African Studies* 2(2):115–136.

Gordon, David M. 2008. "Rebellion or Massacre? The UNIP-Lumpa Conflict Revisited." In *One Zambia, Many Histories: Towards a History of Post-Colonial Zambia*, ed. Jan-Bart Gewald, Marja Hinfelaar, and Giacomo Macola. Leiden: Brill, chapter 3, pp. 45–76.

Gould, David J. and Tshiabukole B. Mukendi. 1989. "Bureaucratic Corruption in Africa: Causes, Consequences, and Remedies." *International Journal of Public Administration* 12(3):427–457.

Greary, William N. M. 1927. *Nigeria under British Rule*. London: Frank Cass and Co. Ltd.

Greene, Abner S. 1994. "Checks and Balances in an Era of Presidential Lawmaking." *University of Chicago Law Review* 61(1):123–196.

Greif, Avner. 2008. "The Impact of Administrative Power on Political Development: Toward a Political Economy of Implementation." In *Institutions and Economic Performance*, ed. Elhanan Helpman. Cambridge, MA: Harvard University Press, chapter 1, pp. 17–63.

Greif, Avner and David D. Laitin. 2004. "A Theory of Endogenous Institutional Change." *American Political Science Review* 98(4):633–652.

Grumm, John G. 1958. "Theories of Electoral Systems." *Midwest Journal of Political Science* 2(4):357–376.

Haber, Stephen. 2006. "Authoritarian Government." In *The Oxford Handbook of Political Economy*, ed. Barry R. Weingast and Donald A. Wittman. New York: Oxford University Press, chapter 37, pp. 693–707.

Hakes, Jay E. 1970. "The Parliamentary Party of the Kenya African National Union." PhD thesis. Duke University, Durham, NC.

Hakes, Jay E. and John Leonard Helgerson. 1973. "Bargaining and Parliamentary Behavior in Africa: A Comparative Study of Zambia and Kenya." In *Legislatures in Comparative Perspective*, ed. Allan Kornberg. New York: David McKay Company.

Harding, Robin. 2015. "Attribution and Accountability: Voting for Roads in Ghana." *World Politics* 67(4):656–689.

Hassan, Mai. 2014. "A State of Change: The Kenyan State after Multi-Party Elections." PhD thesis. Harvard University, Cambridge, MA.

2017. "Strategic Shuffle: Ethnic Geography, the Internal Security Apparatus, and Elections in Kenya." *American Journal of Political Science* 61(2):382–395.

Heilbrunn, John R. 1993. "Social Origins of National Conferences in Benin and Togo." *Journal of Modern African Studies* 31(2):277–299.

Helgerson, John Leonard. 1970. "Institutional Adaptation to Rapid Political Change: A Study of the Legislature in Zambia from 1959 to 1969." PhD thesis. Duke University, Durham, NC.

Henderson, Ian. 1975. "Early African Leadership: The Copperbelt Disturbances of 1953 and 1940." *Journal of Southern African Studies* 2(1):83–97.

Herbst, Jeffrey. 1990. "Structural Adjustment of Politics in Africa." *World Development* 18(7):949–958.

2000. *States and Power in Africa: Comparative Lessons in Authority and Control*. Princeton, NJ: Princeton University Press.

Heston, Alan, Robert Summers, and Bettina Aten. 2002. "Penn World Table Version 6.3." Center for International Comparisons at the University of Pennsylvania (CICUP).

Hjort, Jonas. 2010. "Pre-Colonial Culture, Post-Colonial Economic Success? The Tswana and the African Economic Miracle." *Economic History Review* 63(3):688–709.

Hodgkin, Thomas. 1961. *African Political Parties: An Introductory Guide*. Baltimore, MD: Penguin Press.

Hodgkin, Thomas and Ruth Schachter. 1961. "French-Speaking West Africa in Transition." *International Conciliation* 3:375–436.

Holmstrom, Bengt and Paul Milgrom. 1991. "Multi-task Principal–Agent Analyses: Incentive Contracts, Asset Ownership and Job Design." *Journal of Law, Economics and Organization* 7:24–52.

Holt, James C. 1992. *Magna Carta*. Cambridge: Cambridge University Press.

Hornsby, Charles. 1985. "The Member of Parliament in Kenya, 1969–1983: The Election, Background and Position of the Representative and Implications for His Role in the One-Party State." PhD thesis. University of Oxford, Oxford.

Horowitz, Donald. 1985. *Ethnic Groups in Conflict*. Berkeley, CA: University of California Press.

Huntington, Samuel P. 1968. *Political Order in Changing Societies*. New Haven, CT: Yale University Press.

Hyam, Ronald. 1987. "The Geopolitical Origins of the Central African Federation: Britain, Rhodesia and South Africa, 1948–1953." *The Historical Journal* 30(1):145–172.

Hyden, Goran and Colin Leys. 1972. "Elections and Politics in Single-Party Systems: The Case of Kenya and Tanzania." *British Journal of Political Science* 2:389–420.

Idowu, H. O. 1968. "The Establishment of Elective Institutions in Senegal, 1869–1880." *Journal of African History* 9(2):261–277.

Izuakor, Levi I. 1983. "Kenya: The Unparamount African Paramountcy, 1923–1939." *Transafrican Journal of History* 12:33–50.

Jackson, Robert H. and Carl G. Rosberg. 1982. *Personal Rule in Black Africa: Prince, Autocrat, Prophet, Tyrant*. Berkeley, CA: University of California Press.

Jeffries, Charles. 1972. *Whitehall and the Colonial Service: An Administrative Memoir, 1939–1956*. Number 15 in "Commonwealth Papers." London: University of London.

Jensen, Nathan M., Edmund Malesky, and Stephen Weymouth. 2014. "Unbundling the Relationship between Authoritarian Legislatures and Political Risk." *British Journal of Political Science* 44(3):655–684.

Johnson, G. Wesley. 1966. "The Ascendancy of Blaise Diagne and the Beginning of African Politics in Senegal." *Journal of the International African Institute* 36(3):235–253.

Jones, Hilary. 2013. *The Metis of Senegal: Urban Life and Politics in French West Africa*. Bloomington, IN: Indiana University Press.

Joseph, Richard. 1987. *Democracy and Prebendal Politics in Nigeria: The Rise and Fall of the Second Republic*. Cambridge: Cambridge University Press.

Kanogo, Tabitha. 1987. *Squatters and the Roots of Mau Mau 1905–63.* Athens, OH: Ohio University Press.

Kanyinga, Karuti. 1994. "Ethnicity, Patronage and Class in a Local Arena: 'High' and 'Low' Politics in Kiambi, Kenya, 1982–1992. In *The New Local Level Politics in East Africa: Studies on Uganda, Tanzania and Kenya,* ed. Peter Gibbon. Uppsala, Sweden: Nordiska Afrikainstitutet, Chapter 4, pp. 66–86.

1998. "Contestation over Political Space: The State and the Demobilisation of Opposition Politics in Kenya." In *The Politics of Opposition in Contemporary Africa,* ed. Adebayo O. Olukoshi. Uppsala: Nordiska Afrikainstitutet, chapter 2, pp. 39–90.

Kariuki, James. 1996. "'Paramoia': Anatomy of a Dictatorship in Kenya." *Journal of Contemporary African Studies* 14(1):69–86.

Kenyatta, Jomo. 1965. *Facing Mt. Kenya: The Tribal Life of the Gikuyu.* New York: Vintage.

Kim, Young Hun and Donna Bahry. 2008. "Interrupted Presidencies in Third Wave Democracies." *Journal of Politics* 70(3):807–822.

King, Tony. 2008. Partnership and Paternalism: The Federation of Rhodesia and Nyasaland (1953–1963). In *Defunct Federalisms: Critical Perspectives on Federal Failure,* ed. Emilian Kavalski and Magdalena Zolkos. Burlington, VT: Ashgate Publishing, chapter 4, pp. 47–58.

Kirk-Greene, A. H. M. 1980. "The Thin White Line: The Size of the British Service in Africa." *African Affairs* 79(314):25–44.

Kjekshus, Helge. 1974. "Parliament in One-Party State: The Bunge of Tanzania, 1965–70." *Journal of Modern African Studies* 12(1):19–43.

Koter, Dominika. 2013. "King Makers: Local Leaders and Ethnic Politics in Africa." *World Politics* 65(2):187–232.

Kramon, Eric. 2018. *Money for Votes: The Causes and Consequences of Electoral Clientelism in Africa.* New York: Cambridge University Press.

Krehbiel, Keith. 1991. *Information and Legislative Organization.* Ann Arbor, MI: University of Michigan Press.

Kroeger, Alex. 2018. "Dominant Party Rule, Elections, and Cabinet Instability in African Autocracies." *British Journal of Political Science,* pp. 1–23.

Kuper, Adam. 1983. "The 'House' and Zulu Political Structure in the Nineteenth Century." *Journal of African History* 34(3):469–487.

Kuran, Timur. 1991. "The East European Revolution of 1989: Is it Surprising That We Were Surprised?" *American Economic Review* 81(2):121–125.

Kyapoya, Vincent. 1979. "The Politics of Succession in Africa: Kenya after Kenyatta." *Africa Today* 26(3):7–29.

Kyapoya, Vincent. 1988. "Moi and Beyond: Towards Peaceful Succession in Kenya." *Third World Quarterly* 10(1):54–66.

Lange, Matthew K. 2004. "British Colonial Legacies and Political Development." *World Development* 32(6):905–922.

Larmer, Miles. 2005. "Unrealistic Expectations? Zambia's Mineworkers from Independence to the One-Party State, 1964–1972." *Journal of Historical Sociology* 18(4):318–352.

2006. "A Little Bit Like a Volcano: The United Progressive Party and Resistance to One-Party Rule in Zambia, 1964–1980." *International Journal of African Historical Studies* 39(1):49.

Lebas, Adrienne. 2011. *From Protest to Parties: Party-Building and Democratization in Africa.* Oxford: Oxford University Press.

Lee, David S. 2008. "Randomized Experiments from Non-random Selection in U.S. House Elections." *Journal of Econometrics* 142(2): 675–697.

Lee, David S. and Thomas Lemieux. 2010. "Regression Discontinuity Designs in Economics." *Journal of Economic Literature* 48(2): 281–355.

Levi, Edward H. 1976. "Some Aspects of Separation of Powers." *Columbia Law Review* 76(3):371–391.

Leys, Colin. 1976. "The Overdeveloped Post Colonial State: A Re-Evaluation." *Review of African Political Economy* 3(5): 39–48.

Lindberg, Steffan I. 2010. "What Accountability Pressures Do MPs in Africa Face and How Do They Respond? Evidence from Ghana." *Journal of Modern African Studies* 48(1):117–142.

Lindberg, Steffan I. and Yongmei Zhou. 2009. "Co-Optation Despite Democratization in Ghana." In *Legislative Power in Emerging African Democracies,* ed. Joel D. Barkan. Boulder, CO: Lynne Rienner, chapter 5, pp. 147–176.

Lindeman, Stefan. 2011. "Inclusive Elite Bargains and the Dilemma of Unproductive Peace: A Zambian Case Study." *Third World Quarterly* 32(10):1843–1869.

Loewenstein, Karl. 1949. "The Presidency Outside the United States: A Study in Comparative Political Institutions." *Journal of Politics* 11(3):447–496.

Londregan, John B. 2000. *Legislative Institutions and Ideology in Chile.* Cambridge: Cambridge University Press.

Lonsdale, John. 1992. "The Conquest State of Kenya, 1895–1905." In *Unhappy Valley: Conflict in Kenya and Africa,* ed. Bruce Berman and John Lonsdale. Vol. 1: State and Class. Athens, OH: Ohio University Press, pp. 13–44.

Lonsdale, John. 2006. "Ornamental Constitutionalism in Africa: Kenyatta and the Two Queens." *Journal of Imperial and Commonwealth History* 34(1):87–103.

Lonsdale, John M. 1968. "Some Origins of Nationalism in East Africa." *Journal of African History* 9(1):119–146.

Lugard, Frederick D. 1922. *The Dual Mandate in British Tropical Africa*. London: William Blackwood and Sons.

Lund, Michael and Carlos Santiso. 1998. "National Conferences." In *Democracy and Deep-Rooted Conflict: Options for Negotiators*, ed. Peter Harris and Ben Reilly. International IDEA, chapter 4.8, pp. 252–272.

Lust-Okar, Ellen. 2005. *Structuring Conflict in the Arab World: Incumbents, Opponents, and Institutions*. Cambridge: Cambridge University Press.

   2006. "Elections under Authoritarianism: Preliminary Lessons from Jordan." *Democratization* 13(3):456–471.

Macola, Giacomo. 2008. "Harry Mwanga Nkumbula, UNIP and the Roots of Authoritarianism in Nationalist Zambia." In *One Zambia, Many Histories: Towards a History of Post-Colonial Zambia*, ed. Jan-Bart Gewald, Marja Hinfelaar, and Giacomo Macola. Leiden: Brill, chapter 2, pp. 17–44.

   2010. *Liberal Nationalism in Central Africa: A Biography of Harry Mwaanga Nkumbula*. New York: Palgrave MacMillan.

Macpherson, Fergus. 1976. "British Annexation of Northern Zambezia, 1884–1924: Anatomy of a Conquest." PhD thesis. University of Edinburgh, Edinburgh.

Maddicott, John R. 1994. *Simon de Montfort*. Cambridge: Cambridge University Press.

   2010. *The Origins of the English Parliament, 924–1327*. Oxford: Oxford University Press.

Madison, James. 1788. "These Departments Should Not Be So Separated as to Have No Constitutional Control over Each Other." *The Federalist Papers*, No. 48.

Magaloni, Beatriz. 2006. *Voting for Autocracy: Hegemonic Party Survival and Its Demise in Mexico*. Cambridge: Cambridge University Press.

Mahoney, James and Kathleen Thelen, eds. 2010. *Explaining Institutional Change: Ambiguity, Agency, and Power*. Cambridge: Cambridge University Press.

Malesky, Edmund and Paul Schuler. 2011. "The Single-Party Dictator's Dilemma: Information in Elections without Opposition." *Legislative Studies Quarterly* 36:491–530.

Mamdani, Mahmood. 1996. *Citizen and Subject: Contemporary Africa and the Legacy of Late Colonialism.* Princeton, NJ: Princeton University Press.

Mani, Anandi and Sharun Mukand. 2007. "Democracy, Visibility and Public Good Provision." *Journal of Development Economics* 83: 506–529.

Manin, Bernard. 1997. *The Principles of Representative Government.* Cambridge: Cambridge University Press.

Mann, Kristin and Richard Roberts, eds. 1991. *Law in Colonial Africa.* Portsmouth, NH: Heinemann.

Mann, Michael. 1984. "The Autonomous Power of the State: Its Origins, Mechanisms and Results." *European Journal of Sociology* 25(2): 185–213.

Manning, Patrick. 1998. *Francophone Sub-Saharan Africa, 1880–1995.* Cambridge: Cambridge University Press.

Marshall, Monty G. and Keith Jaggers. 2009. *Polity IV Project: Political Regime Characteristics and Transitions, 1800–2008.* Boulder, CO: Technical Report, Center for Systemic Peace and Colorado University.

Martinelli, Cesar. 2006. "Would Rational Voters Acquire Costly Information?" *Journal of Economic Theory* 129:225–251.

Martinez, Luis. 2000. *The Algerian Civil War, 1990–1998.* New York: Columbia University Press.

Mayhew, David R. 1974. *Congress: The Electoral Connection.* New Haven, CT: Yale University Press.

Mazrui, Ali A. 1970. "Leadership in Africa: Obote of Uganda." *International Journal* 25(3):538–564.

   1979. "The Cultural Fate of African Legislatures: Rise, Decline and Prospects for Revival." *Presence Africaine* 112:26–47.

Mbithi, Philip and Rasmus Rasmusson. 1977. *Self Reliance in Kenya: The Case of Harambee.* Uppsala: Scandinavian Institute of African Studies.

Mboya, Thomas. 1965. *Freedom and After.* London: Andre Deutsch Limited.

McCrary, Justin. 2008. "Manipulation of the Running Variable in the Regression Discontinuity Design: A Density Test." *Journal of Econometrics* 142(2):698–714.

McKechnie, William Sharp. 1914. *Magna Carta: A Commentary on the Great Charter of King John.* New York: Burt Franklin.

Meebelo, Henry S. 1971. *Reaction to Colonialism: A Prelude to the Politics of Independence in Northern Zambia, 1893–1939.* Manchester: Manchester University Press.

Mezey, Michael L. 2013. *Presidentialism: Power in Comparative Perspective.* Boulder, CO: Lynne Rienner.

Mijere, Nsolo. 1988. "The State and Development: A Study of the Dominance of the Political Class in Zambia." *Africa Today* 35(2): 21–36.

Mijere, Nsolo N. J. 1985. "The Mineworkers' Resistance to Governmental Decentralization in Zambia: National-Building and Labor Aristocracy in the Third World." PhD thesis. Brandeis University Waltham, MA.

Mill, John Stuart. 1861. *Considerations on Representative Government.* Amherst, MA: Prometheus Books.

Minikin, Victor. 1973. "Indirect Political Participation in Two Sierra Leone Chiefdoms." *Journal of Modern African Studies* 11(1):129–135.

Momba, Jonathan C. 2003. "Democratic Transition and the Crises of an African Nationalist Party: UNIP, Zambia." In *African Political Parties: Evolution, Institutionalism and Governance*, ed. M. A. Mohamed Salih. London: Pluto Press, chapter 1, pp. 37–65.

2005. "Evolution of Parliament-Executive Relations in Zambia." In *African Parliaments: Between Governance and Government*, ed. M. A. Mohamed Salih. New York: Palgrave MacMillan, chapter 6, pp. 101–119.

Morgenthau, Ruth Schachter. 1964. *Political Parties in French-Speaking West Africa.* Oxford: Oxford University Press.

Mosley, Paul. 1983. *The Settler Economies: Studies in the Economic History of Kenya and Southern Rhodesia, 1900–1963.* Cambridge: Cambridge University Press.

Mozaffar, Shaheen. 1998. "Electoral Systems and Conflict Management in Africa: A Twenty-Eight-State Comparison." In *Elections and Conflict Management in Africa*, ed. Timothy D. Sisk and Andrew Reynolds. Washington, DC: United States Institution of Peace, chapter 5, pp. 81–98.

Mueller, Susanne D. 1984. "Government and Opposition in Kenya, 1966–9." *Journal of Modern African Studies* 22(3):399–427.

Mukwena, Royson M. 1992. "Zambia's Local Administration Act, 1980: A Critical Appraisal of the Integration Objective." *Public Administration and Development* 12(3):237–247.

Mulford, David C. 1967. *Zambia: The Politics of Independence, 1957–1964.* Oxford: Oxford University Press.

Mumeka, Lundondo. 1987. "The Role of the State in Capital Accumulation and Class Formation in Zambia." Monograph. American University, Washington, DC.

Musambachime, M. C. 1991. "Dauti Yamba's Contribution to the Rise and Growth of Nationalism in Zambia, 1941–1964." *African Affairs* 90(359):259–281.

Mutua, Makau. 2001. "Justice under Siege: The Rule of Law and Judicial Subservience in Kenya." *Human Rights Quarterly* 23(1):96–118.

Mwangola, Mshai S. 2007. "Leaders of Tomorrow? The Youth and Democratisation in Kenya." In *Kenya: The Struggle for Democracy*, ed. Godwin R. Murunga and Shadrack Wanjala Nasong'o. London: Zed Books, chapter 5, pp. 129–163.

Mwiria, Kilemi. 1990. "Kenya's Harambee Secondary School Movement: The Contradictions of Public Policy." *Comparative Education Review* 34(3):350–368.

Myerson, Roger B. 2008. "The Autocrat's Credibility Problem and Foundations of the Constitutional State." *American Political Science Review* 102(1):125–139.

Ndegwa, Stephen N. 1998. "The Incomplete Transition: The Constitutional and Electoral Context in Kenya." *Africa Today* 45(2):193–211.

N'Diaye, Boubacar. 2002. "How Not to Institutionalize Civilian Control: Kenya's Coup Prevention Strategies, 1964–1997." *Armed Forces and Society* 28(4):619–640.

Ndulo, Muna. 1974. "The Nationalization of the Zambian Copper Industry." *Zambia Law Journal* 6(55):55–73.

Nkrumah, Kwame. 1957. *Ghana: The Autobiography of Kwame Nkrumah*. New York: Nelson.

North, Douglass C. and Barry R. Weingast. 1989. "Constitutions and Commitment: The Evolution of Institutions Governing Public Choice in Seventeenth-Century England." *Journal of Economic History* 49(4):803–832.

North, Douglass C., John Joseph Wallis, and Barry R. Weingast. 2009. *Violence and Social Orders: A Conceptual Framework for Interpreting Recorded Human History*. Cambridge: Cambridge University Press.

Nwajiaku, Kathryn. 1994. "The National Conferences in Benin and Togo Revisited." *Journal of Modern African Studies* 32(3):429–447.

Ochieng', Cosmas Milton Obote. 2007. "Developing through Positive Deviance and its Implications for Economic Policy Making and Public Administration in Africa: The Case of Kenyan Agricultural Development, 1930–2005." *World Development* 35(3):454–479.

Odinga, Ajuma Oginga. 1967. *Not Yet Uhuru*. Nairobi: East Africa Publishers.

O'Donnell, Guillermo. 1998. "Horizontal Accountability in New Democracies." *Journal of Democracy* 9(3):112–126.

O'Donnell, Guillermo and Philippe Schmitter. 1986. *Transitions from Authoritarian Rule: Prospects for Democracy*. Baltimore, MD: Johns Hopkins University Press.

Ogot, Bethwell A. 1963. "British Administration in the Central Nyanza District of Kenya, 1900–60." *Journal of African History* 4(2):249–273.

1995. "The Decisive Years." In *Decolonization and Independence in Kenya, 1940–93*, ed. Bethwell A. Ogot and William R. Ochieng. Athens, OH: Ohio University Press, chapter 3, pp. 48–82.

2003. "Mau Mau and Nationhood: The Untold Story." In *Mau Mau and Nationhood: Arms, Authority, and Narration*, ed. Elisha Stephen Atieno-Odhiambo and John Lonsdale. Nairobi: East African Education Publishers, chapter 1, pp. 8–36.

Ojwang, Jackton B. 1980. "The Residue of Legislative Power in English and French-Speaking Africa: A Comparative Study of Kenya and Ivory Coast." *International and Comparative Law Quarterly* 29(2): 296–326.

Okafor, Samuel O. 1981. *Indirect Rule: The Development of Central Legislature in Nigeria*. Surrey: Nelson Africa.

Okoth-Ogendo, H. W. 1972. "The Politics of Constitutional Change in Kenya Since Independence, 1963–69." *African Affairs* 71(282):9–34.

Ollawa, Patrick. 1977. "On a Dynamic Model for Rural Development in Africa." *Journal of Modern African Studies* 15(3):401–423.

Omosule, Monone. 1974. "Political and Constitutional Aspects of the Origins and Development of Local Government in Kenya, 1895–1963." PhD thesis. Syracuse University, Syracuse, NY.

Opalo, Ken Ochieng'. 2012. "African Elections: Two Divergent Trends." *Journal of Democracy* 23(3):80–93.

2014. "The Long Road to Institutionalization: The Kenyan Legislature and the 2013 Elections." *Journal of Eastern African Studies* 8(1): 63–77.

2016. "Constitutional Protections of Electoral Democracy in Africa: A Review of Key Challenges and Prospects." In *Annual Review of Constitution-Building Processes: 2015*. ed. Sumit Bisarya. Stockholm: International IDEA, chapter 1, pp. 9–30

2017. "Legislative Strength and Incumbency Effects in Africa: Evidence from Parliamentary Elections in Kenya, 1963–2007." Working Paper.

2019. "Constrained Presidential Power in Africa? Legislative Independence and Executive Rulemaking in Kenya, 1963–2013." *British Journal of Political Science*.

Osborn, Emily Lynn. 2003. "'Circle of Iron': African Colonial Employees and the Interpretation of Colonial Rule in French West Africa." *Journal of African History* 44(1):29–50.

Parpart, Jane L. and Timothy M. Shaw. 1983. "Contradiction and Coalition: Class Fractions in Zambia, 1964–1984." *Africa Today* 30(3): 23–50.

Pelizzo, Riccardo and Rick Stapenhurst. 2004. "Legislatures and Oversight." *WBI Working Papers*, pp. 1–67.

Persson, Torsten, Gerard Roland, and Guido Tabellini. 1997. "Separation of Powers and Political Accountability." *Quarterly Journal of Economics* 112(4):1163–1202.

Phiri, Bizeck Jube. 1991. "The Capricorn Africa Society: A Study of Liberal Politics in Northern Rhodesia/Zambia, 1949–1972." PhD thesis. Dalhousie University, Halifax, Nova Scotia.

  2001. "Colonial Legacy and the Role of Society in the Creation and Demise of Autocracy in Zambia, 1964–1991." *Nordic Journal of African Studies* 10(2):224–243.

Pierson, Paul. 2004. *Politics in Time: History, Institutions and Social Analysis*. Princeton, NJ: Princeton University Press.

Pike, Phillip E. H. 1951. "East Africa." *Journal of Comparative Legislation and International Law* 33(1):107–131.

Pincus, Steve. 2009. *1688: The First Modern Revolution*. New Haven, CT: Yale University Press.

Polsby, Nelson W. 1968. "The Institutionalization of the U.S. House of Representatives." *American Political Science Review* 62:144–168.

Posner, Daniel. 2005. *Institutions and Ethnic Politics in Africa*. Cambridge: Cambridge University Press.

Posner, Daniel and Daniel J. Young. 2007. "Institutionalization of Political Power in Africa." *Journal of Democracy* 18(3):126–140.

Power, Greg and Rebecca A. Shoot. 2014. "Global Parliamentary Report: The Changing Nature of Parliamentary Representation." Technical report. United Nations Development Program, New York.

Proctor, J. H. 1965. "The Role of the Senate in the Kenya Political System." *Parliamentary Affairs* 18(4):389–415.

Proctor, Jesse H. 1968. "The House of Chiefs and the Political Development of Botswana." *Journal of Modern African Studies* 6(1):59–79.

Punder, Hermann. 2009. "Democratic Legitimation of Delegated Legislation: A Comparative View of the America, British, and German Law." *International and Comparative Law Quarterly* 58(2):353–378.

Quinlivan, James T. 1999. "Coup-Proofing: Its Practice and Consequences in the Middle East." *International Security* 24(2):131–165.

Ranger, Terence. 1983. "The Invention of Tradition in Colonial Africa." In *The Invention of Tradition*. Cambridge: Cambridge University Press, chapter 6, pp. 211–262.

Reed, Michael C. 1987. "Gabon: A Neo-Colonial Enclave of Enduring French Interests." *Journal of Modern African Studies* 25(2):283–320.

Remmer, Karen L. 1989. "Neopatrimonialism: The Politics of Military Rule in Chile, 1973–1987." *Comparative Politics* 21(2):149–170.

Riedl, Rachel Beatty. 2014. *Authoritarian Origins of Democratic Party Systems in Africa*. Cambridge, MA: Cambridge University Press.

Riker, William H. 1980. "Implications from the Disequilibrium of Majority Rule for the Study of Institutions." *American Political Science Review* 74(2):432–446.

Robinson, Amanda Leah. 2017. "Ethnic Diversity, Segregation and Ethnocentric Trust in Africa." *British Journal of Political Science*, pp. 1–23.

Robinson, Pearl T. 1991. "Niger: Anatomy of a Neotraditional Corporatist State." *Comparative Politics* 24(1):1–20.

Robinson, Pearl T. 1994. "The National Conference Phenomenon in Francophone Africa." *Comparative Studies in Society and History* 36(3):575–610.

Rodney, Walter. 1982. *How Europe Underdeveloped Africa*. Washington, DC: Howard University Press.

Roelker, Jack R. 1976. *Mathu of Kenya: A Political Study*. Hoover Colonial Studies, Stanford, CA: Hoover Institution Press.

Roessler, Philip. 2011. "The Enemy Within: Personal Rule, Coups and Civil War in Africa." *World Politics* 63(2):300–346.

Rohac, Dalibor. 2008. "It is by Unrule That Poland Stands: Institutions and Political Thought in the Polish-Lithuanian Republic." *The Independent Institute* 13(2):209–224.

Rotberg, Robert I. 1965. *The Rise of Nationalism in Central Africa: The Making of Malawi and Zambia*. Cambridge, MA: Harvard University Press.

1977. *Black Heart: Gore-Browne and the Politics of Multiracial Zambia*. Berkeley, CA: University of California Press.

Rouyer, Alwyn Rudolph. 1971. Political Recruitment in Kenya: The Legislative Elite, 1957-1968 Manuscript Tulane University New Orleans, LA:.

Saad, Elias N. 1983. *Social History of Timbuktu: The Role of Muslim Scholars and Notables, 1400–1900*. Cambridge: Cambridge University Press.

Saiegh, Sebastian M. 2011. *Ruling by Statute: How Uncertainty and Vote Buying Shape Lawmaking*. Cambridge: Cambridge University Press.

Salih, M. A. Mohamed, ed. 2005. *African Parliaments: Between Governance and Government*. London: Pluto Press.

Sandbrook, Richard. 1993. *The Politics of Africa's Economic Recovery*. Cambridge: Cambridge University Press.

Sassoon, Joseph. 2012. *Saddam Hussein's Ba'th Party: Inside an Authoritarian Regime*. Cambridge: Cambridge University Press.

Scarritt, James R. 1979. "The Decline of Political Legitimacy in Zambia: An Explanation Based on Incomplete Data." *African Studies Review* 22(2):13–30.

Schachter, Ruth. 1961. "Single-Party Systems in West Africa." *American Political Science Review* 55(2):294–307.

Scott, Ian. 1976. "Party Politics in Zambia: A Study of the Organization of the United National Independence Party." PhD thesis. University of Toronto, Toronto.

    1980. "Party and Administration under the One-Party State." In *Administration in Zambia*, ed. William Tordoff. Manchester: Manchester University Press, chapter 6, pp. 139–161.

Siavelis, Peter M. 2002. "Exaggerated Presidentialism and Moderate Presidents: Executive-Legislative Relations in Chile." In *Legislative Politics in Latin America*, ed. Scott Morgenstern and Benito Nacif. Cambridge: Cambridge University Press, chapter 4, pp. 79–113.

Simutanyi, Neo. 1996. "The Politics of Structural Adjustment in Zambia." *Third World Quarterly* 17(4):825–839.

Sin, Gisela. 2015. *Separation of Power and Legislative Organization: The President, the Senate, and Political Parties in the Making of House Rules.* New York: Cambridge University Press.

Sindab, N. Jean. 1984. "The Impact of Expatriates on the Zambian Development Process." PhD thesis. Yale University, New Haven, CT.

Sissokho, Oumar and Melissa A. Thomas. 2005. "Liaison Legislature: The Role of the National Assembly in Senegal." *Journal of Modern African Studies* 43(1):97–117.

Spear, Thomas. 2003. "Neo-Traditionalism and the Limits of Invention in British Colonial Africa." *Journal of African History* 44:3–27.

Spencer, John. 1985. *KAU: The Kenya African Union.* New York: Rosberg and Nottingham.

Squire, Peverill. 2012. *The Evolution of American Legislatures: Colonies, Territories and States, 1619–2009.* Ann Arbor, MI: University of Michigan Press.

Stamp, Patricia. 1986. "Local Government in Kenya: Ideology and Political Practice, 1895–1974." *African Studies Review* 29(4):17–42.

Stasavage, David. 2003. *Public Debt and the Birth of the Democratic State: France and Great Britain, 1688–1789.* Cambridge: Cambridge University Press.

    2005. "Democracy and Education Spending in Africa." *American Political Science Review* 49(2):343–358.

Stokes, Susan C. 2001. *Mandates and Democracy: Neoliberalism by Surprise in Latin America.* Cambridge, MA: Cambridge University Press.

Stultz, Newell M. 1968. "Parliaments in Former British Black Africa." *Journal of Developing Areas* 2(4):479–494.

1969. "Parliament in a Tutelary Democracy: A Recent Case in Kenya." *Journal of Politics* 31(1):95–118.

Svolik, Milan W. 2009. "Power Sharing and Leadership Dynamics in Authoritarian Regimes." *American Journal of Political Science* 53(2):477–494.

2012. *The Politics of Authoritarian Rule.* Cambridge: Cambridge University Press.

Szeftel, Morris. 1982. "Political Graft and the Spoils System in Zambia: The State as a Resource in Itself." *Review of African Political Economy* 24:4–21.

2000. "'Eat With Us': Managing Corruption and Patronage under Zambia's Three Republics, 1964–99." *Journal of Contemporary African Studies* 18(2):207–224.

Szeftel, Morris and Carolyn Baylies. 1992. "The Fall and Rise of Multi-Party Politics in Zambia." *Review of African Political Economy* 19(54):75–91.

Taagepera, Rein. 1972. "The Size of National Assemblies." *Social Science Research* 1(4):385–401.

Taagepera, Rein and Bernard Grofman. 1985. "Rethinking Duverger's Law: Predicting the Effective Number of Parties in Plurality and PR Systems – Parties Minus Issues Equals One." *European Journal of Political Research* 13:341–352.

Tamarkin, Mordechai. 1978. "The Roots of Political Stability in Kenya." *African Affairs* 77(208):297–320.

1979. "From Kenyatta to Moi: The Anatomy of a Peaceful Transition of Power." *Africa Today* 26(3):21–37.

Thelen, Kathleen. 2004. *How Institutions Evolve: The Political Economy of Skills in Germany, Britain, the United States and Japan.* New York: Cambridge University Press.

Thompson, Faith. 1953. *A Short History of Parliament, 1295–1642.* Minneapolis, MN: University of Minnesota Press.

Thomson, Virginia and Richard Adloff. 1960. *The Emerging States of French Equatorial Africa.* London: Oxford University Press.

Throup, David. 1993. "Elections and Political Legitimacy in Kenya." *Journal of the International African Institute* 63(3):371–396.

Thurston, Anne and Alan Donovan. 2015. *A Path Not Taken: The Story of Joseph Murumbi.* Nairobi: The Murumbi Trust.

Tibenderana, Peter K. 1988. "The Irony of Indirect Rule in Sokoto Emirate, Nigeria, 1903–1944." *African Studies Review* 31(1):67–92.

Tignor, Robert L. 1971. "Colonial Chiefs in Chiefless Societies." *Journal of Modern African Studies* 9(3):339–359.

Tordoff, William. 1962. "The Ashanti Confederacy." *Journal of African History* 3(3):399–417.

1965. "Parliament in Tanzania." *Journal of Commonwealth Political Studies* 3:85–103.

1977*a*. "Residual Legislatures: The Cases of Tanzania and Zambia." *Journal of Commonwealth and Comparative Studies* 15(3):235–249.

1977*b*. "Zambia: The Politics of Disengagement." *African Affairs* 76(302):60–69.

1980. "Rural Administration." In *Administration in Zambia*, ed. William Tordoff. Manchester: Manchester University Press, chapter 8, pp. 185–212.

2002. *Government and Politics in Africa*. Bloomington, IN: Indiana University Press.

Tordoff, William and Robert Molteno. 1974. "Parliament." In *Politics in Zambia*, ed. William Tordoff. University of California Press, chapter 6, pp. 197–241.

Tsubura, Machiko. 2013. "The Politics of Constituency Development Funds (CDFs) in Comparative Perspective." APSA 2013 Annual Meeting Paper.

Turok, Ben. 1981. "Control of the Parastatal Sector of Zambia." *Journal of Modern African Studies* 19(3):421–445.

Twaddle, Michael. 1969. "The Bakungu Chiefs of Buganda under British Colonial Rule, 1900–1930." *Journal of African History* 10(2):309–322.

Uppal, Yogesh. 2009. "The Disadvantaged Incumbents: Estimating Incumbency Effects in Indian State Legislatures." *Public Choice* 139:9–27.

Uzoigwe, G. N. 1983. "Uganda and Parliamentary Government." *The Journal of Modern African Studies* 21(2):253–271.

van Binsbergen, Wim. 1987. "Chiefs and the State in Independent Zambia – Exploring the Zambian National Press." *Journal of Legal Pluralism and Unofficial Law* 19(25–26):139–201.

van Donge, Jan Kees and Athumani J. Liviga. 1986. "In Defence of the Tanzanian Parliament." *Parliamentary Affairs* 39(2):230–240.

van Zanden, Jan Luiten, Eltjo Buringh, and Maarten Bosker. 2012. "The Rise and Decline of European Parliaments, 1188–1789." *Economic History Review* 65(3):835–861.

Vansina, Jan. 2004. *How Societies Are Born: Governance in West Central Africa before 1600*. Charlottesville, VA: University of Virginia Press.

Vickery, Kenneth P. 1985. "Maize Control in Northern Rhodesia." *Journal of Southern African Studies* 11(2):212–234.

Vincente, Pedro C. 2014. "Is Vote Buying Effective? Evidence from a Field Experiment in West Africa." *Economic Journal* 124(574):356–387.

Vinnai, Volker. 1974. "The Creation of an African Civil Service in Kenya." *Law and Politics in Africa, Asia and Latin America* 7(2):175–188.

Walzer, Michael. 1992. *Regicide and Revolution: Speeches at the Trial of Louis XVI.* New York: Columbia University Press.

Wanjohi, N. Gatheru. 1985. "The Politics of Land, Elections, and Democratic Performance in Kenya: A Case Study of Nakuru District." Working Paper 412, Institute for Development Studies, University of Nairobi.

Wantchekon, Leonard. 2003. "Clientilism and Voting Behavior: Evidence from a Field Experiment in Benin." *World Politics* 55(3):399–422.

Wasserman, Gary. 1976. *Politics of Decolonization: Kenya Europeans and the Land Issue, 1960–1965.* Number 17 *in* "African Studies." Cambridge: Cambridge University Press.

Weingast, Barry R. and William J. Marshall. 1988. "Industrial Organization of Congress or Why Legislatures, Like Firms, Are Not Organized as Markets." *Journal of Political Economy* 96(1):132–163.

Welch, Claude. 1972. "Praetorianism in Commonwealth West Africa." *Journal of Modern African Studies* 10(2):203–222.

Weymouth, Stephen. 2011. "Political Institutions and Property Rights: Veto Players and Foreign Exchange Commitments in 127 Countries." *Comparative Political Studies* 11(1):211–240.

Widner, Jennifer. 1992. *The Rise of a Party-State in Kenya: From Harambee! to Nyayo!* Berkeley, CA: University of California Press.

Wight, Martin. 1947. *The Gold Coast Legislative Council.* London: Faber and Faber Limited.

Willis, Justin, Nic Cheeseman, and Gabrielle Lynch. 2018. "Voting, Nationhood, and Citizenship in Late Colonial Africa." *The Historical Journal,* pp. 1–23.

Wilson, Matthew Charles and Joseph Wright. 2015. "Autocratic Legislatures and Expropriation Risk." *British Journal of Political Science* 47:1–17.

Wipper, Audrey. 1989. "Kikuyu Women and the Harry Thuku Disturbances: Some Uniformities of Female Militancy." *Journal of the International African Institute* 59(3):300–337.

Worden, Blair. 1971. "The Bill for a New Representative: The Dissolution of the Long Parliament, April 1653." *English Historical Review* 86(340):473–496.

World Bank Group. 2013. *World Development Indicators.* Washington, DC: The World Bank.

Wright, Joseph. 2008. "Do Authoritarian Institutions Constrain? How Legislatures Affect Economic Growth and Investment." *American Journal of Political Science* 52(2):322–343.

Wright, Joseph and Able Escriba-Folch. 2012. "Authoritarian Institutions and Regime Survival: Transitions to Democracy and Subsequent Autocracy." *British Journal of Political Science* 42(2):283–309.

Wrigley, Christopher. 1996. *Kingship and State: The Buganda Dynasty.* Cambridge: Cambridge University Press.

Zelniker, Shimshon. 1971. "Changing Patterns of Trade Unionism: The Zambian Case, 1948–1964." PhD thesis. University of California, Los Angeles, CA.

Zucco, Cesar. 2007. "Where's the Bias? A Reassessment of the Chilean Electoral System." *Electoral Studies* 26:303–314.

Index